PRAISE FOR
THE GHOST CHRONICLES

"Ron and Maureen are the perfect combination for a paranormal investigation. Ron brings his skepticism and his belief in equal measure, as his dowsing crystal and EMF meter testify, and Maureen is one of the most genuinely gifted mediums I know. Together they inform, entertain, and intrigue their guests, both on this side of the veil as well as those looking on from the other!"

—David Wells, *Most Haunted*

"Not since Hans Holzer and Sybil Leek has there been such a perfect ghost hunting team!"

—Christian Day, witch, Salem, Massachusetts

"If my experience in Gettysburg with Ron and Maureen is any indication of their other forays into the world of the paranormal, the reader is in for a thrill-filled ride!"

—Mark Nesbitt, author, historian, and paranormal investigator

"I've had the pleasure of taking part in a couple of investigations with the New England Ghost Project. I like to think I maintain a healthy skepticism, but Maureen Wood's abilities have left me seriously impressed. Ron Kolek manages to display a wry sense of humor while keeping a professional attitude toward his work. Together, they're entertaining, profoundly thought-provoking, and fun."

—Jeremy D'Entremont, author, historian for
the American Lighthouse Foundation

"Reading *The Ghost Chronicles* is like taking a joyride with your crazy uncle and favorite aunt—you know your parents probably wouldn't approve, but you can't wait to see what they'll do next."

—Lesley Bannatyne, author of
Halloween: An American History

the Ghost chronicles

A MEDIUM AND A PARANORMAL SCIENTIST INVESTIGATE 17 TRUE HAUNTINGS

MAUREEN WOOD & RON KOLEK

 SOURCEBOOKS, INC.®
NAPERVILLE, ILLINOIS

Published by Sourcebooks, Inc.
P.O. Box 4410, Naperville, Illinois 60567-4410
(630) 961-3900
Fax: (630) 961-2168
www.sourcebooks.com

Library of Congress Cataloging-in-Publication Data

Wood, Maureen.
  The ghost chronicles : a medium and a paranormal scientist investigate 17 true hauntings / by Maureen Wood and Ron Kolek.
      p. cm.
  1. Ghosts. 2. Haunted places. 3. Channeling. 4. Parapsychology. I. Kolek, Ron. II. Title.
  BF1461.W66 2009
  133.1--dc22

2009025669

Printed and bound in the United States of America

CHG 10 9 8 7 6 5 4 3 2 1

CONTENTS

Deep in the basement of the Windham Restaurant, Maureen trance channels an angry spirit. A confrontation develops between Ron and the spirit while reporters from Boston.com look on.

On her first investigation, Maureen joins Ron and the New England Ghost Project at the Windham Restaurant. This is the first of a four-part series with reporter Brian Bates and WNDS News.

The second in the four-part WNDS News series, the Ghost Project visits a B&B that was once the home of the niece of one of the ill-fated witches of Salem.

In the third of the four-part WNDS News series, Ron and Maureen visit Tortilla Flats in Merrimac, New Hampshire, a restaurant believed to have been a part of the Underground Railroad.

FOREWORD

Don't tread lightly into the realms of the paranormal, because it can be a dangerous place. There are so many other subjects that intersect with and overlap the topic of ghosts and hauntings, including psychological issues, religious beliefs, history, science, legends, and even popular culture. Don't think you know everything there is to know about ghosts because you watched a television program or two.

Do read on.

All over the planet there are individuals and groups whose passions involve paranormal investigation. These are folks who spend a great deal of time and their own money digging through old buildings, historical documents, and sometimes through the spirit world, looking for evidence of things that go bump in the night and answers to their own spiritual questions. Ron Kolek and Maureen Wood are two such people.

Think you have what it takes to hunt the supernatural? The demands often include all-night vigils in cold weather, waiting for something to happen. You hear a strange noise above you, and your senses come alive as the adrenaline courses through your veins. You think you're about to find indisputable proof of a haunting, only to discover it's just a raccoon in the attic. It's all part of the job. But once in a while, when conditions are right—and with a little bit of luck—something happens while you're watching and your cameras are rolling. It's these moments we all live for, when we brush the plane that exists between life and death, where ghosts—and sometimes darker forces—dwell. We gaze into the abyss, and the abyss gazes back.

What you're holding in your hands are some of the documented experiences and evidence collected by the New England Ghost Project. I've had the pleasure of knowing Ron and Maureen and working with them for several years now, and I can tell you that they bring total dedication to the subject of the paranormal.

Through hosting their popular radio show, their myriad investigations, and being out in the field for many years doing research, these folks are well-qualified to be your paranormal tour guides through some of their more fascinating cases.

New England is ripe with hauntings. Some paranormal legends go back generations and seem to hover over certain areas like a morning fog. When the stories become more than just tales, witnesses and families go looking for help, so they can better understand their situation or, worse, protect themselves from potential harm. In New England, when people ask around for someone who looks into these kinds of things, they often discover the New England Ghost Project.

When Ron, Maureen, and their team walk into a potential haunt, they're trying to establish contact. Maybe there's a mundane explanation for the phenomena, but maybe there isn't. Being psychic, Maureen will reach out to what may be waiting in any given location as Ron, with his EMF meters, cameras, and other equipment, attempts to scientifically validate any oddities in the environment. When his EMF meter beeps, and Maureen's face gets that faraway look, you know something is happening. I've watched Maureen's shoulders slump and her head drop, and I've heard her voice deepen as she takes on a new personality—channeling someone the rest of us can't see. Ron has seen this before and immediately reacts, asking questions of the "entity," but always mindful of Maureen's safety. If events turn violent, if Maureen starts to shake or swing her fists, Ron is there to subdue her, to bring Maureen back to our world, and to help her drive the entity back out.

When the information Maureen channels can be later verified by historical documents, you have what we in paranormal research call a home run. By combining scientific acumen with psychic intuition, Ron and Maureen bring you a complete picture of a haunting investigation. From lighthouses to spooky mansions, from ancient sites to private homes, this book takes you inside the haunts and into the world of a real paranormal investigation team.

Don't tread lightly as you read through the chronicles of the New England Ghost Project. Do know there are forces and realms we don't fully understand just yet.

—Jeff Belanger,
author of *The World's Most Haunted Places*
and founder of Ghostvillage.com

ACKNOWLEDGMENTS

MAUREEN

Dear Reader, thank you for taking this journey through *The Ghost Chronicles* and walking beside us as we encounter what may seem like surreal paranormal events. However, truth be told, these glimpses into our world, as the saying goes, are often stranger than fiction. So sit back and buckle yourself in, because you're in for a wild ride.

I'd like to thank a few of the special people in my life:

To my mother, Lorraine Couture, I thank you for quieting my fears while growing up as a medium and telling me without a shadow of a doubt that despite society's interpretation of *normal*, I was normal just the same. If it hadn't been for your acknowledgment of my gifts, I may not be as psychically open as I am today.

Jim and Marie Apitz, friends and family of my heart, thank you for being there in my tumultuous youth and believing in not only me, but also my blossoming, sometimes horrific, psychic abilities. It was through you both that I met my metaphysical mentor, Carol Waldie White, a woman who studied under Laurie Cabot, the official witch of Salem, Massachusetts, and who played an important role in teaching me how to control and not fear my gifts.

To the past and present members of the New England Ghost Project, you have always accepted me for who I am—thank you! Ron Kolek, my partner in crime, thank you for your open-mindedness, your strong faith, and for having my back when the going gets tough…and oh boy, can it get tough!

To my family and friends too numerous to mention, I thank you from the bottom of my heart for supporting me in all I do. Yet there are a few I must mention: To my sisters Donna Fereira and Evon Tudisco, thank you listening to my spirited tales and loving me all the same. And to my friends Bety Comerford, Debbie D'Orazio, and Marky Gibson, thank you for your guidance, love, and encouragement, and for helping to solidify my vision.

Deidre Knight, our agent: you are amazing! Thank you for your keen insight and persistence. Shana Drehs, thank you for sharing our vision in our quest to bring our stories to print and for having the patience of a saint to see it through.

Most importantly, I want to thank my husband, Stephen, and my children, Sabrina and Joshua. Stephen, I thank you for your warmth of spirit, for your patience and understanding, for your support, and for your unending encouragement in all my endeavors. But most of all I thank you for being my balance, for catching the occasional glimpse of my paranormal life (as, Reader, you will later attest to) and, to my amazement and my unyielding gratitude, still welcoming me by your side. I love you.

Sabrina and Joshua, thank you for believing in me. You are the light that guides me through any storm. I love you both with all my heart.

RON

When I founded the New England Ghost Project, I had no idea where it would take me. After all, my degree was in environmental science—who'd ever thought I'd be chasing ghosts? But it happened. Perhaps it is my scientific background that pushes me to find the truth. Whatever it is, it has become my mission. Like so many other people before me, I really don't care what others say or see; I want to experience it for myself. I want proof! It is that goal to which I strive. But what constitutes proof?

It would be great to be able to walk up to one of these spirits, touch its substance, and converse with it without the aid of a medium or psychic, but chances are, it ain't going to happen. So I strive for the next best thing: photographic, video, and audio evidence. It is these physical things that we are more apt to believe, and yet to the unbeliever, no amount of evidence will suffice. Therefore, it is my goal not to try to convince you, but rather to share my experiences as I walk along the thin line between the living and the dead.

I cannot say enough about the people who have helped me in my quest. From scientists to witches, from psychics to skeptics, they have all opened my eyes to the many paths I have traveled. I would especially like to thank Maureen Wood, my partner in this journey, who taught me the ways of the metaphysical; Janet, my faithful wife of thirty-six years, for putting up with me; Dr. Karen Da Silva, who saved my life and started me on this journey; the many members and former members of the New England Ghost Project, who have assisted me with this voyage; Brian the Monk and Jeff Belanger, my spiritual and literary mentors; Shana Drehs and Sourcebooks for giving me the opportunity to share my story; and most of all, my mother, Catherine Kolek, who never stopped praying for me.

So as you travel with me through the pages of this book, you will see what I have seen, hear what I have heard, and feel what I have felt. Is this proof of the existence of ghosts? You be the judge.

INTRODUCTION

Come with us on a journey to the unknown, the unexplained, and the unbelievable. Enter a world in which science and religion clash...or do they? The episodes in *The Ghost Chronicles* will test your senses and challenge your thinking. You will meet real people and hear real stories. But what will you believe?

Let the New England Ghost Project take you on a new kind of paranormal adventure, with investigators Ron Kolek and Maureen Wood leading the way.

Before we dive into the ghostly case files, there are a few things you may want to know:

Q: What is the New England Ghost Project?

RON: It's a select group of people who volunteer their time to investigate the paranormal. Our goals are to assist those in need and to educate the public.

Q: How did the Ghost Project start?

RON: It all started with me, New England's own Van Helsing, as I like to call myself. Back in the late 1990s, I cut my fingers off in an industrial accident. The doctors at the hospital were able to reattach them, but one of the doctors had a "feeling" that something was not quite right, so she sent me for a CAT scan. They discovered a pulmonary embolism, a blood clot that had traveled to my lungs, which usually results in death. But they rushed me to the ICU and saved my life. While in the ICU, I had a strange experience: I saw the light, if you will. Everything was bright white. I felt warm, as if I had come home, and there were people all in white (not doctors) and angelic music. Then all of a sudden, it all disappeared, like the closing of an iris. The bright white light was replaced by the dim lights of the ICU, the "people in white" were gone, and the pleasant sounds were replaced by the beat of my heart on the monitor.

When I was released by the hospital, I was no longer able to work, so I took a course in TV production. One of the course projects was to produce a show, and I decided to do the show on ghosts. It aired on local cable television and was so successful that WNDS in Derry, New Hampshire, picked it up. The more I investigated the paranormal, the more addicted I became to it. I started a website (it is the number one result when you Google "New England Ghost") on which I published my findings. As my notoriety grew, I began to meet various people who wished to join me in my quest for the unknown. Each person that I have accepted into the Ghost Project along the way brings a special skill or talent, making the Ghost Project a strong and resilient organization.

Q: How does the Ghost Project differ from other ghost-hunting groups out there?

RON: Some of the other ghost-hunting outfits focus primarily on debunking, using only scientific methods, whereas we capitalize on the unique pairing of a medium and a paranormal scientist, using both spiritual and scientific methods to investigate the paranormal. The Ghost Project goes into an investigation open-minded, using all of our equipment and techniques to discover the truth. We provide the client with the evidence we uncover, and it is ultimately up to him or her to make a decision as to what to do next and what to believe.

Q: Who's on the team?

RON: My partner is Maureen Wood, our psychic investigator and trance medium, and my co-host of the *Ghost Chronicles* radio show. My family is also involved—my son, Ron Jr., and my wife, Janet (also known as Saint Janet by most people, for putting up with my antics), help out as investigators. Various folks will float in and out of the episodes in this book: previous members of the team include Bob Corey and his wife, Gay, photographer Leo Monfet, and electronic voice phenomenon (EVP) specialist Karen Mossey. Current members include photographer Laura Wooster, EVP specialist Jim Stonier, tech manager Clay Rucker, thermal imaging specialist Dan Parsons, case manager Stacylynn Caira, and director of research Janet Rucker.

Q: How did Maureen get involved with the Ghost Project?

MAUREEN: Although I have been communicating with spirits all of my life, up until the day I joined the Ghost Project, I'd never worked with a paranormal investigative team. At a time in my life when the call to communicate with spirits could no longer be ignored, I happened across an article in a local New Hampshire newspaper. It featured a paranormal investigative team called the New England Ghost Project. After reading the article, and being a big believer that everything happens for a reason, I quickly emailed Ron. Curious, he invited me to tag along on the first of a four-part series with WNDS television in Derry, New Hampshire. Episode Two depicts that first investigation with Ron's team: my "audition," if you will. I guess I did something right, because not long after I was invited to join. And as Ron frequently says, the rest is history.

RON: I didn't believe in psychics when I started the Ghost Project. In fact, I always thought they were charlatans. But once I started working with Maureen, I began to realize that there was more truth to psychics and mediums than I had first believed. With a degree in environmental science, I still consider myself a skeptic, but open-minded enough to investigate the possibilities.

In fact, that's why I call myself New England's own Van Helsing. The real Van Helsing comes from Bram Stoker's *Dracula*—like me, he was a man of science, yet well versed in the arts and crafts. I didn't believe in a lot of the metaphysical techniques that you'll read about later in this book, but I have come to understand and accept and even use them.

Q: What's the deal with the typeface changing?

RON: Throughout the book you'll notice two different fonts: one for Maureen's voice, and one for mine. Telling our stories in the first person makes for a much more visceral experience, but we wanted it to be clear who was doing the talking.

Q: How did Maureen know she was a psychic? What is a trance medium, anyway?

MAUREEN: I've been seeing and hearing spirits all my life, but it was difficult to realize what was going on. Think of how many little kids have imaginary friends. That's not to say those imaginary friends are all spirits, but I wouldn't rule it out. When we're young, our minds are completely open. It's not until well-meaning teachers, parents, media, etc., tell us that what we are experiencing is not real that we begin to think it's nothing more than our imagination. That we need to show them proof, you know, they-will-believe-it-if-they-see-it syndrome.

I love *Ghost Whisperer*, but medium work is not as Hollywood as the show. Let me start by explaining the differences between a medium and a trance medium. Being a trance medium means having the ability to share the spirit's energy. A trance medium can allow spirits to enter and speak through her, which is called "channeling" or "trance channeling." On the other hand, a medium picks up information from the spirits and relays it—they are not actually using her voice to speak.

It's difficult to explain exactly what happens when I trance channel, but when we are investigating, I open myself up. Sometimes the spirits are timid, not strong enough, or not cognizant of how to share energy, to allow me to trance channel. Other times, the spirit is all too eager to speak through me.

Most times, I have control of who I channel. But when I open myself up to spirits, it's possible for another, not so nice spirit, to jump in.

I'm also empathic. Which means I can feel the spirit, their energy, and, sometimes, how they died. Ron calls me the Queen of Pain, because sometimes those experiences can be extremely painful.

Q: How does the Ghost Project find new investigations?

RON: We're often contacted through referrals, our website, and the Ghost Line (as we refer to the phone number for the New

England Ghost Project). Ninety percent of our cases are those in which people are looking for verification that they aren't crazy. They just want to know if they have ghosts or not. Sometimes we're contacted by the media, who want to see what we do.

Q: What tools do you use to conduct an investigation?

RON: On one hand there's the research arm of the Ghost Project. Janet Rucker, who holds a degree in library science, heads up that end of the investigating, which involves discovering the details of a particular location or person—the history of a property, genealogies, etc.

But that takes place back at the office. On location, we have two types of tools. The first is Maureen, who uses her abilities to discover any paranormal activity. One of her methods is dowsing, a centuries-old way to use your own sixth sense, an extension of yourself, to tap into various energies. When you read about her using a pendulum or L-rods, that's what's going on. Although she doesn't need a device to speak to the spirits, she uses it as a visual tool for those present during communication with a spirit.

From the paranormal science perspective, we use a lot of equipment: a thermal imaging camera (which is used to view temperature differences), an electromagnetic field (EMF) meter (used to measure fluctuations in electromagnetic fields), and ultraviolet (UV) lamp (used to detect bodily fluids and dust particles in an environment). We also use infrared (IR) camcorders to see in low light, along with still cameras, both digital and 35mm, with infrared film (it's believed that spirits dwell in the infrared range). Infrared film is expensive, however, and it has to be treated very carefully. Because it's heat sensitive you need to load and unload the film in a black bag and the film has to be refrigerated. We also use hand-held digital recorders to gather EVPs.

Q: What exactly is an EVP?

RON: EVP stands for electronic voice phenomenon, also known as "voices of the dead." We cannot hear EVPs as they happen; we can only hear them played back on a recorder. The spirits use the white noise in a recorder to manipulate energy to manifest their voices. Any digital or analog recorder will work. Ironically, the more inexpensive recorders are better, since they have more static/white noise. The recordings are then cleaned up and amplified through a software program like Cool Edit, allowing the listener to decipher the words more clearly.

Q: How much do you charge for an investigation?

RON: I've heard this question numerous times so I've almost come to expect it. The simple answer is: we don't charge.

Now you might be wondering how we get paid.

The truth is we don't. It's voluntary. Since I started the Ghost Project, I made the decision that we shouldn't profit at the expense of someone in need. We all have day jobs: I'm an author and radio show host, Maureen is an author, radio host, and a technical instructor. My wife, Janet, and Stacy are both administrators, Ron Jr. is a manager, thermal Dan is an assistant fire chief, Jim and Clay both work with computers, and Janet Rucker is a librarian. However, we do run lectures, seminars, and classes throughout the year to help cover the cost of our websites, the Ghost Line, film, equipment, and so forth.

Q: What do you consider a successful investigation?

RON: When we go into an investigation, we never know what we're going to encounter. The EVPs, photos, psychic impressions, video, and any other evidence collected during an investigation are reviewed, and we provide our clients with the results, whether there is paranormal activity or not.

Some cases may require special treatment, including spirit removal and/or exorcisms. At the NEGP, we want to help both the living and the dead, but it's our belief that everyone has free will. Unless a spirit is crossing the "karmic line," which we consider to be interfering with the living, we don't force them to leave. But we do ask the spirits if they want to leave. Believe it or not, most times they don't.

To be honest, we can never be 100 percent sure why spirits are here. Maureen can tell you what she's feeling and what she's picking up on. But it's conjecture. What if a spirit is here to help another, living or dead? What if that spirit is part of a bigger master plan? We don't want to interfere by forcing an entity to do anything. So while many people might consider eradicating the ghosts as a successful operation, that's not what the NEGP sets out to do.

Q: And you have a radio show?

RON: As I mentioned before, part of the goal of the New England Ghost Project is to educate the public. To do this we always accept offers to appear on various radio and TV stations. One day after an appearance on WCCM radio in Lawrence, Massachusetts, the station asked me if I would be interested in having my own show. Never shy, I jumped at the chance and on Friday the thirteenth, 2004, *Ghost Chronicles* was born. For three years Maureen and I entertained the rush hour traffic (our motto for the show was, "Rush hour just got scarier"). We were then approached by Ghostvillage (the largest paranormal site on the Internet) and TogiNet (an Internet radio station), and now I produce and host three shows: *Ghost Chronicles*, the podcast on Ghostvillage, iTunes, and Podcast Alley; *Ghost Chronicles Live* on TogiNet and Para-X Radio; and *Ghost Chronicles International*, which is UK–based, on TogiNet and Para-X Radio.

In addition to our studio shows we also take "road trips" and broadcast from haunted locations…which is what the seventeen episodes you're about to read are all about.

Be prepared for the unexpected.

DISCLAIMER

The contents of this book are for informational purposes only. Although these episodes are based on factual events, under no circumstances should they be interpreted as a recommendation for novice or inexperienced paranormal investigators. In no way will the New England Ghost Project or any of its entities be held liable for misinterpretation of this book or any companion websites.

BOOK BONUS EXTRA

To enhance your reading experience, go to www. ghostchroniclesthebook.com. This site includes bonus features such as photographs, video, history, and additional information on the places and incidents described in each episode of this book.

CHANNELING THE DEAD

CASE FILE: 6242684
WINDHAM RESTAURANT

Location: Windham, New Hampshire.

History: An 1812 farmhouse, once owned by the Dinsmore family, has been occupied by several businesses and now houses the Windham Restaurant.

Reported Paranormal Activity: Ghostly apparitions, glasses shattering, objects moving and disappearing, and unexplained noises.

Clients: Lula (owner), Vess (owner).

Investigators: Ron (lead investigator), Maureen (trance medium).

Press: Melissa (reporter from Boston.com), Jen (Melissa's photographer).

*The sign over the door of the Windham Restaurant reads
"Food and Spirits," and it may be truer than you think.*

Bruce Preston

TRANCE MEDIUM

An individual who allows the spirit of a dead person to take
over his or her body for the purpose of communication.

I could scarcely breathe.

The beating grew louder and louder. I thought my heart might burst.

I gasped for breath.

Then I felt a hand on my chest. It was oddly familiar, and I realized it was my own. My breathing was heavy. Raspy.

I clung to the banter between Ron and the reporters from Boston. com, who were standing a few feet away from me, but the crisp, clear syllables of their words became nothing more than an echo in the distance. Even my fear of spiders in the dank cellar was slipping away. I could no longer focus. There was no turning back.

I had reached the "in between," the place where heaven barely touches earth. I knew because I could feel it. The air was charged, sizzling with electricity. The way it always felt when "they" arrived. An ominous presence swirled around us, bringing with it a sense of foreboding. I had a feeling this night was a bad idea. It was Friday the thirteenth after all.

Playing a tug of war with my consciousness, I struggled to recapture Ron's voice.

"You ready to communicate?" I barely heard his words over the electromagnetic field (EMF) meter, its continuous beeping an indicator of an energy shift in the room.

The immediacy in his voice anchored me. For the moment.

"Yeah, sure," I said.

EMF (ELECTROMAGNETIC FIELD) METER

A handheld electronic device used to measure electromagnetic radiation in milligauss. This instrument is widely used by paranormal investigators to identify normal sources of EMF, such as fluorescent lights and electrical wiring, as well as unexplained sources of EMF associated with paranormal activity.

I could tell by the look of concern on Ron's face that my response sounded a little flippant. What could I say? I was getting punchy. It was nearing the midnight hour, and this was the second event of my evening. Just prior to coming to the Windham, I'd given a lecture for the Ghost Project at a fundraiser for the Dracut Republican Town Committee. The long hours working with the NEGP, coupled with my nine-to-five, could sometimes be a bit much.

My energy was waning. The last thing I felt like doing was attempting to communicate. Yet I could tell by the sudden onset of energy that this spirit was just as eager to converse with us as Ron was to talk with him. The energy surge was so full and heavy it felt as if the walls themselves were closing in on me.

Suddenly feeling claustrophobic, I took a step back and widened the space between the reporters and myself, with Ron closer to me. I bumped into a white restaurant-sized freezer, tucked away in the basement, the storage area of the Windham. I clutched a pendulum between my thumb and forefinger.

Then it happened.

The weighted crystal began to swing to and fro. My third eye tingled. Vibrated. A pinwheel of energy enveloped my face. The spirit wanted more. More than just to speak *to* us. He wanted to speak *through* me. As someone who has channeled and spoken with the dead for much of my life, it was a difficult demand for me to ignore. Just then, my breath caught in my throat as my body struggled to adjust to the presence pouring through me. To compensate, my chest heaved up. Down. Once again, my breathing turned raspy. Heavy. Labored. The sound of Ron's voice faded into the distance. It was like being given anesthesia, that final countdown as you prepare to go under into the abyss of unconsciousness. Ten, nine, eight…I breathed in and out, adjusting as best I could. No matter how many times I allow a spirit access to my body, I always take the prospect very seriously. Truth be told, dealing with the unknown is a risky business. I never know what I will come up against. Will it be a nice, benevolent spirit just wanting to communicate? A negative spirit intent on doing harm to others or myself? Or even worse, a demonic entity, attempting to steal my soul? It's my belief, however, that for the greater good, it's worth the risk.

I closed my eyes, and began to say a silent prayer. "Saint Michael the Archangel, defend us in battle." Gasping for breath, I continued. "Be our protection against the wickedness and snares of the Devil. May God…rebuke…him, we…"

It was too late now. My consciousness vanished into the darkness. My body was no longer my own. Jacob was here.

* * *

Even though the red light of my EMF meter lit up Maureen, because she was bent at the waist, I couldn't see her eyes, and that physical sign is crucial when she's channeling. "Who am I speaking with?" I exclaimed urgently. "Is it Maureen or Jacob?"

Bruce Preston

Bent over in the corner of the cellar of the Windham Restaurant, Maureen attempts to make contact with a spirit named Jacob.

Her only response was a deep moan, followed by a succession of slow, arduous breaths.

I crouched low and looked up at her face. As if Jacob was reading my mind, Maureen brought her head up, slowly. Her stare burned. Her eyes were deep. Piercing. It was a look that would rip a hole through the soul of any man. I was looking into the sinister abyss. I had no doubts. It was Jacob.

"Ah, Jacob, how are you, sir?" I said in greeting.

As he spoke through Maureen, his guttural tone grated on my ears. "Why are you back?"

"Don't you like us here?" I asked.

Through drawn eyebrows, Jacob glared at me. "No." I shivered, as the chill in his voice mirrored the sudden drop in the room's temperature.

"Why?" I prodded.

Maureen spoke, but it was Jacob's voice. "Speak when you are spoken to!"

Any of my team will tell you I'm never one to back down during tense investigations—not even in the face of an irritated spirit like this one—and Jacob's resistance only added fuel to my resolve. Undaunted, I challenged him. "Jacob, what is your last name?"

Ignoring my inquiry, Maureen continued to gasp for breath.

Still bent over to avoid the low-hanging pipes, she slowly turned her head and stared across the cobweb-laden beams to where Vess cowered behind rusty shelves.

"Why do they hide?" A sneer crossed Maureen's lips. "They've seen me before."

Vess's eyes grew wide. Realizing he was the focus of Jacob's wrath, he staggered backward, swiping at a rack of wait staff uniforms obstructing his path. He made a hasty retreat, stumbling up the stairs to the safety of the restaurant's bar. Or so he thought.

Maureen slammed the side of the cooler with her fist. "I have papers buried here."

"Where?" I asked, grateful that we were finally getting somewhere.

"In this basement."

Still crouching on the floor, I looked up once again at Maureen, seeing the intensity in her eyes. Her raspy breathing abruptly turned to painful moans. Concerned for her well-being, I hesitated for a moment. You see, Maureen and I have had numerous discussions regarding her safety, about how far is too far, and when it's time to end communication in order to protect her—both spiritually and physically. Almost always, she tells me that I break her channeling line too soon, so despite the increasing tension of this particular situation with Jacob, I decided to take the risk and forged ahead, despite her apparent discomfort.

Wait. *Buried in the basement*? My excitement fizzled as I looked at the concrete floor. There would be no digging through that. "Do you want us to find them?" I asked, realizing the absurdity of my question.

Maureen clenched her teeth, seemingly seething in pain. The eerie silence of the moment shattered as another tormented groan echoed off the walls.

That's it. I'd had enough. Deep in the recess of my mind, somewhere in my subconscious, dwelled an unspeakable fear: that one day we'd confront such evil that no matter how strong my resolve, Maureen would be lost. This would not be that day. Whether she liked it or not, we were done.

"Push him out!" I exclaimed. "Maureen, push him out."

Once more I commanded as I reached for her arm. "Push—him—out."

Jacob became enraged by my interference. Taking advantage of my awkward crouch, he shoved me and the powerful thrust hurled me on my ass. Momentarily stunned, I pushed myself up off the cold floor and brushed away the gravel embedded in my palms.

Undisturbed by his attack, I turned my focus to Maureen's dilemma. "Push him out, Maureen. Push—him—out."

The sudden whoosh of Maureen's forearm sent me flying against the uneven surface of the stone wall. Ignoring the stabbing pain in my back, I forced myself to regain my stance. More determined than ever, I grabbed her arm. She attempted to jerk free of my hold, but this time I was ready—I held my ground.

"I need my—" Jacob stopped mid-growl.

"You need what? You have something to say, than say it!"

Maureen's body stiffened. Then: "This is my house!"

"Fine," I replied. "Do you have anything to say? If you don't, then leave this body—now. I command you. Leave. This. Body. Now. It's not yours!"

Maureen stood bent over, her nails digging into her faded jeans. And, as always, I waited for the sign, the indication that she'd returned to the living. And then I got it: she raised her head and leveled her stare, and the piercing eyes were gone. Jacob had left.

Her breathing became less labored. "Are you all right?" I asked, my heart still pounding.

"Yes." Although in her early forties, she flexed her fingers like a sixty-year-old woman stricken with arthritis. Still grasping the pendulum, and slowly gathering strength, she avoided eye contact. Through several more deep breaths, she sighed, "He's still around."

"Yeah, I know." Although my EMF meter had gone deathly silent, somehow I knew that Jacob was still here. The eight years of working with Maureen had opened me up to instinct more than I care to admit.

Drawn to the sound of shattering glass, we suddenly remembered our audience. Melissa, the reporter from Boston.com, and her photographer, Jen, had knocked over some extra dinnerware. Cautiously they stepped over the shards of broken glass and approached us.

"Is she all right?" Melissa asked, her voice not but a whisper. On the hunt for a Halloween story, they had stumbled upon the New England Ghost Project website and called the Ghost Line to see if they could tag along to document an investigation. Perhaps we'd given them more than what they were looking for.

"Yeah. But give us a minute."

Eager to leave, Maureen took a step toward the stairs, but one leg buckled beneath her. I grabbed her arm and slowly guided her across the cellar. As we reached the stairs I turned to find the two reporters sheepishly following behind. Even in the faint light of the basement their pale faces spoke volumes. "Are you two okay?"

Silently, they turned to each other, exchanging a fleeting look. Almost in unison they answered, "Yes." Their voices said *yes* but their eyes said *no*. I smirked.

Lula, Vess's partner in crime, greeted us at the top of the stairs, "What did you do to Vess? He came running up the stairs like a little girl!" she exclaimed in a rich, Greek accent.

We followed Lula down the hallway to the restaurant's bar. As we approached the staircase that led to the second floor, Maureen sat down on the steps. "I'll join you guys in a minute."

Vess was tucked into the farthest corner of the room, a distraught look on his face. "What's the matter, old man?" I called. "Looks like you've seen a ghost."

"I'll tell you, Ron, you've been in here quite a few times, and I've never been scared. But tonight…I've never seen Maureen like that. If she would have come near me, I would've hit her with a two-by-four and gladly gone to jail."

Maureen poked her head around the corner and peered into the room. "Excuse me, Vess," Maureen paused. "You were going to do what?"

Stunned, Vess turned around to face Maureen as she stepped closer to him. "I—I—I—You don't understand. You should have seen how you looked at me. I know it was you. But it wasn't," he said.

"You would have hit me? Then what?" Maureen asked, her lips twitching slightly into a smile.

"I would have hit you, then dealt with the consequences later."

We all burst out laughing.

"Can I ask you a couple of questions?" Melissa asked, timidly approaching Maureen. "I must say, I was a little nervous down there in the basement. I've never witnessed someone channel a spirit before." She paused. "I'm curious. When did you first discover that you could speak to ghosts?"

"My mother tells me that the ability to hear and see spirits has been in our family for generations. But I also think my near-death experience at the age of three opened me up to the paranormal even more."

"At three years old? You were so young. How could you possibly remember the experience?"

"I realize I was young, but even now, the memories of that day are extremely vivid." Maureen cleared her throat. "I had come down with spinal meningitis. While in the hospital, I remember the joy I felt at leaving the excruciating pain behind in my heavy, weighted body. The body that felt separate from me. Distant even. It was then that I realized that I'd floated toward the ceiling. I looked on as the doctor and his nurses worked frantically over my pale, still form laying face down on the gurney. Just as a priest began to administer last rites, I thought of my parents and suddenly found myself hovering above them. There they were, huddling beneath a flickering fluorescent light, staring into space. I moved in closer to get their attention, but instead, they looked right through me, as tears streamed down their cheeks. I tried to reach out to them, to tell them I was okay, that I was there. That they shouldn't cry. Then, without pause, I felt myself careening backward. Pulled back into the emergency room, and into my body. The sudden onset of pain was so horrific, I blacked out. When I awoke, I felt different somehow. Older."

"That's unbelievable," Melissa said. "But, how do you know it wasn't a hallucination?"

"Like I said, it was so vivid. Years later, still plagued by the experience, I told it to my parents. To all of our surprise, they validated what I had seen, the description of the doctor, the priest, and even down to the colors of the drab green tiles lining the emergency room. While growing up, I would often tell my mother about the 'friends' that were visiting me at all hours of the day and night. She comforted me by giving me a hug, a bottle of holy water, and telling me not to worry about it, that I was normal. I believed her. Until I got older that is and realized that not everyone was experiencing what I was. At least not to the same extreme."

HOLY WATER

Ordinary water that has been sanctified by a priest or bishop for the purpose of blessing persons, places, or things. It is most notable for its use in baptism but it can also be used for protection, whether safeguarding equipment from malfunctioning or batteries from draining, or preventing unwanted spirits from following one home by blessing the windows of a car. A blessing is done by dipping ones finger in the holy water, making the sign of the cross, and saying, "Bless and protect this vehicle and all those who occupy it from all unwanted energies. In the name of the Father, Son, and Holy Spirit, Amen." Holy water can also be used in healing and in exorcisms.

"So, getting back to what I witnessed downstairs," Melissa said. "Maureen, could you tell me what it's like when you channel?"

"Well, when I'm sensing them, my third eye is going crazy." Maureen placed her index finger to a spot between her eyes. "My whole face and head get tingly. When the energy gets really strong, and I'm letting them trance channel through me, I open a part of me up that lets them come through. But when they do, sometimes the energy is so strong that my arms go numb. My legs go numb. Because the energy is just so intense. It's almost as if they have a chance to be alive again. So whenever they can, they love to go into a body."

I chimed in, "Imagine if you couldn't talk for a hundred and fifty years and you had the opportunity, wouldn't you be all over it?"

Melissa thumbed on her digital camera, and started scrolling through shots of the night.

"So what are you going to do with this stuff?" Maureen asked.

"We're going to put together an audio slide show which will permanently be on Boston.com."

"Cool," I said, excited that it would be so widely available, and then I saw the look of shock on Maureen's face. "Oh. Did I forget to tell you that?"

"It'll be up forever? Great," Maureen replied. Her reaction reminded me, once again, of her sensitivity about what she does. While an article on the Internet meant "forever" coverage for me, for Maureen it unearthed a host of concerns in terms of her name and reputation being "out there."

"You two sound like an old married couple," Melissa said.

"I don't *think* so," we blurted out in unison.

The corners of Melissa's mouth twisted up in a smile. "Yeah," she laughed. "Anyway, let's get serious. How did you guys meet?"

As if in response to Melissa's question, the EMF meter I had left lying on the bar began to blink and beep wildly. I couldn't help but notice Vess out of the corner of my eye as he fumbled for his shot glass and threw down another one. I looked to Maureen and she to me. We didn't need words—Jacob had joined us again.

Melissa's voice quaked over the incessant beeping of the meter. "Is this normal?"

"Define normal." I placed my hand on my chin, like Sherlock Holmes in *The Hound of the Baskervilles*. "Actually, let me tell you about the first time Maureen joined the New England Ghost Project on an investigation and the first time we met the spirit named Jacob. It was right here at the Windham Restaurant..."

RESULTS OF THE INVESTIGATION

Maureen's trance channeling of the spirit referred to as Jacob revealed that he had papers
buried in the basement. Now that the floor is
concrete, there is little chance of ever finding
them. Additional investigations of the Windham
would be required to learn more about Jacob and
his papers. But Boston.com got what they were
after, their Halloween story.

You can see and hear Melissa's slideshow pre-
sentation of *Channeling the Dead* on Boston.
com by going to: http://www.boston.com/travel/
explorene/specials/halloween/newenglandg-
hostproject/ or by going to the New England
Ghost Project site at www.neghostproject.
com and clicking on the photo of the Windham
Restaurant.

FIRST CONTACT

CASE FILE: 6231963
WINDHAM RESTAURANT

Location: Windham, New Hampshire.

History: An 1812 farmhouse, once owned by the Dinsmore family, has been occupied by several businesses and now houses the Windham Restaurant.

Reported Paranormal Activity: Ghostly apparitions, glasses shattering, objects moving and disappearing, and unexplained noises.

Clients: Lula (owner), Vess (owner).

Investigators: Ron (lead investigator), Maureen (trance medium), Leo (photographer), Ron Jr. (investigator), Bob (investigator/videographer), Gay (Bob's wife/investigator).

Press: Brian Bates (news reporter from WNDS television), Tom (Brian's cameraman).

It was late at night when we arrived at the Windham for our first Ghost Project investigation with Maureen. We were accompanied by Brian Bates, a reporter for WNDS in Derry, New Hampshire, who wanted to do a four-part series on haunted places in New England. Because I had worked with WNDS television in the past, he asked if he could accompany us on an investigation.

The Windham has an unsettling eeriness to it, which is reflected in the wooden sign hanging above its sturdy white door. "Food and Spirits," it simply reads. *How damn appropriate*, I thought the first time I saw it.

As we approached the nearly two-hundred-year-old building, a feeling of apprehension swept over the group, and a rather large group it was. In addition to Maureen and me, the Ghost Project contingent included our photographer Leo, our investigator Bob and his wife, Gay, Ron Jr., and our two special guests from WNDS television, Brian and his cameraman Tom.

As we reached the front door, it suddenly swung open. The lights from inside cast a shadow, revealing the silhouettes of our hosts. Lula, although dwarfed by her partner Vess's presence, beamed with life. She gave me a hug and invited us in. I introduced myself to Vess and shook his hand. One touch of his uncalloused hand, and I knew without a doubt that he was the chef.

Vess had heard about the Ghost Project from one of his patrons. Anxious to verify his and his partner's belief that the building was indeed haunted, they called the Ghost Line. Our initial research of the building revealed that the restaurant was located in an old farmhouse built around 1812 by the Dinsmore family. Isaac Dinsmore and then his son, Horace, lived in the house for many years. Later it was occupied by several businesses before finally becoming the Windham Restaurant. We were as anxious to investigate it as Vess and Lula were.

As I entered the restaurant I scanned for a place to set up base camp. I couldn't help but notice the warm glow of a fireplace through a set of French doors. The chill in my bones made my decision easy: we'd use the dining room.

BASE CAMP

A control station that remotely monitors and records the activities of the investigation in real time. This is done by placing remote temperature gauges, video cameras, and other recording equipment throughout the investigation site, prior to doing a building-wide sweep to check for paranormal activity. The base camp is in constant contact with the investigators via two-way radios.

I slid a chair in front of the fireplace. Brian and Tom, taking my cue, set up their camera for the shoot, as did Bob, our videographer.

"Can I get you guys something to drink?" Vess asked.

"No, thanks. I think we'll just get started." I looked around. "Are the waitresses here?"

"Nah. They're too shy to talk on camera. So I'm it."

Not wanting to be influenced by the interview, Maureen left the room, closing the French doors behind her.

Sitting in a chair, a glass of Merlot in his hand, Vess began to tell his story as the fire crackled behind him.

"My name is Vess Liakas, and I'm the owner of the Windham Restaurant. Since I've owned this place, many strange things have occurred here that I can't explain."

"Like what?" I asked.

"The chairs on the second floor would be turned around facing the window, like somebody was watching a parade coming up the street. Other times we would find the silverware and place settings on some of the tables out of place or gone missing." Taking a moment, he sipped from his wine glass.

"After locking up in the evening, we would return in the morning to find windows opened, faucets running, and lights on." He shook his head in disbelief. "We even lost an expensive set of dishes in the kitchen when they flew off the rack and smashed on to the floor."

"Has anybody else seen anything unusual?"

"Customers and the wait staff have seen a little boy, a girl, and a man in a blue suit that the staff named Jacob. In fact, one night my partner Lula saw a man fall down the stairs, and when she ran to help him, he was gone. Vanished into thin air. Now she refuses to be here alone."

"Anything else?"

"Oh, yeah. Pagers and deodorizers are constantly having their batteries drained with no logical explanation. Sometimes when the staff needs to go into the basement to get something, they hear a man clear his throat when no one is down there." Vess rolled his eyes. "I can even remember a time when I was in the kitchen preparing a meal and the shrimp disappeared off the plate. I looked everywhere, but I couldn't find it. It was gone. In seconds."

As I listened, I couldn't help but have my doubts about *that* story. Just as I finished the interview, I could feel a surge of cold air rush by me, causing the little hairs at the base of my neck to stand at attention.

"Something's here!" Bob said with a broad grin. He felt it too.

We didn't have to be told. But just as quickly as it had appeared, it was gone.

It was time to see if we could find any evidence to validate the stories we had just heard. Maureen rejoined us and we gathered up our equipment to do a sweep of the building, while Ron Jr. monitored base camp. During a "sweep," we go from room to room looking for evidence of ghostly activity, such as EMF spikes, unexplained temperature fluctuations, psychic impressions, EVPs, as well as video and photographic evidence.

EVP (ELECTRONIC VOICE PHENOMENA)

When a spirit manifests its voice by manipulating the white noise on a recorder. The voices of the dead are not heard by the naked ear, but are heard later upon playback.

It was now time to try out my brand new EMF meter, something I was pretty excited about.

After assembling the group, with meter in hand, I turned to Maureen. "Okay Maureen, you ready? Let's see what you can do."

* * *

With a sweep of Ron's arm, he indicated I should get a move on. "Where do you want to go?" he asked. "Lead the way."

Lead the way? Was he kidding? Not wanting to look inept, I plastered on a makeshift smile and prayed I appeared more confident than I felt.

The nervous energy I'd been fighting since I'd opened my eyes to start the day continued to gnaw at me. Before leaving my house that evening, I'd pulled a few tarot cards from my Voyager deck to gain some insight on what type of evening to expect.

I've been reading tarot cards all my life as a tool to connect me with other people's pasts, presents, and futures. I don't usually read for myself, but it isn't every day that I'm invited to join a team of paranormal investigators in search of communing with the dead. To gather my nerve, I visualized the two cards I'd pulled: the Sensor, a sign to me that my senses were in overdrive, and the Magician, a card of dreams realized and manifestation. Although it was too early to know for sure, I'd say that the "manifestation" card was right on the mark. I'd known it the second I'd walked into the Windham Restaurant. The air danced with electricity, a sure sign to me that it was haunted, inhabited by an earthbound spirit.

Finishing our sweep of the first floor, we climbed the stairs to the second floor, Ron directly behind me with his EMF meter and the remainder of his team nipping at his heels. As we walked through the second floor of the restaurant, I felt a presence. Intuitively I knew it was a male spirit. By the weight of the energy, the lightness, and the fleeting feel of it, I knew he remained at a distance. His presence wisped around us, darting too and fro, coming close, then retreating just as quickly as he'd come. Having had more than twenty-five years, experience in dealing with the paranormal, I knew this activity meant the spirit was just as curious about us as we were about him.

That all changed a few moments later, when we walked into the room Ron referred to as the wait station, an undersized prep area with coolers, a sink, a counter, and some small appliances. The second we crossed the threshold, the atmosphere became dense and statically charged—it grabbed me like a live wire. It was the same feeling I'd experienced when we had first arrived. I glanced at Ron.

"A male spirit is here, and he is anxious to speak."

We positioned ourselves to make communication. *What was I thinking*? The anxiety I'd been feeling up to now suddenly turned to claustrophobia as each member of our party filed in one by one. Ron stood to my right, Brian Bates to my left, Leo beneath the entranceway, and Tom, the cameraman, kneeling between us, the light of his camera burning my retinas.

"You ready?" Ron asked.

Gingerly I nodded my head. With all eyes on me, I began to feel a bit self-conscious. I'd never been on an outing with the group, and I was terrified of failing them. Although Ron hadn't expressed any fears about the evening's success, I sensed the New England Ghost Project had a lot riding on this investigation, especially with the television cameras rolling. I didn't want to let them down.

Whether I liked it or not, there was no turning back. I pulled out my pendulum.

Although the spirits communicate with me in numerous ways, spiritual dowsing acts as a visual tool for those who are present to take an active role in the communication, so I'd decided to start with that.

SPIRITUAL DOWSING

Using a pendulum (a weighted bobber on a string or chain) to communicate with the dead via a series of rotations. The various rotations indicate "yes," "no," and "maybe" responses, and they vary from person to person depending upon each one's own energy.

I lifted my pendulum between my thumb and forefinger, waiting for it to sway.

"How does that thing work?" Ron asked. By the eagerness in his voice, I knew I'd captured his attention.

"I'm using my psychic ability to tap into the energy around us. You know, that sixth sense that so many people forget about. First I make a connection. I mentally open myself up to energy that is reaching out to me. When my third eye begins to pulsate we begin to ask the spirit questions."

I started off with the usual questions.

"What is a yes?"

The pendulum swung counterclockwise, indicating what a yes response would be.

"What is a no?"

The pendulum slowed, stopped, and began its circular swing to a clockwise rotation, indicating a no response.

"What is a maybe?"

Once again, the pendulum indicated its response; it slowed its movement then swung to and fro in a back and forth motion.

"Is there someone here with us?" I asked.

The pendulum swung counterclockwise. A yes.

But I didn't need a pendulum to tell me that. I already knew.

"Are you a woman?"

The response was clockwise: no.

"Are you a man?"

The brass bobber rotated counterclockwise once again.

"Is your name Jacob?"

I knew intuitively it was, and then the pendulum gave a resounding yes.

"Can you feel this?" I asked Ron, excited that the spirit seemed to have been touched by the last question. Almost as if the mere mention of the name Jacob had garnered the ghost's undivided attention.

"Feel what?"

"The air. It's different. Heavy." It wasn't just heavy; it was inhabited. But how could I tell Ron that? It was the first night out with the group, and I wanted to be on my best behavior. Well, at the very least, I didn't want him to think I was crazy.

"You don't feel that?" I asked, sensing the weight of energy hovering above us.

Like a minnow chasing a shiny fishing lure, Ron became distracted by the sudden blaring of his EMF meter.

My attention returned to the spirit reaching out to us. My third eye pulsated with energy. It was spiraling, consuming my whole face in sizzling electricity. The heavy energy sapped my breath as if stones had been laid upon my chest.

A random thought popped into my mind, and with it a feeling of rage. Gathering strength, I moaned, "He's not happy with the changes in the restaurant." I turned to meet Ron's glare over the glowing red light of his EMF meter. "This is his home. He doesn't like what's going on."

"Tough. Tell him to get over it."

My mouth said, "Be nice," but my mind thought, *What a jerk.* Was he serious? Weren't we here to help the spirits too?

An oddly familiar voice entered my mind, diverting my attention away from Ron's momentary lack of respect. It was the reporter, Brian Bates. I could feel his thoughts; his unspoken words burned me to the core. He thought this was all a sham and that I was completely nuts. Not that I'm unfamiliar with this type of reaction to what I do, since I'd faced it all my life, but for some reason, this time I took it to heart. Maybe it was because I'd wanted to make such a good impression with the New England Ghost Project . I suddenly felt like a fool in front of the camera. The fact that Brian didn't believe me really pissed me off.

As if *my* thoughts were being flashed on a neon sign, an awkward silence filled the room. Once again Jacob's energy grew stronger, and in a flash, I felt his anger reach out to me. Brian's refusal to acknowledge Jacob's existence had gravely insulted him. On some twisted level, I couldn't help but agree. The silence erupted as a voice crackled over the radio.

It was the base camp. "The temperature's dropped to 66.6 degrees!"

I felt his presence gathering more strength. Then—*bam.* Jacob's energy tore through my abdomen like a freight train, doubling me over in pain. My body was a conduit, channeling a surge of supernatural energy. Instantaneously, the force barreling through me triggered the coffeemaker on the counter, turning it on. We jumped at the sound of suddenly spurting coffee.

Ron Kolek

An infrared photo taken at the time of the incident captures an energy spike surging through the coffee machine.

The faint aroma permeated the air. Feeling like I'd just been knocked over with a wrecking ball, I clutched my abdomen in an attempt to catch my breath.

"What the hell was that?" Brian shouted. He bolted for the door, not even waiting for a reply.

Over the buzzing in my ears, the frantic chatter of the rest of the group became nothing but a jumble in my mind.

Although Ron and I had worked together for no more than several hours at this point, he sensed my agony. "That's it. Let's get out of here."

Ron grabbed my arm and guided me out of the wait station. His well-meaning efforts irritated me though. As he patted my back to comfort me, I inwardly shrugged him away, wanting nothing more than to cower in the corner and ride out the residual energy left like a fingerprint on my soul.

"Why don't we go outside and get some air? You look a little pale."

I hesitated. Jacob's voice was still dogging me. "Wait. Wait, Ron."

I closed my eyes in an attempt to hear Jacob's weakened whisper. He wanted me back in the room. I'd had enough and mentally told him so. Undaunted by my refusal to return, he said, *Leslie.*

Leslie?

"Is there a Leslie here?" I called out. "Jacob's calling your name."

Ron immediately said, "No," but was quickly corrected by Gay, Bob the videographer's wife, as she scurried out from the adjacent dining area, straight toward Ron.

"My name is Leslie," she said. Adjusting her Red Sox cap, she looked at me. "But I don't use that name. What does he want?"

Even though I sensed that Jacob was already gone, I could see her excitement and didn't want to hurt her feelings. I thought quickly. "He wants you to take pictures," I lied. I suspected Jacob only really wanted to prove he existed by whispering a name to me that I couldn't possibly have known.

* * *

Brushing by me and Maureen, Gay entered the wait station, snapping away. The click, click, click of the camera and the buzzing of the group filled the hallway. They were still shocked at what we had just witnessed. I stood transfixed for a moment while I attempted to digest what had just transpired between Maureen and Gay. Leslie was Gay's real name—but Maureen could not have known that, since it was the first time they had met. What an amazing connection.

Maureen's first spiritual contact with Jacob had been swift, and laden with pain. But there was no way we could call it a night now. The house certainly had paranormal activity, and I wanted to see the scope of it. Some spirits inhabit their favorite rooms, while others roam. If we left before completing our investigation and doing a walkthrough of each room in the house, we might have never known if the house had any other spiritual communication to offer.

I turned to stare at Maureen. Happy to see the color returning to her face, I asked, "Are you ready to continue with the investigation?"

She nodded.

We first entered the dining room to the right of the wait station, making our way in a continuous loop from room to room with little else happening but the creaking of the floors. Not having worked with a psychic before, I looked at Maureen to gauge her reaction. "Are you picking up anything?"

She narrowed her stare, as if she read my thoughts. "No," she replied abruptly.

We made our way toward the narrow stairs to the third floor. Maneuvering past the ill-placed vacuum cleaner, we climbed the stairs. I hesitated as I reached the top of the landing and pointed above us. I directed my question to our photographer. "Right here. Remember the picture that Jean Pierre showed us, Leo?"

"Oh yeah. The Christmas packages, I wish I'd been there to see it in person."

I then realized the group had no clue what we were talking about. Leo was referring to another incarnation of the restaurant, when Jean Pierre, the previous owner, had had a strange experience. "The previous owners had these empty boxes wrapped up like Christmas packages," I explained. "When they came in one day, they found the boxes stretched out like a bridge from wall to wall. Hanging in mid air."

Leo chimed in, "Yeah. You'd need a lot more than a ladder and a couple of guys to pull off that stunt."

We walked to the end of the hall and entered the room on the right with Maureen in the lead. Turning the corner, she jumped back, slamming into me. "What the hell is that?"

I scanned the room and saw the source of her terror. There, in front of us, stood a life-size statue of a chef. Encased in shadows, it had an ominous presence, becoming more than just a statue. It took on the persona of a doll from one of those horror flicks. I half expected to hear, "Hi, I'm Chucky, wanna play?"

We laughed, breaking the tension that had clung to us since Jacob's visit.

Just then I glanced down at my EMF meter. Although we were picking up fluctuations in the electromagnetic field, they were minimal at best. Disappointed, I changed tack. "Okay, let's go to the basement."

The basement door creaked when we opened it, like it was crying out in agony. Was this a sign of what was to come? We weaved our way through the old cellar; with a flick of my hand I brushed away cobwebs as we went.

"Ewww. I hate spiders," Maureen said, as she followed close behind.

"You aren't afraid of ghosts, but you're scared of a little spider?" I asked with a laugh.

After ducking under heating pipes, we reached the back of the basement where the cellar door was. Almost immediately my meter began flashing. Its eerie red glow illuminated the expression of pain in Maureen's face.

"He's here. Right between us."

Maureen's words confirmed what my meter was already telling me.

Once again Ron Jr. reported a temperature drop, and Maureen told us that she could feel electricity filling the basement. We attempted to make contact via the pendulum, but to no avail.

"He's agitated," she said. "No...he's pissed and getting more angry by the moment...He doesn't like you, Ron," Maureen said, as if afraid to tell me.

Great, I've got another fan, I thought sarcastically. I swear, if there's a post office on the other side, my picture is hanging in it. It seems some of the nastier spirits resent my lack of respect for them. However, just as in the real world, I believe respect is earned. And this was no different.

I heaved a heavy sigh. I looked at Maureen's drawn face, and since it was our first investigation together, I wasn't sure how much more pain and discomfort she could withstand. Given that Jacob seemed to be hostile, I thought it best to end the investigation.

All in all, though, it was a successful night. It even left the skeptic reporter Brian Bates shaking his head. That was a good sign, since we had agreed to provide WNDS with a weekly series, a spotlight on the newscast. A four-week haunted crescendo with a Halloween night finale meant we still had three more investigations to go. I chuckled to myself when I thought of Brian's reaction to the coffee-pot incident. Hmmm. Maybe I'd make a believer out of him yet.

There was also the question of Maureen. I thought she would be a great addition to the staff of the Ghost Project, but I wanted to see a little more of her work.

I wouldn't have long to find out. I had another test for her next week, when we investigated the Phillip Knight House.

RESULTS OF THE INVESTIGATION

To Vess and Lula's delight, we were able to verify that the Windham was indeed haunted. Infrared photos taken during the investigation revealed an energy spike going through the coffeemaker as it turned itself on during Maureen's communication with the spirit named Jacob. Even more interesting, later research into the property revealed that a German immigrant who once owned the land was named Jacob. The owners were impressed by the results of the investigation and, because of those results, coupled with the rate of paranormal activity there, requested we return.

THE PHILLIP KNIGHT HOUSE

CASE FILE: 6251867
THE PHILLIP KNIGHT HOUSE

Location: Middleton, Massachusetts.

History: Phillip Knight Jr. built the home in
1692 for his bride, Rebecca Towne. She was
the niece of Mary Estey and Rebecca Nurse,
who were convicted and executed for witch-
craft in the Salem Witch Trials. This house
was in the Knight family for two hundred
years, later becoming the Blue Door Inn Bed
and Breakfast.

Reported Paranormal Activity: Apparitions, unexplained noises, and moving and disappearing objects.

Clients: Ethel (owner).

Investigators: Ron (lead investigator), Maureen
(trance medium), Ron Jr. (investigator).

Press: Brian Bates (reporter WNDS), Tom (Brian's
cameraman).

Ron, are sure you know where you're going?" Maureen asked. This was the first time she'd questioned my directional skills, but sure as shooting, it wouldn't be the last.

"Of course I do," I said. I was trying to put on an air of confidence, but truth be told, I hate driving. If I could just beam myself somewhere, like they did in *Star Trek*, I'd be happy.

"Here it is," I cried, slamming on the brakes and taking a sharp left through a narrow opening between tall hedges. As the old Subaru crept down a hidden driveway, the harvest moon cast menacing shadows on the poorly lit pavement. At the end of the driveway, we stopped in front of a quaint wooden building with dark brown cedar shingles. It was the Phillip Knight house.

I stopped the car and shut off the engine. Mesmerized for the moment, we sat in stillness staring at the skulking structure.

After a minute Maureen turned to look at my son in the backseat, then at me. "Do you feel anything, Ron?" she asked me.

"Yeah, hungry, but then again, when don't I?" I turned the question back to her. "Why...do you?"

"I sense someone looking out the window," she replied.

"Yeah, you don't have to be psychic to see that. That would be Ethel. She's our host."

Just then we were flooded by the headlights of an approaching vehicle. As I raised my arm to shield my eyes, I heard a familiar voice call out to me. It was Brian and his cameraman, Tom, from

WDNS, ready for the second investigation of the four-part series. I'd chosen the Phillip Knight house, a place I'd investigated before for *The New England Ghost Project* television show. But back then, Maureen hadn't been with us. This time, with her here, we might be able to get some psychic verification of paranormal activity.

Our group now complete, we walked across the windswept pavement to the porch, which was embellished with various Halloween decorations. The seasoned wooden door creaked slowly open, and there stood Ethel, a short older woman with a heartwarming smile.

"Hello, Ron," she said in a slight Yankee accent. "How are you?"

"Better than nothing," I quipped as the aroma of fresh-baked bread drifted out of what must have been the nearby kitchen.

Turning, I introduced the rest of my ensemble one by one as they filed past us and into the kitchen—and back in time. Well, it felt like that, anyway. The warm glow of a cast-iron stove filled the room. A heavy wooden table was surrounded by hunter green ladder-back chairs. Pewter candlesticks, a snuffer, and a wicker basket filled with pistol-grip silverware sat atop a white hand-crocheted tablecloth.

"Wow, Ethel, where did you get all these antiques?" I asked.

Ethel looked wistful for a moment. "I picked them up here and there. My husband and I used to enjoy antiquing. But he passed away years ago."

I caught a faint whiff of candle wax. But there were no candles lit in this sea of nostalgia. "Ethel, do you have any candles burning?"

She smiled knowingly. "No. However, it's funny you should say that. Many guests have reported the smell of candles burning and the pungent odor of tobacco."

"Ron, I know you like to take the scientific stance," Maureen said. "But are you sure you're not becoming more sensitive, and picking up on things?"

I frowned at Maureen. "I doubt it. I'm about as psychic as a brick."

"Never say never," she chuckled.

I was itching to get started. Since I had been there previously to film a television episode of *The New England Ghost Project*, I knew I wanted to start in the living room, or Victorian Room, as Ethel liked to call it.

We got Ethel settled in a blue Queen Anne chair beside the red brick fireplace.

"So, Ethel," Brian began. "What's the history of this house?"

Maureen and I joined Brian on the sofa, while Ron Jr. and Tom stood, each with a camcorder rolling.

"The original house, a four-room cottage, was built in 1692 by Phillip Knight Jr. as a wedding gift for his bride, Rebecca Towne of Topsfield. She was the niece of Mary Estey and Rebecca Nurse, who were hung as witches during the Salem Witch Trials." Ethel paused for a moment. "As you know, Middleton was formerly part of Old Salem Village. Phillip Knight Jr. and his bride moved into the house. Unfortunately, he died an untimely death at the early age of twenty-seven."

"How long have you owned the house, Ethel?" Brian asked.

"Twenty-three years," she replied. "A psychic told me I was going to buy a dark house. The minute I walked over the threshold, I knew I belonged here."

"Well, as Ron can testify, I am somewhat of a skeptic. But tell me, what kinds of things have happened here?" Brian asked.

"Lots of things. Most notably, previous guests have reported seeing a ghostly apparition of what appeared to be a sea captain.

In fact, one of the guests captured his image in a photo. The likeness in the photo is a mirror image of a portrait we have of captain Henry Quiner. Henry Quiner was not a captain; however, he did come from Marblehead, Massachusetts, to live here in Salem Village, and everyone in town called him the captain." She smiled. "Would you like to see the photo?"

"Yes, I would, but not right now." He paused. "Ethel, would you like to add anything else?"

"Yes. The captain is not the only spirit that has been seen. White figures have been seen walking the grounds, and a woman in brown period dress has been seen in this room. I think her name is Rosemary, because I could swear I heard her name whispered in my ear."

The lights flickered, as if someone or something were acknowledging the name. Ethel visibly shuddered, then briskly rubbed her arms. "Did you feel that?"

"Yes," Ron Jr. answered. "It felt like a cold draft just swept through the room."

Tom nodded in agreement.

Brian cleared his throat, seemingly a little nervous, almost intent on ignoring what had just transpired. "Ethel, please continue."

"There have been so many strange things that have happened here…one time a couple visiting from England wrote in the guest book, 'We awoke to find a figure of a man with gray hair and spiffy mustache standing over our bed. Had we known this place was haunted, we would have never stayed here.' Even my brother-in-law saw a ghost in a window. Guests have also heard the sound of people running up and down the stairs. Items disappear. Glasses spill by themselves. And the doorbell rings, before anyone can press the button. It's as if the spirit is alerting us to their approach."

"Interesting," Brian said, shaking his head. "But Ethel, have *you* ever been really scared?"

"Oh yes," Ethel said with a nod. "One night I woke up with a heavy pressure on my chest, like somebody was pushing down on it, but nobody was there." She raised her hand to her chest to demonstrate what she was saying. "A psychic friend of mine told me that if it happens again, just tell them to stop it. It did, so I told them to stop. Since then I haven't had any problems."

"Okay, that's good. For the rest of the interview, I'd like to follow the Ghost Project as they do their investigation." Brian nodded in my direction. "You'll hardly know we're here."

As we walked down the hallway, the wide plank floors creaked beneath our feet, adding an air of creepiness to our tour through the historic bed and breakfast.

We entered a room painted in rich pumpkin shades, with cream trim surrounding an oversized working fireplace.

"This place is amazing, Ethel." Maureen said, her mouth agape.

"Yeah, terrific. You picking up anything?" I asked, ignoring Maureen's apparent fascination with the surroundings.

"Actually, not really."

"Then let's move on," I said, glancing at my silent EMF meter.

Ethel walked past the group, taking the lead. She guided us up through a set of winding stairs, until we reached what she'd said was the oldest part of the house. It was the only room, in fact, that still had its original flooring.

Brian, the next in line behind Ethel, turned the corner into the room and jumped. "What the hell is that!"

Ethel laughed. "That's one of my dolls," she said, pointing to a four-foot-tall doll with large green eyes. Just like the doll at the

Windham, it looked more like a creature from a horror flick than a child's toy. "Did Ron tell you the story behind it?"

"No, Ethel, I saved it for you." I looked at Brian, whose color was just returning.

"As you can tell, I like to keep my dolls in period clothing. But for some reason, I have found her numerous times with just one of her shoes missing." Ethel moved closer to the doll, lifting the skirt slightly. "You can see that the stand she's on doesn't allow for it to be removed easily."

She turned to face us. "One Christmas, at a family gathering, I found her again with one of her shoes missing. I said aloud, 'Where is that darn shoe?' then nearly choked on my own spit when the shoe, out of nowhere, slid across the floor toward me."

"Seriously?" Brian asked.

"Yes. It happened right in front of everyone."

"Is there anything else significant about this room?"

"Yes. As a matter of fact, I really don't like sleeping here." She walked over to the window on the far side of the room. "This is the window that Phillip Knight was believed to have fallen through and broken his neck."

"Is this the room where your brother-in-law saw the ghost in the window?" I asked.

"No, that's the '20s room," she said, as she made her way toward the door.

"Why do you call it that?" I asked.

"Come on, I'll show you."

* * *

I followed Ron and Ethel into the '20s room. It had a large poster bed with Duco Gold trim and amber-colored beads dangling from the cloth lampshade. But it was the chintz material on the dressing table chair that gave it away. It was the *roaring '20s* room. "Hey Ethel, how come there are no windows in this room?" I asked.

"This used to be a Masonic Temple," she said, with a knowing smile. "That's why I think there's a lot of activity in here. Because of all the rituals they did." She turned to Ron. "Do you remember when Brian the Monk was here? He went nuts."

"Ron, sorry to interrupt, but who the hell is Brian the Monk?" asked Brian Bates.

"Brian is a Franciscan monk who was doing a thesis in the seminary on spirits. He had heard about a ghost book written by Bob Cahill, and he decided to go with Bob on an investigation and prove that he was full of crap." Ron hesitated for a moment. "Instead he photographed six spirits that night and has been hooked ever since. I met him through Bob when Bob retired. I kind of picked him up on waivers. You know, like they do to professional baseball players when they're no longer needed."

Brian grinned. "So, is Brian the Monk a member of the Ghost Project?"

"Unofficially. He works with us sometimes, when our schedules don't conflict. The last time we were here, he was almost positive that a ghost was going to materialize right over there," Ron said, pointing to the far end of the room. "In fact, this is the room where we saw the name Rosemary on the ceiling." Ron walked up to the dressing table and touched the lamp. "Light emanating from this lamp filtered through jewelry lying atop the dresser and projected the name on the ceiling." He hesitated, his voice rising in excitement. "As Ethel said during the interview, Rosemary is one of the spirits believed to haunt this house."

As they were talking, I couldn't help but feel the level of energy escalating in the room. It swirled around me, rising from the floor, drawing closer and closer. Like a moth to a flame, the spirit called to me. It somehow knew I was listening. I called out, "Ron, there's someone here."

With the last of my words, Ron's EMF meter sprang to life.

"I think they want to make contact. Now."

"Okay, okay, don't get so huffy," Ron grumbled as he circled me with his meter.

Barely in time for my pendulum to be ready, names and images quickly ran through my mind, almost too quickly. A young girl's face. A familiar room. A favorite toy. The doll I'd just seen. Fragmented images bombarded my consciousness. As I closed my eyes to block out any distractions, I took a moment to sort out the onslaught of information. Then I blurted out, "It's a little girl. Ten years old." Once again, I struggled, focusing on the impressions in my mind's eye. "Her name. It's—Rebecca. No, Becky."

"I thought you can only get yes and no answers with the pendulum. Where is this stuff coming from?" Ron growled, disbelief evident in his voice.

Some things were just hard to explain. Ron and I had only been working together for a short time, so on some level I understood his confusion, although I didn't like having to justify what I was getting. "It's hard to explain," I said. "It's like someone is putting messages in my mind."

"So, it's like tapping into their consciousness?" Ron asked.

"Yeah, that's a good way of looking at it," I replied as Ron's meter went silent.

"They're gone," Ron stated.

"No, *they're* not. *She's* over there," I said, pointing to the top of the stairs.

Following my lead, we walked to the top of the stairs, the meter blinking on and off, like a child flipping a light switch. "She's playing a game with you," I said, cloaking the satisfaction in my voice.

Brian spoke up, "Maureen, ask her if she's the one playing with the doll."

Echoing his question the pendulum swung wildly, a big yes.

A stabbing pain at the base of my skull suddenly broke my concentration. I cringed in pain, clutching the back of my neck. "What the heck?" The swirling energy had returned.

"What's up?" Ron asked, with a look of concern on his face.

"I don't know. My head is killing me," I said, still holding my neck. "I think the pain is coming from Becky. She must have died from a head injury."

"There's a lot of that going around," Ron Jr. snickered from behind the camera.

"Ha, ha." *The apple doesn't fall far from the tree*, I thought. "You know it's not easy being empathic."

"Empathic?" Brian asked.

"Yeah. I tend to feel how the spirits have passed."

"Good to know," Ron quipped. "Sure glad it's you and not me."

Typical, another Ron-ism, I thought. The throbbing pain began to recede, along with the spirit of the little girl. "Either she's gone or she's moved to another spot in the house," I said, tucking my pendulum into the safety of my pocket.

Ron stood for a moment, silent, pondering what had just transpired. "This makes sense. It has to be the same little girl that Brian the Monk captured on infrared film, the last time I was here."

Brian the Monk

An infrared photo by Brian the Monk of the spirit of a little girl
(upper left hand corner)

He grinned at me. "Good catch." He waited for a moment. "Are you picking anything else up? Is she still here?"

I closed my eyes and concentrated on my surroundings, opening myself up one more time. Nothing. "No. I'm afraid she's gone. And I'm not picking up anything else."

Ron frowned. "Fine." Then he visibly sniffed the air, winking at Ethel. "That banana bread's calling my name. Let's go back to the kitchen."

Within moments we were at the kitchen table, scarfing down the fresh-baked goodies. "Hey, why don't we pull some cards on the house? Would you be up for that, Ethel?" Ron asked.

"Sure, do you need some playing cards?"

I glanced from Ron, who had offered my reading services, to Ethel. "No, I have my own cards and crystal ball." I reached into the black bag I'd left on the table when we arrived and pulled out my tarot deck.

"Crystal ball?" Ron said, mockingly.

"Well, it's not what you think it is—well, okay, it is," I said with a chuckle. I reached into the bag once again and retrieved a four-inch round crystal. "See here," I said, rotating the quartz for everyone to see. "All these fractures in it were caused by the energy of my clients when I do readings."

"Yeah, I can see, it's fractured like your mind." Ron said, giggling like a schoolgirl at his own witticism.

I handed the crystal ball to Ethel, even though what I really wanted to do was crack Ron over the head with it. "Hold this for a minute, it'll help me connect with your energy." I looked at the way she scrunched her forehead, taking it as a sign that she was confused. "Ethel, there are lots of ways I use to connect with the energy of someone. This is just one of them. Think of it as nothing more than a tool."

"A tool, just like you." Ron piped in.

Man, he was on a roll. I decided to ignore him. It was better that way. Turning toward Ethel, I smiled and then continued, "When I do a series of readings in a row, it works as a way to break the energy from one person to another."

"Okay. Now what?"

"Shuffle the cards for me, then draw six."

Ethel handed them to me facedown, one right after the other. I laid them on the table in two neat rows. I turned each card over and studied them carefully. "Ethel, I can see you're emotionally attached to this house. Which is why you're so torn about your recent thoughts." I glanced at Ethel. "You're making a decision about whether or not to sell this place."

"Yeah, you hit the nail right on the head." Ethel shifted in her seat, looking a little uncomfortable.

I pointed at the card depicting a black cat and a collage of spiritual images. "See, this is the Sensor card. I believe this is why you felt the presence in the bedroom and heard the name Rosemary whispered in your ear."

"What?"

"I think you're a bit more psychically sensitive than most people, which is why you've had these experiences."

I raised my head and caught the blank stares of the group, their faces suddenly unreadable. *Are they bored?* I just had a feeling they weren't buying this.

"Thank you, Maureen," Ethel said. "That was great."

"Wait a minute." I suddenly had an overwhelming feeling of unfinished business. "Let's pull one more card." With that, I spread the cards facedown on the table, accordion style. I lightly slid my hand across the cards, drew one out of the deck, and flipped it over.

Immediately the image of a little girl hugging a doll jumped out at me. I now realized why I had to pull that extra card. "Look, it's Becky!"

Instantaneously I felt the crush of the group at my back, as everyone fought to get a better look.

"Oh my God," Ethel said, excitedly. "Would you look at that?"

Brian, the skeptic, glanced at the card. "Tom, take a shot of that."

As Tom stood over my shoulder with his camcorder, Brian said, "Ethel, you'll be able to catch this episode tomorrow night on the ten o'clock news on WNDS."

After all was said and done, I'd survived the second of four investigations with WNDS, and I thought they had gone pretty well. With two more to go, I couldn't help but wonder what Ron had in store for me. I shuddered to think.

RESULTS OF THE INVESTIGATION

During our investigation, the spirit of a child made herself known to us through various means. The infrared photo taken by Brian the Monk on a previous investigation, combined with Maureen's contact with the child in the '20s room and the tarot card drawn at the end of the investigation, all pointed to the conclusion that this was the spirit believed to be called Becky, the same little girl thought to be responsible for removing the shoe on Ethel's doll. Later research into the property revealed that a young Rebecca Knight once lived there and was believed to have died there. Ethel was pleased that her beloved home was once again focus of a television documentary.

episode four

THE MEXICAN STANDOFF

CASE FILE: 6271975
TORTILLA FLATS RESTAURANT

Location: Merrimac, New Hampshire.

History: Two separate houses were joined to create this restaurant. During the Civil war, one of the structures provided a safe haven for fugitive slaves as part of the Underground Railroad.

Reported Paranormal Activity: While dining, patrons have seen an image of a woman in the reflection of a window. The voices of children and footsteps have been heard. Objects move of their own accord, and people report an overwhelming feeling of being watched.

Clients: Amy (dining room manager), Katie (waitress), Jenny (waitress).

Investigators: Ron (lead investigator), Maureen (trance medium), Leo (photographer), Bob (videographer), Gay (Bob's wife/investigator).

Press: Brian Bates (reporter for WNDS), Tom (Brian's cameraman), Eric Baxter (editor for the *Salem Observer*, Salem, New Hampshire), Bruce Preston (photographer for the *Salem Observer*).

Beep, beep, beep, beep…

"Maureen, they're here!" I yelled over the aimless chatter and mundane noise flowing from other rooms of the now-closed Tortilla Flats Restaurant. She hurried into the room and stopped at my side. The depth of her pained eyes revealed that she now knew it too. She reached into the pocket of her green-print fleece top, removed her pendulum, and sprang into action, a scene that would be replayed so many times in our lives together.

Taking a deep breath, she asked, "Is there someone here with us now?" The brass bobber spun counterclockwise, indicating a yes.

"Oh yeah," she said smugly, as the members of the Ghost Project, along with the wait staff, reporters, and news crews, began to drift into what the staff referred to as Room #1. It was the third install-ment of the WNDS series on haunted places in New England, and we'd called Tortilla Flats to see if we could check the place out, as it had a reputation for being haunted.

Ron Kolek

A fireplace and stained glass window in Room #1 at Tortilla Flats.

A quick flash of light temporarily blinded us. My eyes regained focus to see Bruce Preston, photographer for the *Salem Observer*, kneeling in front of the old brick fireplace, camera in hand, shutter aimed at us. Other media people were tagging along this time as well. Trying not to get distracted by the ever-growing clamor in the room, we continued our query of the unknown entity.

Maureen took another deep breath, this time expelling it much more slowly. "Did someone commit suicide in this room? I think someone hung themselves in here."

Once again the spinning chain and brass bobber confirmed her question.

"Was it a man?" she asked.

"Yes," she answered quickly, visibly trembling. Her answer seemed to come with a price.

"Is there more than one of you?" I asked, pushing my quest for the facts.

Maureen echoed my question and quickly said yes as my meter screamed in a never-ending series of beeps.

She paused briefly for a moment and looked up at me, as if searching for my approval. "Zechariah." Shaking her head, listening for an undistinguishable voice, she repeated the name once again, "Zechariah." Suddenly she winced in pain, placing her right hand on her chest. She breathed deeply and exhaled more quickly.

"Do you want to tell us something?" I asked Zechariah, pushing my concern for Maureen's well-being to the side.

Gritting her teeth, she replied, "Yes."

I took a step closer, our forearms nearly touching. A quick jolt of what felt like static electricity charged up my arm, causing the hairs on the back of my neck to stand. I shuddered. "Maureen, did you feel that? It was like I stuck my finger in a light socket!"

"You stepped into the energy I was picking up on." Maureen looked at me and grinned. "I think you just felt Zechariah."

All eyes on us, I decided to turn my attention back to the questioning.

"Are you unhappy?" I asked.

More pain evident in Maureen's face, another yes.

I reached out and placed my hand on her arm in a halfhearted attempt at comfort. "Do you want us to leave?" I asked.

A long pause, and just for an instant, a small smile slid across Maureen's lips. She raised her head and slowly moved it from side to side. "No." Her smile faded away, replaced with a look of agony.

"Will you appear for us?" By the tormented look on her face, I could only assume my questions were becoming more and more irritating to our unseen visitor. Overlooking her discomfort, my quest for knowledge so great, I pushed for answers.

Again, a long pause, as Maureen swayed to and fro, unsteady on her feet. "Yes."

I thought for a moment and asked, "Do you want us to go into the basement?" A deadly silence fell over the room.

In response, the bobber pulled straight down as if some invisible force was yanking it.

"He's leaving now," Maureen said, breathing a sigh of relief. The pain had lessened.

I grabbed her arm, and like a bride and groom on their wedding day we walked down the corridor and out the front door into the cold crisp October night air.

We were safe—for the moment. Free from Zechariah's reach. It appeared this spirit was a grounded spirit, unable to leave the house.

"Are you okay?" I asked, my concern for her now pushed to the forefront.

"Yes." Her words were a mere whisper between the heavy breaths. "Do you have your St. Michael card?" She looked up at me with pleading eyes.

"Is the Pope Catholic?" I replied, using my humor to soothe my concern.

I pulled the worn laminated card from my back pocket. She placed one hand on it, our voices resonating as we began together, "Saint Michael the Archangel, defend us in battle, be our protection..."

* * *

After I had gathered my composure, Ron and I returned to the restaurant. Almost as soon as I walked through the door, I could feel the presence. "What's next, Ron?" I asked, already knowing the answer.

"We've got to go into the basement," he replied in an almost apologetic tone.

The tranquility I'd felt just moments ago on the porch of the restaurant was now replaced with a sense of apprehension. This was only my third investigation with the Ghost Project, and since this was the second angry spirit we'd encountered in such a short span of time, I was beginning to wonder if I had made the right choice by teaming up with them.

When I'd been invited to accompany them to the Windham Restaurant, I'd been overjoyed. It finally felt as if I'd found a place where I fit in: a team of paranormal investigators who shared similar interests, and who didn't think I was crazy for doing what came naturally.

But now I was torn. I'd joined so that I could put my abilities to good use, assisting spirits in need. Unfortunately, there were times like today, when a spirit didn't play nice. The physical pain and drain on my energy made the investigation difficult to endure. I'd suddenly been reminded why all those years ago I'd taken a break in communicating with the dead. Now, I was back. What the hell had I been thinking? A dull ache weighed heavily on my chest, a lingering effect of my encounter with Zechariah. Gritting my teeth, I followed Ron into the left-hand side of the restaurant, to base camp, in the room referred to by the staff as Room #3.

Eric Baxter, a reporter for the *Salem Observer*, approached me. "Are you all right?" he asked.

"Yeah, sure," I replied, not revealing that I was still a little shaken.

"By the way, thanks for letting us tag along."

"No problem. How did you find out about us, anyway?"

"I saw the piece on WNDS News and thought it would be a good story. Typically, I try to remain objective, but—you're not going to believe this," Eric mumbled, looking as if he'd seen a ghost. "Earlier, when you were in contact with Zechariah, Brian and I were standing over there near the door." He ran a hand through his thick chestnut curls, and then pointed to a spot just inside the doorway to Room #1. "Well, just as you said, 'He's leaving,' both Brian and I felt a cold breeze brush between us." He paused. "Then, for no reason, the battery on my camera drained all at once." Looking a little befuddled, he said, "I just charged it. I, uh, there's no way…"

Our conversation was cut short when Ron piped in, "Does anybody know anything about the basement?"

"I do," said Amy, the dining room manager, a tall blonde with shoulder-length hair.

"Do you want to tell us about it?" Ron continued.

"Sure," she replied as she took up a position in front of the stained-glass window next to the fireplace in Room #1. Illuminated by the lights of the cameras, she seemed a little stunned, uncomfortable in the spotlight.

In a quiet tone she began, "Well, I have heard lots of stories. There's a hidden room off the back that was rumored to be part of the Underground Railroad, where slaves used to hide. I have also heard that when children lived here, they played in the cellar." She hesitated for a moment as if to get her thoughts in order. "When people from the restaurant have gone down there, they hear voices. From where, I'm not sure. I have heard lots of stories about things moving on their own, and when people stay in the basement for any extended period of time, we tend to have more ghostly activity over the next couple of weeks in the regular part of the restaurant."

"So that seems to stir things up," Ron interrupted.

"It seems so."

As she spoke I couldn't help but notice the expressions of terror on the faces of the other waitresses who were huddled together in the corner of the room, like children in fear of the bogeyman.

"Anything else you want to tell us?" Ron asked.

"No. Would you like to go to the basement?"

"Without a doubt. Let's rock," Ron replied.

Gathering our equipment, we followed her into the hall and through the swinging doors of the kitchen. Ron and I were directly behind her, with the rest of the group trailing us in what seemed to be an endless conga line.

We passed through the kitchen, then through another door and down a set of well-worn stairs into the basement. As we entered, the irritating hum of coolers, refrigerators, and fluorescent lights filled the room, triggering Ron's EMF meter. His meter picked up the electrical activity, while I felt a different kind of activity—spirit energy. It was following our every move. This presence, it seemed, was almost as anxious for us to get to the hidden room as we were. Following Amy to the very rear of the basement, we came upon a narrow tunnel. She pointed into the darkness. "Hey, where's the light for the tunnel?" she cried.

Jenny, a short waitress with dirty blonde hair, answered her. "The light's on, but the bulb's not lit. That's not right, it was fine earlier. I guess it's a mystery."

Coincidence? I think not. I had only been with Ron for a short time, and I was already beginning to think like him. *Now that's scary*, I thought to myself.

Amy turned to me and, with a look of apprehension and a quiver in her voice, said, "Do you want to go first?"

"No, that's okay. I'm not in any hurry," I replied, even though I could sense that the spirits were in a hurry for us to join them.

"I'll go first," Ron spoke up, never shy to throw himself into the limelight.

The cement floor soon turned to dirt as we made our way through the narrow passageway. As we reached the end, we turned right, and I nearly gagged when I caught a whiff of the dampness. The stone foundation was cluttered with wires, old hewn beams, and, of course, spiderwebs. I hate spiders. As I entered the hidden room that Amy was referring to, my attention was drawn from the cobwebs to the energy that was now swirling strongly around me.

I took up a position in the center of the room away from the hanging webs. Though light was coming in from the outside room, when I looked at Ron he was nearly in darkness. He was crouched over, scanning the area with his meter. As he swung the meter around to me, it lit up like a Christmas tree. They were here; I knew it, and Ron's meter confirmed it. Moving my pendulum in front of me, I began to make contact.

"Ron, I feel a difference in the energy here. It's somebody else." Taking a deep breath, I asked, "Are you a woman?"

Once again the pendulum confirmed what I was already feeling: yes. It was a much more pleasant energy than the one I had faced earlier. I turned my head to the right, half expecting to see her standing there. Her energy was so thick, it was as if I could reach out and touch her.

"Who's got an infrared? Who's got an infrared? Take some shots," Ron commanded, playing off my feelings.

Almost immediately, the group responded with a barrage of flashes.

I became a bit self-conscious in the assault of camera flashes. It felt like my every move was under scrutiny. Ron seemed oblivious to it as he continued his questioning of our newfound friend; all the while his EMF meter continued its incessant beeping.

"Did you die here?" he asked.

"Yes," I replied with an inner knowing, not fully waiting for the pendulum to answer.

"Did you live here?"

His question went unanswered, as I felt the familiar sinister force from earlier in the evening beginning to slither in.

"There is something else here now," I cried. I clutched my chest, gritting my teeth in reaction to the pain coursing through me. The same, contentious energy that had plagued me in the upstairs dining room was pushing away the weaker spirit. With total disregard for my well-being, it stepped in once again. My chest still raw, sore, from our previous encounter, I mentally pushed back at the uninvited energy; I was not willing to be accosted by this particular spirit. Nearing my breaking point, I bent over and dug my fingers into the flesh of my lower thigh, something I do to ground myself in the present. A little of my own pain, at least for me, brings me back to reality.

"Are you okay?" Ron asked.

I nodded quickly and blurted out, "Yes." I lied.

Once again a dead silence fell over the room. This was becoming a theme. I wanted to end contact with this angry spirit as soon as possible, so I asked, "Does anybody have a question?"

Katie, another waitress, spoke out, "Does it bother you when we come down here?"

I repeated her question, and audibly heard the spirit's whisper of defiance. "No."

Brian chimed in, "Will you appear for us?"

I grabbed my chest and winced in pain, feeling the spirit's anger growing. "Maybe."

"It's the suicide one, the hanged man, isn't it?" Ron asked, somehow tapping into my brain.

Still wincing in pain, I nodded my head. Again I slowly turned to look over my shoulder. If I hadn't known any better, like the woman before him, I'd have sworn he was standing right beside me.

Ron raised his camera and took a picture without even turning his head or aiming. "How many spirits are here, are there more than five?" he asked.

I felt an instant dislike, almost a loathing for the questions being asked. With that thought the pain intensified. "Yes. But he's the strongest one," I added.

"Are you related?" Ron asked.

"Yeah, some of them are anyway," I replied. "But not him."

Not to be left out, Eric added a question of his own. "Are the spirits here from the Underground Railroad?"

"Yes," I answered as I bent over, clutching my abdomen, suppressing the pain ravaging my body.

Jenny threw out another question. "Are the spirits slaves?"

I paused for a moment, when someone suddenly muttered, "Shit!" It was Tom. The battery on his camcorder had just drained itself completely.

I stood upright once again and repeated Jenny's question.

The pendulum confirmed what I was hearing. "Yes. But not all of them."

Shifting my weight from one foot to another, my eyes pleaded to Ron to hurry this up.

"Are there any other questions?" Ron asked.

"Are there any children here?" asked Katie from the back of the crowd.

I shook my head and answered yes, finding it more and more difficult to endure the agony that was now enveloping my body.

"Do you want something from us?" Ron asked.

The bobber pulled straight down, a sign to me that our "friend" had had just about enough of our questioning. As had I. I followed the pull of the energy with my mind's eye; instinctively, I felt he had fled through the opening in the wall. "He's gone. He went that way," I said, nodding in the general direction.

"What's over there?" Ron asked.

Amy spoke up, "If you follow the wall to the right there's a staircase, but it's boarded off."

Ron and Leo, our photographer, scurried over to where I had seen the spirit disappear. Leo raised the camera, clicking wildly. "Damn it, it won't let me take a picture," he cried.

Within seconds the charge in the air dissipated, a sign to me that the spirit had left. At the same moment, Leo said, "Would you look at that, now it's working again."

"I'd say we're done here," Ron said. "Let's get back to base camp."

As we weaved our way through the kitchen, everybody was excitedly talking about what had just transpired. Everyone, that is, except for Jenny and Katie, who walked arm in arm with petrified looks on their faces.

We hung around the base camp trying to decide our next move, when Ron turned to Amy and asked, "Is there an upstairs to this place?"

No sooner had he gotten the words out of his mouth, when the base camp monitor went to static. Gay, who was sitting by the monitors, cried, "Ron, look at this."

Flippantly he dismissed her remark. "That's nothing. It's just some kind of natural interference." Just then, the screen returned to normal. I, on the other hand, wasn't so sure that the "static" was natural at all.

Once again, Ron asked, "Can we see the upstairs?"

As if on cue, the static returned.

Just like I thought. This was no "natural interference," more like, "para-natural."

As we opened the door to the second story, I could sense a spirit lingering at the top of the stairs peering down at us. In a zigzag motion, we ascended the dilapidated stairs, stepping over bottles, bags, brooms, and various cleaning supplies. If that wasn't enough of a challenge, we gingerly stepped over missing floorboards, careful not to plunge through to the room beneath us. The spirit retreated as we drew closer.

Ron made his way to the front room with the rest of us behind him. It was extremely tight quarters. He turned to me and waved his silent meter, saying, "I'm not getting very much here."

"Go to the right, Ron," I told him, becoming somewhat frustrated. "No, my right."

Turning, he went deeper into the room until he reached a window that overlooked the parking lot. As he did, his meter went off. "Oh yeah," he said triumphantly. "Lucy, I'm home." A reference to the *I Love Lucy* show. *Sometimes he's such a nut,* I thought.

When I entered the room, the atmosphere was much lighter, an indication to me that the spirit was much younger. Intuitively, I knew it was a little girl. I could barely contain my smile. This was so much more pleasant than the "hanged man," as Ron referred to him. "It's a woman, a young woman."

I paused for a second. "Jenny, her name is Jenny," I said, repeating what I heard psychically.

"What does she want?" Ron asked.

I chuckled, "She just wants to be with us."

"You mean like hanging with us?" Ron continued.

"Yeah," I said, my voice mirroring her emotions.

"That's cool; does she like us?" Ron asked.

My emotions felt bubbly, light, euphoric even. "Yes, look how fast my pendulum is going. She likes you." Go figure. "It's not the negative one," I said to Ron, trying to explain what I was feeling. "I don't have the same pain, which is a good thing," I added.

"Are you happy?" Ron asked of the little girl spirit.

Yes, answered the pendulum

"Are you happy we are here?"

The answer, a resounding yes.

"You just want attention, don't you?" Ron asked, teasing the spirit.

Eric asked, "Are you part of the Underground Railroad?"

A strong yes.

"Are you white?" Ron inquired.

The pendulum swung counterclockwise, indicating a yes.

"I thought so," Ron stated, straining his voice to be heard above the beep, beep, beep of his EMF meter.

"Did you help with the Underground Railroad?" I said, asking a question of my own.

Yes, the pendulum responded, but I already knew the answer.

Seemingly out of nowhere a rush of cold air blanketed the room.

The rapid fire of Ron's EMF meter was suddenly transformed to a slow, rhythmic beep.

Beep—beep—beep.

A familiar pain invaded my chest.

The energy was dark, heavy, almost touchable, like mist rolling over a cold gravestone.

"He's back," I said, fighting my way through a wave of nausea.

Ron's beaming smile was gone.

"Go away," he commanded. "We don't want you here. We want to talk to Jenny." The lightness in his voice of moments ago was now replaced with a newfound gravity.

Ignoring Ron's command, the energy only thickened. "No," I said.

Doubling over in pain, I clutched my legs for support. "He doesn't want us to talk to anybody but him. He's the dominant one," I said in a low tone, a sound that was grating, even to my own ears.

"I don't want to talk to him, let's stop," Ron said, trying to wrestle control of the situation from the vile spirit.

"Yes, it works for me, but you know he can follow us," I added.

"Not outside," Ron said with a smug look on his face.

I felt the hanged man's anger. Being the obvious bully that he was, he did not like Ron. After all, he thought *he* was in charge.

As we made our way back to base camp, I could still feel the pull of his energy. He was not used to being dismissed, so he continued to dog us. Tapping my shoulder, ignoring my obvious rush to leave, Brian asked, "Why can't he go outside?"

"It's difficult to say," I replied, stepping over a missing floorboard. "But it seems that some spirits are tied to a specific house or property. Almost like they are stuck there." Still making my way down the stairs, I glanced over my shoulder and said, "For instance, this restaurant is comprised of two houses joined together. On one side, I don't feel any spiritual activity whatsoever, while the other side is overly active." Still feeling the hanged man's noose gripping my body, I said, "Sorry, Brian, I have to go. Ron, I'm going outside for some air."

"Do you want me to go with you?" he replied.

"Nah, I'll be okay," I said as I sped to the door.

* * *

I watched Maureen as she exited the building.

"Ron," Eric turned to me. "You know, when the second spirit came in, I was looking through my camera and noticed a light appear at the top right of the view finder. I don't know what it was, but it might have been something."

"That's cool; you probably picked up on him," I said.

I was interrupted when I heard Amy yell from the other room, "Ron, I just thought of something else."

Eric and I rushed to Room #1, where we saw Amy, hands on her hips, standing by the fireplace, in front of the stained-glass window. "I have two stories for you. First, you see the window I am standing in front of? Well, it was a regular window at one time, but customers began to complain when they would see the image of a woman in it instead of their own reflections, which really freaked them out. So the owner replaced it with this stained glass, which has no reflection."

"Wow," I interjected, although my mind was drifting to Maureen and how she was doing. "And what's the second story?"

"Well, sometimes I would hear noises upstairs almost like foot-steps, so I would open the door and peek my head in the stairway, and to my surprise I would see…like, little white clouds moving across the room. I tried to debunk them, but couldn't. That really scared me."

"Wait a minute," Bob said.

"What's wrong?" I asked.

"The camera keeps going in and out of focus. There's something by the fireplace, near the bookshelf."

I went over to investigate. Pushing the books aside, I found a se-cret shelf. On it was an old book hidden from view. I pulled it out, and to everyone's amazement, there in bold print on the cover was the number 666. No one could tell us where the book came from. *Is this a message from the hanged man? Or just another attempt to intimidate us?* I was betting on the latter of my thoughts. Was it evil? Possibly. More often than not, our experience has shown that when we're confronted with "evil" spirits, they usually use the "666," the mark of the Devil according to Biblical references, as an attempt to intimidate.

I turned at the sound of footsteps on hardwood and saw Maureen standing in the doorway. By the look of exhaustion on her face I knew it was time to wrap it up.

On the way home, my thoughts turned to next week's investiga-tion with WNDS. I really wanted to scare the crap out of Brian this time. After all, it was taking place on All Hallows Eve. *Hmmm. Where could I go? Aha! I've got it: a cemetery. What could be scarier than that…?*

RESULTS OF THE INVESTIGATION

Tortilla Flats lived up to its reputation and provided us with another gripping episode for WNDS News. We made contact with several spirits, including slaves and a young girl whose family aided the fugitive slaves. However, the strongest, most dominant spirit was the "hanged man," whose name is thought to be Zechariah. And although we could find no historical record of him, the restaurant staff confirmed that a man did hang himself in Room #1.

episode five

THE CRYPT KEEPER

CASE FILE: 6231963
OLD HILL CEMETERY

Location: Newburyport, Massachusetts.

History: Established in 1729, the oldest cemetery in Newburyport. The resting place of sea captains and revolutionary soldiers.

Reported Paranormal Activity: Ghostly images and alleged possessions.

Clients: The viewers of WNDS News.

Investigators: Ron (lead investigator), Maureen (trance medium), Pete (Ron's friend).

Press: Brian Bates (reporter WNDS), Tom (Brian's cameraman), Beth (Brian's intern).

It was Halloween and the final night of the four-part WDNS series, and I was glad it was almost over. After all, we had spent the past month together exploring some of New England's most haunted places, and the original curiosity, which they had first shown, had now been replaced with a weird sense of camaraderie.

The frozen ground crunched beneath our feet as Maureen and I stumbled between the broken gravestones of Old Hill Cemetery in Newburyport, Massachusetts. It was cold, but I didn't need a thermometer to tell me that. The stinging of my nose spoke volumes.

The faint flicker of dancing lights radiating in the distance slowly morphed into the flashlights and camera of the WNDS News crew. We had reached our destination. It was Brian, Tom, and a young woman, an intern whom I had never seen before. Judging from the beaming smiles on their cherry-red faces, they were glad to see us as well.

"Hi Ron, give me a minute, I just have to tape the opening to the show," said Brian.

We stood back a few feet to give them some room. With a signal from Tom, Brian walked out of the darkness, into the light of the camcorder, and began. "You know, cemeteries during the day can be eerie enough, never mind at night. So what better place to be on All Hallows Eve, the spookiest night of the year, than at a cemetery, one of the oldest and most haunted along the coast. In the historic seacoast town of Newburyport, Massachusetts, a town filled with stories of horror and hauntings, including those from the grave."

Barely waiting for him to finish, I blurted out, "Hey guys, you ready to go?" Not waiting for a reply, I said, "Good, let's rock."

With Maureen at my side, we slowly slipped back into the darkness, with Brian and the crew trying to keep up. As we walked amongst the headstones, Maureen turned toward me, and before she could speak, I knew what she was going to say.

"So what's the plan?" No, I wasn't psychic. She always says that.

"I'm looking for a special grave. One with holes in the ground where you can see the bones and skull. You know, the one where I got slimed."

"You got slimed?" Brian exclaimed as he darted up to my side. He reached into his pocket and pulled out a recorder. "Tell me more."

"You never heard about that? Hmm, I must be slipping." With the click of Brian's recorder, I continued. "We were supposed to go on an investigation to a deserted island, but it got cancelled. In fact, that was to be Maureen's first investigation with the group. Since we already had the cameras loaded with infrared film, we decided to use it in another investigation. After all, infrared film, which is heat sensitive, doesn't last very long. So, Brian the Monk brought me here instead. He said this was a good place to use up the film. He showed me the photo that he took here, of a head coming out of the ground."

"Do you have a copy of it?" Brian asked.

"No. But you can find it in Bob Cahill's book, *Haunted Happenings*."

"So, where did you get slimed?"

"Somewhere there's a grave here…" I said, scanning the desolate parade of tombstones. "You can see the skeletal remains of the person buried there by peering through a hole in the eroding ground." I chose my next words carefully, not knowing how a rational person would react to what I was about to say. "So when I was here with Brian, I stuck my camera in the hole to snap a couple of pictures, when all of sudden my arm from my wrist to my elbow was covered with a thick, black, oozy gook that burned terribly. There was nothing above or below me, it just appeared out of nowhere." As I retold the story, the horror of the moment resurfaced to my consciousness. My heart began to thud wildly in my chest. "I—I just freaked."

"What do you mean you freaked?" Brian asked.

At Brian's question I could feel the anger building in my voice. "Well, what would you do, Brian? One minute I'm taking a picture, and the next minute I'm scraping thick, black, foul-smelling, nauseating crud off my arm. How do you think I felt? I was totally repulsed. Meanwhile, Brian the Monk is standing there, laughing at me. And telling me that I'd been slimed, thinking it was the best thing he'd seen since *The Texas Chainsaw Massacre*."

"What was it? Did you get a sample?" Brian asked.

"Yes, tell me, Mr. Scientist," Maureen said, gesturing with air quotes. "Did you take a sample?"

Glancing at Maureen, I couldn't help but notice her smug smile. I just wanted to smack her. Since she had already heard the story before, she knew that the answer was no. "Well, Brian, I consider myself a man of science. After all, I did graduate with a 4.0 in Environmental Science. But, on that day and at that time, it was all for naught. I guess we never know how we'll react until we face our darkest fears. I was so repulsed by it that I was consumed with the need to remove it as quickly as possible. A decision I'll regret for the rest of my life."

"I guess that makes sense." Brian's voice suddenly escalated with excitement. "So do think you can find this grave?"

Hesitantly, I replied, "I'm not sure. It's been awhile. But I have an idea. Why don't you find it?" I turned toward Maureen, still irritated with her "sample" remark. "You've got the dowsing rods, smart ass."

* * *

DOWSING RODS (DIVINING RODS)

L-shaped brass rods. The handles are approximately four inches long with copper sleeves that allow the rods to swing freely while being held. The rods will point in the direction that an object or place is located. Once the area or object is found, they will either cross over each other or uncross, depending upon the particular user's energy field.

* * *

"Fine," I grumbled at Ron. Grudgingly, I removed my gloves and pulled my dowsing rods from my back pocket. "What are we looking for?"

"You know, the grave with the hole in the ground."

"Okay." I positioned the rods in my hand, closed my eyes and made the request: "Show us where the hole in the ground is." Both the rods spun, pointing the way. Following the direction of the rods I took a step, then plummeted to the ground, my right leg disappearing into a gopher hole. I guess I had found what I'd asked for.

The sound of laughter reinforced my embarrassment. I was now the subject of unwanted attention, being asked to lead the team, only to fall on my face, literally. With one leg swallowed up to my knee, I was unable to stand. Finally, once the laughter subsided and they realized my predicament, both Brian and Ron reached down and pulled me out of my snare.

Doing my best to hide my mortification and regaining my balance, I quipped, "Okay, guys, I guess we'll have to be more specific."

Carefully rethinking my words, I once again repositioned the rods to dowse. This time I focused my intentions and phrased my request appropriately. "Where is the location of the grave?" I paused. "The one where Ron got slimed." I felt both rods begin to vibrate slightly, as they slowly turned in unison, changing direction to the left of where we stood.

Following the rods, we began our search. We snaked our way through the ill-kept cemetery, past the crumbling stones, avoiding the gopher holes. I opened my mind to reach out to any spirits that may be around us. Although I was finding it difficult to concentrate in the bitter cold, I began to feel a low-level energy prickling across my skin, so low it was almost indistinguishable from the numbness I was feeling. But it was there. "Ron, I'm picking up on some energy. But, it feels more like residual energy than anything else."

As we continued to follow the dowsing rods, Brian asked, "Residual energy, what's that?"

"There are different types of energies. Residual energy, or a residual haunting, is like an imprint in time, or memories if you will. An echo of the past. Much like videotape, the event is replayed over and over again, with no intelligent spirit, ghost, or other entity involved. Whereas an intelligent energy or haunting is when a spirit, ghost, or other entity interacts with the living."

"Here it is. I found the grave!" Ron yelled.

"Excuse me...*you* found it?" I asked, unable to squelch the humor in my voice.

"Okay. *We* found it," he reluctantly agreed. Ron glanced at the dowsing rods. "I guess those things really do work."

"So how do you want to do this?" Brian gestured to Tom. "Can you get a shot of the grave?"

"Yeah, I think so." Bending over, Tom placed his camera in the hole. He adjusted the lights to illuminate the grave and began filming.

After a couple of minutes, Tom stood up. Ron quickly took his place. He lay on the frozen ground, shifting a bit for a better vantage point as I knelt down beside him.

* * *

"Maureen, give me one of those, I want to try something," I said, pointing to the dowsing rods.

She handed me the dowsing rod. Then she hesitated in a moment of indecision. "Here, take it. I'll wait over here."

"What? Where you going?"

In a hushed voice she answered, "I already made a fool of myself once; I'm not going to do it again—on camera, no less. Here, you do it," she said as she raised herself off the cold ground and retreated to a nearby tombstone.

I held Maureen's dowsing rod over the hole to see if it would pick up any energy. As if by magic, I felt a pull in my hand as the rod slowly spun from left to right. I wasn't sure what it meant, but it was cool just the same. Putting down the rod, I picked up the EMF meter and was surprised by the lack of readings. I reached for my 35mm camera, stuck it in the opening, and quickly snapped a photo. Seeing the human skull was too much of a temptation for me. Sticking my arm into the hole, I rubbed the uneven surface of the decaying bones. For some inexplicable reason, I slowly removed my hand and brought my half-frozen fingers to my nose and took a sniff. The sickly sweet smell of rotting flesh pervaded my nostrils, but the putrid odor was the least of my worries. By the shocked expressions of those standing around me, I had little doubt this gesture would come back to haunt me.

The excitement of the moment began to wear thin, as the bitter cold penetrated my clothing. Unable to endure it any longer and eager to get my blood circulating again, I decided to move on.

"So what's next, Ron?" Brian asked.

"Well, there's a tomb here that's been broken into several times."

"You're kidding."

"No. Actually, it's pretty bizarre. You want to take a look?"

"Sure. Lead the way."

"No problem. This one I can find."

Within moments we reached the crypt. Eerily, the battery in Tom's camera failed. "That's odd. These are seven-hour batteries and should have had plenty of time to spare."

Maureen and I glanced at each other; a smile crossed our faces. "Coincidence, I think not," I said.

Brian waited for Tom to replace the battery in his camera. "So, Ron, what is so bizarre about this particular crypt? Can you share with me a bit of the history?"

We stood in front of a heavy door with an embossed cross. "The Pierce family crypt has been broken into several times in its history. The first time was back in the 1880s when several youths broke into the tomb. They propped up the corpses, poured liquor down their throats, and had a mock game of cards with them. Later they were arrested in town, wearing the clothes of the deceased." I paused for a moment, sniffled, and then continued. "The most recent time was in 2005, when an inmate performing community service broke into the vault and twisted the skull off one of the corpses. He then proceeded to parade around the graveyard with the skull on his shoulder and even had his picture taken with it."

"Ewww," Maureen said. "I'm sure his mother must have been real proud of that snapshot. That's a nice Kodak moment."

"That's disgusting." Brian paused to gather his thoughts. "So, Ron, why do you think it's been broken into so many times?"

"I'm really not sure. Out of all the tombs in this cemetery, why this one? Always the same one? Do you believe in curses?"

"I don't know. I never really thought about them," Brian answered.

"It's just conjecture on my part, I really can't say for sure, but… What if someone placed a curse on this family? A curse that ensured that they would never rest in peace. And after all that's happened to this one particular crypt over all these years, wouldn't it make sense?"

"Okay, this is good. But we need some action. Any ideas?" Brian asked.

"Ron, this place is dead," Maureen said. "No pun intended. But really, I'm not feeling anything. Other than the residual energy from before, that is."

I shrugged my shoulders. "I don't know, let's take a look and see what we can dig up." I led the group deeper into the burial grounds. We had contacted local law enforcement to ensure a safe and legal investigation, and now we were getting a boring one. I racked my brains for something, anything to salvage this episode. Here we were in one of the most haunted cemeteries, a place where I'd been slimed, no less, on the spookiest night of the year, and it seemed that nobody was home.

As we stumbled through the darkness, we came upon a lone dead tree perched on a barren hill. Large, bulbous, seemingly animated roots stretched out, as if in search of sustenance to quench its unearthly appetite. A creepy feeling crawled up my spine. I half expected to see a hangman's noose dangling from its rotting limbs, casting an eerie shadow in the moonlight. Along with it came an overwhelming feeling of doom. Was this the omen of some forthcoming evil lurking in the darkness, waiting to pounce on us? An unnatural silence fell upon the group.

A dark, hulking figure came out of the shadows, and the sharp, shrill, blood-curdling scream of a female voice startled the group, breaking the deadly silence. It was Beth, Brian's intern, who screamed at the approaching figure, the first utterance we'd heard from her all night.

"What the hell!" I cried, the hairs on the back of my neck standing on end. Tom turned, the light of his camera slightly illuminating the approaching figure. It was Pete, a friend of mine whom I had invited along to try out his new infrared camera. He was so late and I had been so preoccupied with the investigation that I had forgotten that he was coming.

INFRARED CAMERA (IR)

A camera that operates on the infrared range and allows the viewer to see in low levels or the absence of light.

Once everyone regained their composure and the introductions were completed, we continued our investigation. We left the precarious presence of the "hanging tree," as we had aptly named it, and headed down the hill to another portion of the burial ground. Passing old and ill-kept graves, we came upon a large, flat tomb. Focusing the light from our failing flashlights, we struggled to read the etchings on its weather-beaten surface in an attempt to find who had been buried there. "Okay, 1776, that's the date. The name, can anybody make it out?"

Silence was my answer as everyone attempted to decipher the engraving, to no avail. As the light in Tom's camera faded out, he spoke up. "Brian, that's another battery down. How weird is that?"

Still, with little other paranormal activity to note, I decided that we should try an experiment to see what we could conjure up. I turned to Maureen and asked her if she had her tarot cards.

* * *

When Ron asked me if I had my tarot cards, I cringed. "They're in the car, why?" I was just getting to know how Ron thought, and I didn't like where this was going.

"I want to try something. You think you can do a reading on the crypt?"

"Are you crazy?" I can't believe I was actually contemplating doing a reading in a cemetery. Some people would say any tarot reading at all would be consorting with the Devil, let alone doing it over someone's grave. *Oh, I am so going to hell*, I thought to myself. "Fine. Then you go get 'em." With that, Ron disappeared into the darkness.

"Maureen, while Ron's gone, why don't you show me how those things work?" Brian said, motioning toward the dowsing rods. I'd just begun to demonstrate them, when I heard a yelp in the distance. Looking in the direction of the cry, I saw the silhouette of Ron, illuminated by the streetlight. That's when I realized he had also fallen into a hole. Our laughter echoed in the stillness of the night as we watched him stumbling to get out.

Now that's funny. "Are you okay?"

"Fine." His voice vibrated in the distance.

After the laughter subsided, I continued my demonstration until Ron returned.

Taking the cards from their velour pouch, I tentatively laid them on top of the tomb. I removed my crystal ball, which felt more like an ice cube between my chilled palms, and positioned it on a small purple satin pillow.

Ron Kolek

At Ron's request, Maureen attempts to stir things up at the cemetery by drawing tarot cards on an aging tomb while Brian Bates looks on.

"Maureen, what's the crystal ball for?" Brian asked.

"You have a short memory," I chuckled. "Remember last week, when I used it at Ethel's? I use it to help connect with the energy, and when I do multiple readings, it helps to break the connection from one person to another."

"Oh yeah, I forgot." The darkness couldn't hide his embarrassment.

"So, Ron, what do you want me to do?" I asked.

"Here's the deal. How about if we each draw a card, and we'll start by doing a reading for the person buried here?" Ron answered.

"What…are you nuts? You want me to read on top of a crypt? It's over someone's body, for God's sakes. You do want me to go to hell, don't you?"

"Better you than me."

"Somehow I think it'll be both of us."

As I suspected, the cards revealed more about the person who pulled the card and less about the soul buried here. It didn't take long before the group began asking questions. The questions became less and less about our investigation and more about those who were present. Tired with the way the reading was progressing, since it was not revealing anything about the person buried there, and opening my mind's eye once again, I splayed my hands over the cards. This time, I began to feel a surge of energy. It felt thick, weighted. The closer my hands came to the cards, the stronger the pressure repelling them away, like matching poles of a magnet. It was the strongest energy I'd felt all night. "Ron, I'm beginning to feel an intense wave of energy. I just can't place where it's coming from." But just as I finished my sentence, the energy dissipated, as if it didn't want to be discovered. "Wait. Forget it. Whatever it was, it's gone."

"Shit!" Ron said. "The first damn thing we pick up on all night, and it decides to play shy on us." Ron pouted. "Brian, I hate to be the bearer of bad news, but I think this is the best we're gonna do tonight. Investigations are like this sometimes. Unfortunately, spirits don't perform like trained monkeys."

We stood there for a moment, hoping for something to happen, until the cold finally took its toll on us and we decided to call it a night.

We packed up our gear as Brian did his closing piece. "We didn't see any heads coming out of the ground tonight, but it was definitely one of the spookiest places I've been to so far. So if you happen to come across this particular graveyard in Newburyport and you feel a little spooked, there's a good reason. There are over fifty sailors who fought in the revolutionary war buried right here. They've come back a number of times, to haunt not only Ron, but locals as well. Happy Halloween. I'm Brian Bates, News 9 night team."

"I've got one shot left." Ron turned back toward the cemetery and clicked the shutter on his 35mm, ending our night.

Ron's last infrared photo reveals what appears to be an ecto mist in the shape of somebody waving good-bye.

The next day I called Ron. "Did you see the news piece?"

"Yeah," he said, "I thought it was decent."

"I watched it with Stephen," I said, mentioning my husband. "It was too funny. Right in the middle of the broadcast, he turned to me and said, 'Did I see that right? Did Ron just do what I think he did?'" I waited for Ron to respond, which he didn't, so I continued. "I told him, 'No, Steve, you weren't hallucinating. Ron rubbed the skull and smelled his fingers.'" I laughed.

"So what's the problem?" he replied. "You know you have to use all your senses. Well, the nose is just another tool."

"You and your tools." I chuckled. It was only my fourth investigation with the team, and already I had learned to expect the unexpected with Ron, or at least I thought I did. *Never* in the darkest corners of my mind did I suspect that our next case would be to assist a Franciscan Monk in an exorcism.

RESULTS OF THE INVESTIGATION

Old Hill Cemetery is one of the creepiest burial grounds we have ever been to. It contains a crypt that has been broken into several times over the past hundred years, with the corpses defiled in a macabre series of ways. Open graves can be found, where you can rub the skulls of the dead, for those brave—and crazy—enough to try. Photos of a ghostly head coming out of the ground have been taken. And, perhaps the most bizarre occurrence of all was when Ron was slimed with a thick black oozy gook. But on the scariest night of the year, it seemed the dead were off to a Halloween party of their own, and we weren't invited—or so we thought. Ron's final photo revealed a ghostly mist, with one arm raised, waving good-bye—or was it perhaps good riddance?

THE EXORCISM

CASE FILE: 6875624
EXORCISM

Location: Boston, Massachusetts.

History: Old Victorian house on the South Boston waterfront, later converted to a townhouse.

Reported Paranormal Activity: Gas stove that turns on by itself, electric outlets destroyed, objects moving of their own accord, dog tormented by unseen entity, and physical attacks on owner.

Clients: Brenda (homeowner), Duke (Brenda's dog).

Investigators: Ron (lead investigator), Maureen (trance medium), Brian the Monk (the exorcist).

Maureen, Maureen. Wake up." I heard the sound of my husband's voice in the distance. "Wake up. You're having a nightmare."

Heart still pounding in my chest, I bolted upright. Finding it difficult to swallow with the lump in my throat, I stared at Steve. The whites of his eyes were more pronounced, a look of concern etched his face. "Are you okay?" he asked.

"Yes," I lied. Still gasping for breath I looked past him at the clock. 7:00 a.m. I scrambled out of the tangled covers and ran into the bathroom. "If I don't get a move on, I'm going to be late."

"What is up with you lately? Maybe it's all that speaking with the dead you do. You know. Affecting your brain."

Truth be told, the nightmare had scared the hell out of me. As I stood looking into the bathroom mirror, a kaleidoscope of colors and fragments of disjointed images twisted before my eyes. For the moment, I was back, standing on the deserted street of my nightmare. I felt a rush of panic. It was all too close to home. There, in front of me, stood my teenage son. I struggled to make sense of what I had seen. Why had he been in my dream? I'd have never allowed my children to partake in an exorcism. A tear slid down my cheek as I once again saw Josh's wide-eyed stare as he reached out and cried, "Mom—please!" Just as in my dream I was once again forced to helplessly watch as his pale body was being clawed at by dark, soulless figures with unseen hands. They whipped around him, pulling him down, deeper. Deeper. Until the pavement swallowed him whole.

The images of the nightmare were way too vivid, way too colorful, way too coincidental. It must be a warning. My thoughts ran to the discussion I'd had with Ron a few nights ago, when I'd agreed to attend an exorcism with him and Brian the Monk, a friend of Ron's I hadn't met. Brenda, our client, had called for help after finding our website, and we thought Brian's services might be needed.

Steve's voice carried over the sound of running water as I splashed my face. "Don't you think it's time to give this up? I mean, come on. What's it going to take for you to realize this isn't healthy for you?"

I'd known the truth when I first met my husband all those years ago. He was terrified of the idea that souls actually existed after death. I witnessed his fear every time I talked to him about my experiences. His eyes would tear up and his usual jovial demeanor would turn solemn and gruff. Since we'd met so young, he had assumed I'd grow out of it, like the habit of biting nails. Bad assumption. These days, though, our conversations of the dead and dying are few and far between. He likes it that way.

Trying to make myself sound more upbeat, I forced a smile. Smiles have a way of lightening a voice. I don't know why, but they do. "Don't worry about me. I'm fine. Maybe it's that horror flick I saw the other night? Really, I'm fine."

I glanced in the mirror, the terrible visions of moments ago now gone. I gasped at my reflection. Visine for the redness, makeup for the dark circles, but only time would heal the puffiness.

Later that night, after wrestling with the images of the nightmare plaguing my mind, I called Ron. "Ron, I had another nightmare.

I've been thinking…I don't know that I can make it with you and Brian on Wednesday."

"What do you mean? We need you. Brenda needs you."

"Look, I really want to help. But this time 'it' went after my son. I couldn't stop it."

"Maureen, it was just a bad dream. Besides, Brian said for it to work right, he needs the three of us."

My heart thudded in my chest. "My son, Ron. Did you hear me?" My voice cracked as I swallowed back the tears. "Look, to you it's just a 'bad dream'…I do want to help. But at what cost? It was my son, Ron."

"You know, if you have a bad dream and tell someone about it, it'll go away."

Not fully convinced, but on the off chance that he was right, I shared my dream. "I saw the townhouse looming in the darkness in downtown Boston. The house seemed alive. The moment a blonde woman opened the front door, I felt evil oozing out of it. Josh was there. He was being attacked by dark, soulless figures. I was helpless as my legs disappeared into the molten pavement. There was a man standing near the woman, wearing a long, woolen, brown robe. The front of his brown hair was cut short, the back pulled loosely into a ponytail. He had a diamond stud on his left ear and wore wire-rimmed glasses. With a bible in his left hand he started praying over the blonde woman in a foreign tongue. I think it was Latin. *'Exorcizámus te, omnis immúnde spíritus…'*"

The phone went silent when I finished.

"Ron, are you there?"

"Yes. I'm here." He hesitated. "It must have been just a dream, because Brian doesn't wear glasses. And I'm not sure if they pray in Latin anymore."

"What?" I'd never met Brian so I had no way of knowing. Besides, I was just relaying the dream like he'd asked. "Ron, I don't know. I'm just telling you what happened."

"Well, you hit on a couple of things. Brian has dark hair and he does have a ponytail. He wears an earring, but he doesn't wear glasses. So see, you're worrying over nothing. It was just a dream. Actually," Ron's voice faltered, "he's been having dreams of you, too. In fact, he described you to a T."

My blood ran cold. "Okay. Say no more. I'm out of it."

"Brian thought you would feel that way."

"What are you talking about? When were you planning on sharing this little tidbit of information?"

"Don't get all huffy about it. It's just that I didn't want to scare you. Brian figured you'd be calling me to cancel. He told me that it's up to you. But he said that he'd protect us. That the demonic entity is just trying to scare you. You know, like when we've gone on investigations and the number 66.6 appears on the temperature sensors. It's just its way of trying to intimidate us."

I swallowed hard. "Well, it's doing a damn good job of it."

"Maureen, if you don't want to come, I understand. Why don't you think about it, and let me know sometime tomorrow? If you feel you can't go through with it, I'll find someone to take your place. No matter what, Brian and I are still going. We'd prefer it be you with us. But if you can't, you can't." Ron's voice sounded softer somehow. "When I first met you, you told me how much you want to help people with your gift. Don't let this thing get the better of you."

I lay awake all night, tossing and turning. I shivered when I thought of the years I'd spent being a medium for séances. One night, at the age of nineteen, when a negative entity followed me home and tried to suffocate me in my sleep, I'd felt firsthand the evil that lurked, waiting for an open door.

My thoughts turned to Brenda, the woman who contacted us through the Ghost Project website. She needed our help and had nowhere left to turn. As much as I hated to admit it, Ron was right. Not one to be bullied, and suddenly angry that this "thing" would sink so low as to hit me where it hurt, I closed my eyes and said a silent prayer to St. Michael for the protection of my family, for Brenda, and, most of all, for strength.

* * *

Unlike Maureen, I was excited about tonight's adventure. Sitting in traffic, my mind began to wander. I thought about when the movie *The Exorcist* came out. After I'd watched it, I'd had nightmares for weeks, its images festering deep within my mind. Just thinking about it now, though, doubts bubbled to the surface of my consciousness, and a dull panic nipped at my confidence.

But this is what the NEGP had set out to do, and I knew I couldn't back down. Slowly my confidence returned, aided by Tom Petty on the radio: "*You can stand me up at the gates of hell but I won't back down.*"

I had one more stop to make before picking up Maureen. Saint Francis Church. Van Helsing might be brave, but he isn't stupid. I was stopping to get a blessing from the parish priest. One more silver bullet in my arsenal of protection. I tucked the infrared film that I had just purchased into my duffel bag, got out of the car, and made my way through the church basement to the parish office.

I poked my head through his open office door and said, "Good evening, Father, can I talk with you for a moment?"

"Hello Ron," he said with a warm smile. "Come on in. What can I do for you?"

I entered the room and stood in front of his rich mahogany desk. "I need your help, Father."

"Glad to help," he said, smiling. "What's this all about?"

"I'm going to an exorcism, and I need your blessing," I blurted out.

"Exorcism," he said, as his smile disappeared. "What do you mean 'exorcism'?"

"I was contacted by this woman from Boston asking for help, so I called a Franciscan monk that I know, and he's going to perform an exorcism on her—tonight."

"Franciscan," he said, as if it were a dirty word. "What do you know about this Franciscan?"

"I've known him for a while; he's a designated exorcist for the Franciscan order."

"This is serious, Ron. The Church doesn't take this lightly. How do you know he's authorized to do this? Have you checked with the Bishop?"

"I know him, Father. I believe him," I said, ignoring his questions.

He stood up and walked around to the front of the desk. "You know there's a lot that has to be done before an exorcism can be performed. You have to be evaluated by a medical doctor, a psychiatrist, a sociologist, and you have to go before a panel. This all takes time. As I said earlier, the Church doesn't take this lightly."

"I know in my heart I'm doing the right thing and I want—no, I need—your blessing."

"Very well, Ron, if I can't talk you out of it, it is the least I can do," he said with a frown. He made his way across the soft carpet to the desk. Opening a drawer, he removed a purple stole and a small bottle, and returned to my side. He kissed the dark purple cloth and placed it around his broad shoulders. Sketching a cross in the air with his fingers, he uttered a short prayer. He tilted the bottle, moistened his finger, and anointed my forehead. He began to recite the Our Father as I joined in. An instant later it was over.

Despite his earlier dissuasion, any doubts that I had were gone. I felt stronger, confident, and almost invincible. Like I'd explained to Father, I knew in my heart I was doing the right thing. I stood up, thanked him for his blessing, and headed toward the door. As I reached the door, his voice stopped me. I turned to hear him say, "Good luck, Ron, and may God be with you."

"Thank you, Father, but if I have God's blessing, I need no luck." I hurried away to pick up Maureen.

I was pleased and a bit surprised that Maureen had relented and agreed to join us. As she got in the car, I asked, "How you doing? You all right?"

"Yes. Let's just get going before I change my mind."

"Did you bring your scapular like Brian recommended?"

> ## SCAPULAR
> A devotional object used in the Catholic religion, made from cloth, wood, or metal, and usually worn around the neck. It is a silent prayer offered to the Blessed Mother in request for her protection.

"Yes. It's right here." She reached beneath her shirt and slid out a piece of cloth protected by clear plastic, hanging on a dark green ribbon. "It was my father's. My mother gave it to me when he died." With the last of her words, she closed her hand around the devotional artifact and squeezed tightly.

"I'm wearing my scapula and exorcism medal. See here." I slid the medal out from the confines of my Ghost Project shirt to demonstrate. Being the devout Catholic I am and trying to comfort her, I asked, "Do you realize the significance of wearing a scapular?"

She didn't answer, but stared out into the sea of cars as we traveled down Route 93 to 128.

"It's solely of spiritual nature," I said. "A sign of the wearer's readiness to serve." I waited for a moment to see if she was paying attention. When she returned a blank stare, I said, "A defender in the service of God and for the protection of the Blessed Mary."

She gave me a small smile. "Ron, I'll be fine."

Not more than twenty minutes later Brian was in the car.

"So, Maureen," Brian said, "I hear you've been having dreams too."

"Yes." Maureen was usually more talkative than this. She hadn't said more than five words to me since I'd picked her up from her house.

"Since we last spoke, how is Brenda doing?" Brian asked me.

I usually don't like to tell Maureen the details until after an investigation, so she doesn't go in with any biases. However, since this was an exorcism, and we were there to assist, I decided to tell all.

EXORCISM

A ritual for the purpose of forcing a demonic entity to stop obsessing or possessing a body.

OBSESSION

When an evil spirit attacks the body of a human being from the outside.

> **POSSESSION**
>
> When an evil spirit assumes control of a human soul from within the body.

"Like I said earlier, for the past five years she's been dealing with something unseen wreaking havoc in her life. Doors opening of their own accord, electrical outlets destroyed, the jets to her gas oven turning on by themselves, and so forth." I glanced in the rearview mirror at Maureen, her face still blank, revealing nothing, as she stared straight ahead. "Brian, she went to the church for help, but they told her to seek psychological help."

Brian asked. "What about her dog? You had also said that it was affecting her pet? I'm wondering if you'd heard anything more."

I smiled inwardly. Brian was an animal lover through and through. "Brenda said that her dog, for some unexplainable reason, starts whining uncontrollably, like he's in pain."

"Not to worry. He'll be fine," Brian said. "I have a little something for him too."

Maureen broke her silence. "Ron, I know you don't like to share details of the case, afraid that I'll go in with a preconceived notion, but if you don't mind…This once I'd like to hear what's really going on. Is there anything else that you haven't said?"

Maureen was right; I hadn't told her everything. She prefers to be kept in the dark as much as I like to withhold the details, so the fact that she was asking for more information told me she was still feeling nervous. I couldn't blame her. I'd never attended an exorcism either.

I said, "After the church turned Brenda away, she did a little research into ghosts and asked a friend to help her. They 'smudged' the condo. That's when things went from bad to worse."

SMUDGING

A ceremony in which a bundle of herbs, most commonly sage, cedar, and sweetgrass, is burned, used to drive out and keep negative energy from entering a space.

"Two weeks ago, after they smudged and her friend left the house, Brenda was attacked." I took a moment to gather my words. But no matter how much I tried to soften the story, it was no use. "She was up in her bedroom on the second floor. When her dog started whining for no reason, she went to investigate. She'd barely stepped down onto the first floor landing when a spindle hit her. It had worked its way free from the second floor banister, flown down the stairs of its own accord, and struck her in the back of the head. Panicked, fearing she was not alone, she ran from room to room looking for intruders. But no one was there."

We all silently took this in for a minute, then Brian said, "Like I thought, Ron. This is the real deal."

* * *

As we stepped out of Ron's car, I stood, mouth open, staring at the tall, dark building in front of me. "That's Brenda's place?" I stammered.

"I think so. Why?" Ron asked as he squinted, holding up a small piece of paper in the yellow light of the streetlamp. "Yup. That's the one."

My breathing quickened; I nearly choked. "That—that's the house from my dream."

As if not hearing me, Ron and Brian scurried to the front door. Still stunned, I stood gaping at the house, until the sound of their voices carried from across the street.

Ron gazed over his shoulder. "You coming or what?"

I struggled to move. I shuddered as the odd sensation that I had experienced this before chilled me to the bone. Fixated on Ron's voice, I forced myself to move.

I stepped up behind Ron and Brian just as Ron pressed the button to the doorbell.

The bell rang and rang, one continuous ring, not shutting off. The front door flew open. With it, the intense ringing grew louder, deafening, almost ear piercing. A tall woman stood in the open doorway. She raised her hand to her forehead. "You must be Ron." When she stepped into the light, I noticed her thick, shoulder-length, blonde hair and cringed. My heart skipped a beat. The little hairs at the base of my neck stood at attention. This was getting way too freaky. She was a living image of the woman in my dream.

Raising her voice to be heard clearly above the constant shrill of the doorbell, she said, "It's him. He does this all the time. Hurry. Please—come in."

"Brenda, I'm Brian," he said. "Please, show me where the doorbell is."

We hurried after Brenda. Within moments we were staring at the doorbell mechanism.

Brian dropped his brown leather duffel bag on the kitchen table. Retrieving a vial of holy water, he moistened his right thumb. Hurrying over to the doorbell, he made the sign of the cross. The second he did, the sound stopped.

"Brian, you rock. That's so cool," Ron said, as Brenda and I looked on in amazement.

Brian grinned. "In light of what just happened, I'd like to get this show on the road." He reached into his leather bag once again, this time pulling out his 35mm camera.

"Why do you have all that stuff on your camera?" Brenda asked, referring to the extra protection Brian had attached.

Brian held up the black Nikon camera. "I put this *stuff* on here to protect the camera. Before I started using it, the batteries would drain, the shutter would freeze, and more often than not, the film would be ruined. Now it's protected. See here," he said, pointing to the brown wooden beads wrapped around the camera, "I have rosary beads. I bless it with holy water, and more importantly, I have a photo of the Shroud of Turin, because evil cannot look upon the face of God."

SHROUD OF TURIN

A linen burial cloth that is believed to bear the true image of Jesus Christ.

Ron placed his own duffel bag on the kitchen table next to Brian's and began to rummage through it in search of his 35mm camera and EMF meter.

As we waited for Ron to ready himself, Brenda gestured to the small, white stove in the corner of the kitchen. "Did Ron tell you what happened here?"

"No," I replied, my anxiety growing.

"One night, while making supper, I wrapped a couple of russets in tin foil and placed them on the center rack in the oven. Exhausted after a trying day at the hospital, I rested on the couch while they baked. I guess I fell asleep, because I was awakened by the shriek of the smoke alarm. I ran into the kitchen and there was smoke billowing out of the oven. Quickly opening the door, I discovered the potatoes were no longer on the center rack. In fact, they were no longer in tin foil. Somehow they ended up on the bottom of the stove, on the heating element. They were on fire." She sighed heavily. "This is the kind of stuff that I've been plagued with. I haven't added it all up yet, but if I had to guess, it would be thousands of dollars in damages." Eyes watering and voice cracking, she continued, "Please, do you really think you can help me? I'm at my wits' end. I don't know how much more I can take."

Brian drew nearer, placing a hand on her shoulder. "Not to worry, this isn't my first exorcism. It'll be okay."

Ron and I followed Brenda and Brian up a set of stairs. When we reached the second floor landing, I began to sense a heavy energy. The feeling of nervous apprehension swam over me, but it was difficult to tell where it was coming from. *Was I picking up on the entity? Or was it my own fears?* Movement out of the corner of my eye caught my attention. I looked to see Brian raising his 35mm camera; he quickly snapped a shot to our left. It was the same direction from which I'd felt the first surge of energy. *I guess it wasn't my own fear, after all.* Somehow, that thought didn't make me feel any better.

Brian turned to look at me with raised eyebrows. "Maureen, what are you getting?"

I gave him my first impression of the energy. "It's intense, anxious. But I feel that whatever is here is dogging us."

"Not anymore." Brian darted off. Chasing the entity, he ran from room to room, snapping shot after shot.

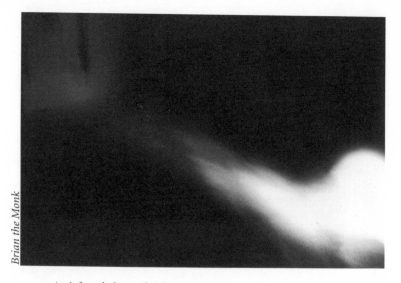

Brian the Monk

An infrared photo taken by Brian the Monk of the entity attempting to escape his camera.

As I stood in the hallway at the top of the stairs, a surge of raw, cold energy, originating from the bedroom off to the far left, the one Brian was now in, whisked through me and descended the stairs. Brian, in hot pursuit, quickly exited the bedroom and ran toward me.

"Maureen, did you feel anything out here?" Before I had a chance to respond, pain-filled moans emanated from below us on the first floor. Brenda, who lived alone with her dog, reacted like a mother hearing her child crying in the middle of the night and hurried down the oak stairs to the first floor. "Oh no. It's after Duke again!" she screamed.

We scurried down the stairs to find Duke, Brenda's dog, whimpering. The black Russian terrier cowered in the corner, shaking uncontrollably.

Brian reached into his pocket and pulled out a small, flat square of plastic with a rawhide tie. He glanced at Brenda, nodded, and then knelt beside Duke. "This is for Duke. It's a picture of the Shroud of Turin," he said, as he attached the rawhide tie to the silver buckle of Duke's collar.

Miraculously, the dog immediately stopped whining and rested his head on Brian's knee. "See, this stuff really works."

Brenda, fidgeting with her hands, sighed. "Thank you. He finally looks peaceful." She wrapped the large dog in her arms and ran her fingers through his fur. "I haven't seen him this relaxed in months."

Brian gestured for Brenda to take a seat on the couch. "Okay, now it's your turn. But first, do you have somewhere I can change?"

Brenda and Brian walked into the kitchen as I looked at Ron. "Now what?"

"How am I supposed to know? I've never been to an exorcism before."

Brenda strode past us, taking a seat on the couch. Brian followed a short time later with his brown leather bag. His jeans and black Rolling Stones T-shirt were now replaced with a brown woolen smock, a rope belt tied around his paunchy waist. He placed his bag on the floor beside the couch. "Brenda, could you please lay back on the couch for me?" he asked. Reaching into the bag, he removed a white sash, unfolded it, and brought it to his lips, then placed it around his neck. Next he took out a heavy-looking, brown, tattered Bible. Its cover was embossed with a golden cross, so faded it nearly blended into the background. Reaching into the bag once again, he retrieved a pair of wire-rimmed glasses and put them on.

I shoved my elbow deep in Ron's ribs.

Ron jerked away, rubbing his side. "Ouch! What was that for?"

"Brian doesn't wear glasses, huh?"

"Oops. My bad," Ron replied, still wincing from the jab.

Brian turned to face us, his words interrupting our bickering. "We're going to open with a prayer. But I need your help. The three of us need to say it together."

"Why is that?" Ron asked.

"Because like the Trinity, it makes the prayer stronger. We'll start off with the Our Father." Then, making a cross in the air with his hand, he said, "In the name of the Father, the Son, and the Holy Spirit."

Our voices resonated as one. "Our Father, who art in heaven, hallowed be Thy name…"

The sweet, pungent aroma of the anointed oil permeated the air as he ran his thumb across Brenda's forehead, and then I heard the hollowness of Brian's voice speaking in a strange tongue. "*Exorcizámus te, omnis immúnde spíritus…*"

An infrared shot of Brian the Monk conducting the exorcism
(client's face obscured to protect her identity).

As in my dream, he moved his head slightly, looking from the Bible to Brenda, then back to the Bible again. I shivered, even as his wire-rimmed glasses slid down his nose. He pushed his glasses back into place and continued his prayers.

Brenda began to moan slightly and shift uncomfortably with each word passing Brian's lips.

As I watched the scene unfold in front of me, tension filled the room. The energy I'd felt at the top of the stairs was now all around me, darting back and forth.

Brenda's body twisted and turned.

Bone-chilling cold encircled our bodies. Brian's voice grew stronger. Penetrating. Powerful. There was no doubt the energy I sensed was demonic. The evil presence's anger grew, escalating with each word. An acrid odor assailed my senses.

Brian sensed it too. His stance became rigid, tall, growing in stature. For a man who couldn't have been more than five foot nine, he seemed like a giant. His voice became unyielding, meeting each invisible thrust of demonic energy with his own determination.

Brenda's body was now the battleground between the demonic energy and Brian's unwavering faith. Her head tilted back and her body followed suit, her spine bowing backward then curling in as a silent scream escaped her lips. Brian quickly laid his hand upon her head. "*Omnis satanica potestas, omnis incursio infernalis adversarii, omnis legio…*"

Evil roiled around me, filling the room. I gasped. As if a vacuum had sucked the air out of the room, I suddenly found it hard to breathe. Coughing, I struggled. My throat tightened, closed, constricted. Unable to swallow, I opened my mouth to scream. But no sound came out.

Brian detected my distress. Still chanting, he stepped away from Brenda for a heartbeat. Sticking his finger in the anointing oil once again, he made the sign of the cross on my forehead. The death grip on my throat lessened. Greedy for air, I inhaled deeply.

A moment later, Brian was once again at Brenda's side. Kneeling, his voice rose and reached a crescendo. "...*Omni infernálium spirituum potestáte, láqueo deceptióne et nequitia nos poténter liberáre, et incólumes custodire dignéris. Per Christum Dóminum nostrum. Amen.*"

With that came a loud bang. Brenda's body stiffened like a corpse, then collapsed. Her chest heaved up and down. A long, exaggerated sigh escaped her as she sunk deeper into the softness of the couch. The fetid odor that had once permeated the room was gone.

Brian stood to face us. "Maureen, are you all right?"

"Yes, I'm feeling better now. Thanks."

"Wow, that was amazing. Brian, what was that sound Brenda made?" Ron asked.

"When you hear that sound, you know the exorcism was successful. The evil spirit is gone."

"Where did it go?" I asked.

"I can't guarantee where's it's gone, but I *can* guarantee it's no longer here."

Brenda slowly sat upright. Grabbing a tissue from her pocket, she dried her eyes.

Brian turned his attention back to her. In a gentle voice he asked, "Brenda, are you feeling any different?"

"Yes, I feel so much lighter, as if my burdens have been lifted." She smiled, genuinely. "Is it just me, or does it feel warmer in here?"

"You know, you're right, I was going to say something about that. It feels so much better in here right now." Ron said.

Brian smiled. "Okay, Brenda, the spirit is gone now, but to ensure that it doesn't come back, I'm going to hang the Shroud of Turin over your doors and on the walls facing each other. Do not take them down for at least thirty days. I'd also like it if you would start going to church."

Brenda sat solemnly on the couch, nodding as Brian relayed his instructions.

"Brian, if you want, I'll help you hang up the printouts and bless the house," Ron offered.

"I'd appreciate that." Brian said.

As Brian and Ron left to hang the pictures, I sat beside Brenda on the couch. "So, Brenda, how are you feeling?"

"I'm feeling worlds better. It's amazing. I'm so grateful for everything all of you have done for me." As Brenda lifted her purse off the floor beside the couch and rummaged for her wallet, I could tell she wanted to offer us monetary compensation.

I placed my hand on top of Brenda's. "Please. We appreciate the offer, but this is volunteer work. We're just happy that you're going to be all right."

Brenda looked a little taken aback. Tears glistened in her eyes. "You're sure?"

"Positively." I smiled. Warmth spread through me. Although I'd been fearful of coming here, one look at Brenda and I was extremely happy that I did.

"Brenda, we're all set here," Brian said as he and Ron stepped off the last step and walked into the living room. "As you can see, Ron and I have finished hanging the images. Also, we've blessed all the doors, windows, and the rest of the rooms with holy water, so you should be all set." He smiled. "Do you have any questions for me before we head out?"

"You feel confident that it's gone?" Brenda asked, her voice sounding a little unsure, afraid to believe the horror she'd been living was now gone for good.

"Yes. But make sure you follow the directions I gave you. If you have any more problems, feel free to give Ron a call and we'll come back out as soon as possible. But truthfully, I know you're going to be just fine."

Two weeks later, while writing an article about protection, I went to my jewelry box for a better look at the scapular that I'd worn that night. The instant my hands came in contact with it, I dropped to my knees. A searing pain pierced my heart. I gasped for breath. My hand on the dresser, I steadied my breathing and pulled myself up and off the floor. It took a moment for my mind to clear. To realize what had happened. The scapular had indeed been my protection, absorbing the negative energy, protecting me, like St. George, shielding me from the dragon's breath. My mistake was not realizing that I should have cleansed it, blessed it with holy water. I'd learned an invaluable lesson. One that I would never forget...

RESULTS OF THE INVESTIGATION

Research revealed that the original owner of the house was a Catholic who had committed suicide by hanging. Brian determined that Brenda was plagued by a demonic obsession, not a possession. It appears the exorcism was successful. Neither Brenda nor Duke required our services again.

While writing this episode we were plagued by odd events: computer and electrical problems, water damage from a pipe bursting, and perhaps the eeriest occurrence of all, the unexplained removal of Ron's scapula and exorcism medal. The medal, the one worn during the exorcism, which was safely secured on a chain, was torn free.

ASHES TO ASHES

CASE FILE: 6281763
ASHES TO ASHES

Location: Chester, New Hampshire.

History: A split level home built in the 1960s, surrounded by woods.

Reported Paranormal Activity: Ghostly figure appearing in photos, noises in the basement, apparitions, and disembodied voices.

Clients: Andrea (owner), Robert (Andrea's husband).

Investigators: Ron (lead investigator), Maureen (trance medium), Leo (photographer), Karen (EVP specialist).

What would you do if you found the ashes of the former owner of a house you just purchased in the closet? Or what if your young daughter came up to you and said, "Tell that man to get out of my bed?" These aren't hypothetical questions. These events really happened to a family in Chester, New Hampshire.

Ring, ring, ring.

"Good afternoon, New England Ghost Project."

"Hello, Ron, this is Andrea. I Googled 'ghosts' and found your website. I was the one who sent you the email about what's going on at our house. Ahhh, you know, the house with the ashes in the basement."

"Oh yeah. Now I remember." *Hmmm, that's a little strange,* I thought. "Whose ashes were they?"

"George, the former owner. And things have escalated since the email."

"What do you mean, 'escalated'?" I asked, hoping my voice didn't sound as apprehensive as I felt.

"There are voices coming from the woods." With the sound of panic in her voice, she continued, "Evil laughter. We can hear a little boy crying, 'Mommy, Mommy, Mommy.' And if that's not bad enough, they're commanding us, 'GET OUT!' Even my husband's starting to hear them. We feel like we're losing our minds. Ron, we don't feel safe here anymore. And I'm really worried about my daughter."

The thought of a child in danger tugged at my heartstrings, and being the sensitive sort, I said, "How about Saturday night?"

Her voice quivered, sounding on the verge of tears. "Thank you. That would be great. I realize it's short notice, but we're desperate."

"Don't worry, we'll be there." As I hung up the phone, a sense of dread assailed my senses, my gut twisting in a knot. I couldn't help but wonder if it was a premonition of what was to come or the kielbasa I ate for lunch. I was hoping it was the lunch, but we would soon find out.

* * *

"Brrrrr." My soul shivered as I stepped out of Ron's car, my foot coming into contact with Andrea's paved driveway. I cringed at the sudden sharp pain boring a hole through my heart. Ron was right; it was apparent to me that the entities had come out to answer the challenge, to check out the fresh meat that dared enter their space.

The hair at the base of my neck prickled to attention. I didn't know about anyone else, but I was ready to call it a night even though we'd only just arrived.

"Maureen, are you coming, or are you going to make a night of it?" Ron sarcastically remarked.

Pushing away the threatening feelings, I pretended to be calm. I was determined to keep up the charade as long as I had to. "Yeah, just a minute," I quipped, doing my best to push my fears to the recesses of my mind. *Ron can be such an ass at times*, I thought. And besides, we'd come to help, and there was no way I was turning back now.

As we reached the front door I turned to look at the remaining members of the NEGP for some sort of sign, any reaction to show me they had picked up on something too. But it looked like I was alone.

"Hi, I'm Andrea, and this is my husband, Robert. Glad you could make it."

First stop on this little tour of horrors would be to find George, or what was left of him. "So, Andrea, what happened to George's ashes?" I asked.

"Well, you see, from what we were told, George wanted his ashes buried beneath the maple tree he had planted in the backyard. But..." She hesitated, giving Robert a cold stare. "But Robert cut it down. That's when we started hearing noises. Doors slamming, boxes being dragged across the floor, and throaty whispers emanating from the basement."

"Oops. So what did you do?" Ron asked.

"To try and appease George, we scattered his ashes in a simple ceremony on Memorial Day weekend, at the site of the former tree."

"Did it work?" I couldn't help wondering.

"For a while. But that's when the voices started, and that's when we contacted you guys for help."

"Do you think you can find the place where you scattered his ashes in the dark?" Ron asked, digging in his pocket for his flashlight.

We followed Robert as he cut a zigzag path through the dried twigs and branches, stumbling over fallen trees and unseen rocks.

Twenty minutes later, briars stuck to my jeans, we stood where Robert thought he had laid George to rest. "Is this the spot?" I asked.

"I don't know. It's dark, and it's been six months."

Judging from the path he cut, I had my doubts.

"Want to try and communicate?" Ron asked eagerly.

With my pendulum held tightly between my thumb and forefinger, I attempted to make contact. "Are there any spirits here with us?" I asked, as Ron began to scan the vicinity with the EMF meter.

Was this the resting place of George's ashes?

My pendulum remained still. No response. Nothing. From what little I could sense, our friend George was not hanging out in the woods with his ashes. If they were even here.

I stuffed my pendulum back into my pocket, while Leo, our photographer, began taking infrared shots.

Ron looked at me. Without even speaking I knew his thoughts: *There's nothing out here.*

I shrugged in response.

Turning our backs on the buzz of the group, we began our trek back, the dim lights of the house acting like a beacon in the star-filled night. Approaching the rear of the house, we stopped momentarily, as if at a crossroads. I closed my eyes, breathing in deeply the frigid night air, and waited for my instincts to kick in. That's when it came to me. We had to go toward the right side of the house. I had no way to explain it. I just knew. Like a magnet to iron, without the time to explain, I took off at a near run. "This way," I said, stepping over weathered landscape timbers and around a child's swing set. Turning, looking over my shoulder, I cried, with a sense of urgency in my voice, "Hurry, over here."

Ron quickly joined me. As we neared the right front corner of the house, the pull became stronger. This was it.

I stopped dead in my tracks.

My third eye pulsated. Energy was everywhere. But I was having trouble discerning who or "what" it was. The beeping of the EMF meter was amplifying the feelings surging through my veins.

The energy grew thick, suffocating, like a storm cloud starting to envelop us. As if reading my thoughts, Ron said, "Yeah, I feel it too." He paused. "What the hell is it?"

"I don't know. I wish I knew," I said, unable to focus. "I just can't make it out." The intensity was growing around us, reaching a crescendo, when—bam—it was gone. The beeping of Ron's EMF meter was quickly replaced by the footsteps of the approaching group, who looked totally oblivious to what had just transpired.

Robert, Leo, and our EVP specialist, Karen, meandered by us, laughing and chatting about something that sounded like ghosts in period clothing and flowing dresses.

"I think we're done here," Ron said. "Let's go in."

Andrea was sitting at the kitchen table, laptop open; Leo and Karen were already perched over her shoulder, mouths agape, apparently enthralled by the photo on the screen.

"What's that?" Ron asked, walking up to the table.

"Check this photo out." She paused, angling the LCD screen so we all could see.

Peeking over Andrea's shoulder I caught a glimpse of the head of a shadowy figure behind a toy Oscar Mayer Weiner mobile. Its eye sockets were intently focused on the toy in front of it. Curious about what I was looking at, I asked, "Where did you take this?"

Andrea pointed to the L-shaped counter top. "Right there. I sell collectibles on eBay, and when I take the photos, these 'things' show up."

"Now, that's something you don't see every day," Ron commented, as we both knew that was good evidence that something was going on here. Looking down at his watch, he continued, "Let's finish up the investigation."

Leo picked up his 35mm, Karen her recorders, and we followed Andrea down the narrow hallway, with Ron and I bringing up the rear. One by one we entered each room with little result, until we reached the daughter's room. I was struck with a familiar feeling as we entered. "Has anything ever happened in here?"

"Funny you should ask. My daughter had an invisible friend she would often play with in here." Andrea paused, carefully considering her words. "But that was before we 'buried' George's ashes."

Ron turned to me, "Isn't this the corner of the house where we picked up our readings?"

I nodded. Now I knew what I had felt—it was the same energy. Although there was energy present, it was fleeting, and unfortunately for us, I had a feeling the worst was yet to come. And oh boy, was I right...

Having checked out all of the rooms, we were done with our investigation of the first floor of the split-level, and we headed to the basement. In single file we traversed the narrow steps to the cellar.

It was chilly. Although the thermostat on the wall read 70 degrees, an unnatural coldness penetrated our bones.

"This is where we found the ashes," Robert said, as he pointed to a small closet in the corner. "And this," he said, grabbing an old office chair gathering dust, and shoving it across the cement floor, "is the chair that always moves around on its own."

Above the sound of Robert's voice I heard Ron yell, "Maureen, come here." I followed his voice. We found ourselves standing just below the daughter's room.

"Karen, you want to try some EVPs?" Ron asked.

"Sure, Ron," she said, adjusting her recorder and pushing her long hair, reminiscent of the sixties, out of her face. "But you need to be quiet."

Ron turned down the volume on his EMF meter.

A dead calm settled over the group.

In a slow drawl, Karen asked, "Is there anyone here wishing to speak to us?"

The light on Karen's recorder sprang to life, indicating it was recording.

Suddenly, with all the intensity of a piranha feasting on a fresh kill, the ugliness I'd pushed away when we'd first arrived had returned. Dumbstruck, I stood there trying to get a handle on what I was sensing. I had the uncanny feeling I was being summoned. And whatever "it" was, it wasn't pretty.

Karen continued her recordings as I reached in and pulled my pendulum from the safety of my jeans. Despite my feelings, I knew once again I needed to attempt to make contact with whatever it was that was haunting this family. Only this time I wasn't feeling as confident. Whatever it was that was waiting was ready to pounce, and I knew that if I left an opening, it would.

Ron, realizing Karen was through recording, turned the volume on his EMF meter back on. As I stood there, my pendulum swinging to and fro, George's thoughts bombarded my consciousness. "He wants you out," I said, as I raised my head, catching the intensity of Robert's stare. All the while the staccato beep, beep, beep of Ron's EMF meter peppered the silence.

"Why?" Andrea asked, her voice trembling with fear.

"It is 'his' house. And, as far as he's concerned, you are intruders."

Ron drew closer to me. "Bbbbeeeeeppppp," the meter screeched, turning from staccato to shrill. "I think we have another visitor," he said. "The needle's off the scale."

In my mind I could feel George's anger, but I sensed something much darker. The evil toying with me since I'd arrived was suddenly upon me. My body struggled for control as the energy intensified tenfold. The invading darkness gave George a karmic push out of the way. Suddenly I was repulsed by the anger, the hatred, and the sins of the undead that clung to me like a foul second skin.

"Hey. Are you with us?"

Unable to respond I doubled over, clutching my ribcage. My mind fought for control, while Ron's words of concern sounded like a garbled voice spoken to me under rushing water. The harder I fought back, the worse it got, until searing pain akin to a hot poker being jammed up and under my ribcage held me temporarily immobile. Just as I felt my knees buckle, I felt Ron's hand on my arm as he held me up.

"Okay, that's enough. Let's go outside."

Stepping through the door, the crisp, cool night replaced some of the burning, but instinctively I knew it wasn't going to be enough. And it was only temporary. This thing, this pariah, had latched itself to me and was sucking my energy, like a bloodsucker on damp flesh. I needed to remedy the situation and fast or, at the very least, risk spending the next few days in bed rethinking my career choice.

"Maureen, where are you going?" Karen said, walking at my side. "Need some help?" Although she was short of stature, I'd learned quickly that she was big of heart.

"Yeah." Not having time to explain, and remembering the added protection I'd left in the car, I took a few deep breaths, inwardly prayed for protection, got my second wind, and headed for Ron's car. The high-pitched, rapid beeping of the EMF meter was indication enough that Ron was close on my heels. *God, give me a break. Sometimes I'd like to take that EMF meter and—.* Ignoring Ron and his damn meter, I turned toward Karen. "Here, hold this for a minute," I said, dropping the pendulum, chain and all, into the palm of her hand. "Ron, you want to give that EMF meter a break for a second and hand me your holy water?"

Reaching into his pocket, he pulled out a vial of holy water and handed it to me.

I blessed the car windows and opened the rear door.

Feeling a momentary sense of safety, I reached into the backseat, digging into my bag of goodies. Pulling out a sage bundle, I stepped away from the car and shut the door. I struck a match, and anxiously waited for the sage to ignite before smudging. The aroma of smoldering sweetgrass bound with sage hung in the air, permeating my senses. Almost immediately I could feel the shift in the energy. The night air had lightened. The evil that had been dogging me was temporarily held at bay. *Amen.*

Ron jabbed the meter within two inches of my chest. "Is it gone?"

"No. It's still here. But it's not stuck to me anymore." I paused, thinking for a moment. "Try moving the meter out a few feet."

Stepping back two feet on the pavement, Ron's eyes grew wide as the meter blinked wildly. "Damn, you're right. It is still here."

"Ron, I'm exhausted. This thing's gotta go." Reaching back into my bag of goodies, I pulled out my ace in the hole, my St. Michael prayer card.

As we recited the prayer, uneasiness filled the air. And a feeling I couldn't quite put my finger on washed over me, making me wonder if this wasn't the calm before the storm.

As I breathed a sigh of relief, I remembered that Karen, who was standing quietly to my left, still had my pendulum. I reached my hand out, palm up. "Thanks for holding it for me."

Karen dropped the pendulum into my waiting hand.

"What the...?" To both our amazement, the chain was missing.

"I—I—I don't know what happened to it, Maureen. It never left my hand."

After searching the driveway and immediate area, we found nothing.

"It's getting late," Ron said. "We can't spend all night here." He headed for the house, calling over his shoulder. "Let's pack it up."

Karen and I quickly joined Ron and our host in the kitchen.

Andrea looked around Ron to where I stood. "Maureen, are you all right?"

"Yeah, fine," I lied.

Andrea turned back toward Ron. "As I told you earlier, I'm scared for my daughter. Just the other day she ran out of her room crying, mumbling about some dark man in her room. She was terrified. With everything else we've been experiencing, I don't think it was just her imagination," Andrea said, her voice laced with desperation. "Is there anything we can do?"

"If you want, I can bless the house," Ron said.

"Thank you. That would be great."

"Maureen, while I'm blessing the house, why don't you see if you can help Andrea pull up the Shroud of Turin on her computer." Ron grabbed the vial of holy water and disappeared into the bedroom.

"Here it is," I said, pointing to the Google listing. "Let's open it up and see if we can print it." I hesitated, thinking how to explain it without scaring her off. "Print out a bunch of copies of these and tape them above each door and window."

"What will these do?"

"The Shroud of Turin, Christ's burial cloth, still holds his image. As Brian the Monk says, 'Evil cannot look upon the face of God.'"

"I think we're all set here." Ron walked back into the kitchen as he tucked a plastic bottle of holy water in the front pocket of his jeans. "It's time to leave."

As we walked to the cars, Andrea approached us. "By the way, I have something to tell you."

Ron stopped. "What?"

"Well, there's a rumor in town about some stuff that had been going on around here. A few people in town said something about Satan worshipers in the woods. Is this possible? Could it all be related to what's been going on here? You know," she said, her voice still shaky, "the neighbors have experienced similar problems too. Even though they try to ignore 'em."

"It's hard to say," Ron replied. "Anything's possible, I guess."

I remained silent. I was just too exhausted. In fact, if I had heard this tidbit of information prior to the investigation, I may have discounted it as nervous gossip. But now, after everything that had just happened, I couldn't discount it at all. Because what I felt was nothing if not pure evil.

All I knew was, I was happy to get the hell out of there. It had been a rough night. And, somehow I knew the ordeal wasn't over. Not by a long shot.

The next day I answered the phone.

"Hey, did you hear what happened to Leo and Karen?" Ron asked.

"No. What?" The knot in my stomach that had been there since the night before suddenly tightened.

"I got a call from Karen's son. Shortly after listening to last night's recordings she got in a freak accident. She broke her arm, scraped her face, and has a concussion."

"You're kidding me. That's awful."

"And that's not all!"

"Oh no. Now what?" I asked.

"Leo was rushed to the hospital last night with abdominal pain. Gall bladder surgery," Ron said. "Not for stones, but for a failed organ!"

"You're kidding! But you know, Ron, they were the only ones who chose not to protect themselves."

"Holy sh—. You're right."

"Aren't you glad that we always do?"

"Yeah, but maybe now Leo and Karen will rethink their protection process."

"You don't think there's any relationship to the ashes, do you?"

"Ashes to ashes, dust to dust." A phrase from the English burial service, sometimes used to denote total finality. Finality? Not likely. At least not for this investigation…

RESULTS OF THE INVESTIGATION

Maureen picked up on two spirits: George, the previous owner, and a hideous dark entity of unknown origins. Although we had no photographic evidence, we did capture some EVPs in the basement, which included "Are you hunters?" and "This ain't no party." But more importantly, Karen and Leo learned the value of protection. As for the homeowners, we later discovered that Andrea had been delving into spiritual communication, which may have contributed to the unrest in the home and perhaps unknowingly invited the evil that lurked in the woods. Unable to cope with the escalating activity, they sold their home and moved out of state.

episode eight

HOUGHTON MANSION

CASE FILE: 6232069
HOUGHTON MANSION

Location: North Adams, Massachusetts.

History: In the early 1890s, Albert C. Houghton, the first mayor of the city of North Adams, built the mansion. It was his third home in North Adams. On August 1, 1914, tragedy struck the Houghton family. They would see the death of four individuals associated with the mansion, all dying within eleven days of each other. In 1926 the Masons purchased the house from William Gallup, the son-in-law of A. C. Houghton. The Masons erected a Masonic Temple on the site of the formal garden, where it still remains today.

Reported Paranormal Activity: Unexplained shadows and footsteps.

Clients: Nick Montello (Mason), Josh Montello (Mason/Nick's son), Sarah Onorato (Nick's daughter), Greg Onorato (Mason/Sarah's husband), Paul Marino (local historian), Scott Cairns (Mason).

Investigators: Ron (lead investigator), Maureen (trance medium), Ron Jr. (investigator), Janet (Ron's wife/investigator), Marc Lemay (videographer).

Press: Ryan Quinn (reporter for North Adams Transcript newspaper).

The Houghton Mansion in North Adams, Massachusetts

For a moment we stood gazing up at the towering Houghton mansion, mesmerized at its appearance. Not at all what I had expected. Looming in the darkness with meager lighting casting shadows over the cracked cement walkway was a large building, paint curling, showing its age. *It seems harmless enough,* I thought. Then I silently chastised myself. I knew better. I had been investigating the paranormal for more than ten years, and if I had learned anything as a paranormal investigator, it was that even the most benign of situations could turn ugly in a matter of seconds. I thought of the long night of investigating that lay ahead and the two-and-a-half-hour ride home from North Adams. No, this definitely was not a night to get careless.

As we unpacked our equipment, the creak of the porch door drew our attention. We turned to see a heavyset man briskly walking toward us. As he approached, the dim light revealed his beaming smile beneath a heavy mustache. "You must be Nick," I said. Up until this point, I had only chatted with him on the phone. A book was being written about haunted places in Massachusetts, and the author wanted to include the Houghton Mansion, so she had contacted Nick. After researching various paranormal investigative groups on the Internet, Nick selected the New England Ghost Project for verification. As first impressions go, I found myself liking him already.

"You must be Ron. It's great to finally meet you guys. This is so cool."

We followed behind as he led us up the granite stairs of the aging mansion and into the foyer.

I looked at a sullen Maureen. "What's wrong with you? You're unusually quiet."

"I don't know. I can't quite explain it." She hesitated. "For the past hour or so I've had the odd sensation that we're being watched."

Without another word, we followed Nick as he veered through a doorway to the right and ushered us into what appeared to be a meeting area. Toward the far side of the wall stood a set of six-foot conference tables and chairs, partially blocking the view of the elegant marble fireplace. Gazing at the ornately carved columns, wainscoting, and antique brass sconces, I said, "Wow, this place is awesome." One look at the surroundings and I found myself momentarily distracted, envisioning what the Houghton Mansion must have been like in its heyday. As I have always said, haunting and history go hand in hand. To find out who the spirits are, you have to look at the history.

Placing my black canvas bag on the table, I eyed my surroundings one more time and smiled inwardly as I thought of all the history this building had witnessed. Something told me that we were going to be in for one hell of a night.

The sudden sound of movement from behind caught my attention, and I turned to find Nick standing amid a small cluster of onlookers.

"Ron, this is my son, Josh, my daughter, Sarah, and her husband, Greg."

The introductions continued with the rest of the group, like a receiving line at a wedding. And just when I thought the introductions were complete, he gestured to a hulk of a man with a pseudo-ZZ Top beard, standing sheepishly in the corner. "I'd like you to meet Paul, our local historian." Judging from his black T-shirt, which read "Local History Rules," I didn't have to be a psychic to figure that one out.

"Paul's not able to stay too long, but he was nice enough to offer to take us to the cemetery and give you guys a short history of the place."

"Sure, how far is it?"

"It's only a couple of blocks away, but at this time of night you want to drive."

Three blocks later we pulled up behind Josh's truck, alongside the wrought-iron gate of the cemetery. Nick, with Paul leading the way, escorted us to the Houghton family plot, while Maureen remained behind in the car. That was when the melodrama unfolded.

The drawl of Paul's monotone voice began, "It was August 1, 1914, when A. C. Houghton, former mayor of North Adams, decided to go for a pleasure drive with his daughter, Mary, and some friends, the doctor and Mrs. Hutton, who was a childhood friend of Mary's." Paul hesitated and then pointed to a smaller headstone, situated behind and to the right of the massive Houghton tombstone. "Over there is where Houghton's chauffeur John Widder is buried. That day, he was at the wheel of A. C.'s brand new 1914 Pierce Arrow, a seven-passenger touring car. He was not as familiar with cars as would have been preferred. He was much more familiar in dealing with horses."

"Is there a point to this?" I asked sarcastically.

Paul, evidently not used to being interrupted, became a bit flustered. "I, ah, I'm getting to that," he answered. Pointing to the distant mountains, he continued, "Driving up what is now Spruce Hill Road, they came upon a work gang. Widder was forced to drive the Pierce around a team of horses, and he hit a soft shoulder. He lost control when the engine began to race, causing them to plunge down a fifty-foot embankment. The car rolled over three times. Everyone with the exception of Mary was thrown from the vehicle. Although the men escaped with minor injures, Mrs. Hutton died immediately when the car rolled over on her. Mary, suffering a number of substantial injuries, including a crushed face, died in the hospital later that day."

"John Widder, distraught with guilt over the accident, committed suicide the next day in the mansion's barn by shooting himself in the head. Mr. Houghton, who was expected to live, just gave up, dying ten days after the accident."

Just when Paul finished with his tale, a shuffling sound startled the group. We turned to see a silhouette materialize out of the darkness, stepping into the glare of my flashlight. It was Maureen.

"How did you know we were done? What are you, psychic?"

"Ha, ha, Ron. You're soooo funny."

Tamping down the grass with our feet we circled the tomb one more time, as I disappointedly glanced at my silent EMF meter. "Picking up anything?" I asked, looking at Maureen.

Swatting at the mosquitoes, she bristled. "Let's make this quick, 'cause I really don't feel a thing. Besides, I'm getting eaten alive."

Maureen was right; this place was dead (no pun intended). Calling it quits, we made the short journey back to the mansion and did what every good investigative team would do: ordered pizza. After all, we planned to stay into the wee hours of the morning to take advantage of the time when the spirits are strongest.

I hadn't finished my last bite before the EMF meter in my pocket began blaring. I took one look at Maureen's vacant stare and knew something was up. Standing by the doorway to the room with the fireplace, I called for the rest of the group. We had to act fast, or we'd miss the connection.

"Nick, we're gonna do it. I don't want to lose it." I sent my wife, Jan, to retrieve the rest of the team.

Over the incessant beeping of the EMF meter, Jan's voice could be heard. "My husband bellows." *Only she would say that*, I thought, as the room quickly filled with people.

* * *

By the time Ron and the rest of the team entered the room, I already had my pendulum in my hand and had begun to feel the first surge of familiar energy. Realizing that Ron understood my plan, I maneuvered myself beneath the entranceway. Closing my eyes, I concentrated on my intent, and reached out with my mind. This is a silent, internal conversation I sometimes have with entities, a way for me to open up, by mentally asking who they are and if they wish to communicate. I placed a karmic phone call, and as I did, I struggled for a moment to push back the awkwardness of having what felt like a million eyes focused on me.

I can't help it. I still feel self-conscious under the watchful eye of new clients.

I turned to Ron. "Can you feel it?" I asked, inhaling deeply, my body adjusting to the sudden onslaught of energy. I looked up into the eyes of Nick and his family, along with the reporter from the local newspaper, who had decided to join us at the last minute.

Is anyone else picking this up?

I sighed, as I gazed into the blank stares of the onlookers. Apparently not, but I knew we were not alone.

With that, it began. My third eye pulsated, the swirling energy so strong it encompassed my whole face. Even as my arms began to throb in pain from the sudden onslaught of energy, my consciousness ebbed and flowed. I felt distant, detached. The sound of disembodied voices rumbled in my brain. The air was charged, sizzling with electricity. There was no disguising it. A spirit had arrived. "Is someone with us right now?" I asked, already knowing the answer. My pendulum responded with a spinning yes.

"Do you want to talk to us?" Ron asked. Without waiting for an answer, he continued, "Is this a male or a female?"

A voice echoed out of the background; Ron Jr. piped in sarcastically, "Yes-or-no questions."

I didn't need the pendulum because instinctively I knew, "Male."

"That works..." Ron responded, ignoring his faux pas.

"Not my..." I stumbled through gasps of breath. It was becoming increasingly difficult to speak. "Not my..." Suddenly I was struck with the overwhelming feeling of grief. But it wasn't mine; it was Mr. Houghton's. His feeling of loss became almost unbearable. "Not my Mary," I spat out, fighting the tears that caused my mascara to run. "It's not my fault. I'm sorry."

"Who was Mary again?" Ron asked, looking for help.

"Mary was Houghton's daughter," Paul said.

"Is this A. C. Houghton?" Ron asked.

The energy became crippling, preventing me from communicating verbally. All the while the pendulum continued to swing to and fro, supplying Ron and the remainder of the group with yes and no answers that I myself was unable to give.

"Hey Ron, something's going on with the camera," Marc stammered. "It's going in and out of focus."

Turning to Marc, Ron said, "*That's typical*, just keep shooting." Sometimes when a spirit passes in front of a lens it interferes with auto focus. Without missing a beat, Ron turned his attention back to me and asked again, "Who are we speaking with? Is it Mr. Houghton?" The pendulum swung a resounding yes.

"Do you want to leave this place?"

The pendulum swung wildly, indicating no.

Ron turned to the group, as if to explain my silence and the change of my demeanor. "Maureen's also an empath. She can pick up on how somebody died."

I found my voice. "I can't feel my arms. They're so heavy," I said, tears running down my face, nearly dropping my grandmother's rosary beads I had clutched in my hand. "The grief, it's so horrible. The pain," I said, grabbing my left arm. "I think he died of a heart attack. I can't feel my arm, it's numb. I have to break the connection."

"Do you want to go outside?"

Mimicking Ron's words, I begged, "I have to go outside." Ron closed the gap between us and grabbed my arm.

Invisible electrified hands pushed up and under my ribcage and shoved me back. In an unnatural motion I doubled over slightly in pain, recoiling from Ron's touch. "Oy, it hurts!" I said, my hand covering my abdomen.

"What the hell was that? You're not going to get outside that way."

"He's trying to keep me here," I said, shoving the pendulum into Ron's hand. Regaining strength I shook off Houghton's advances. With Ron's hand on my arm, we headed for the door.

Stepping into the night, a cool breeze touched my face. With it came a welcome sense of relief that the spirit was no longer with me. Bent over, my hands on my knees, I took several deep breaths to clear what felt like cobwebs in my brain. The last remnants of residual energy finally dissipating, I turned to look up at Ron for his reaction to what he'd just witnessed.

Through furrowed brows, Ron asked, "Are you all right?"

"Yeah, I guess," I lied. Not wanting to look as weak as I felt, I pushed my raw emotions to the recesses of my mind and stood straight and tall. But I really wasn't ready.

"Let's go back in?"

"I'm right behind you." Great.

Drying my eyes and freshening up, I reentered the meeting room, which was alive with chatter, where we wolfed down the last remnants of the pizza and endured interviews with the reporter.

"Ron, now what?" I asked.

"Okay, let's do a sweep of the building."

Nick, all too anxious to start, bolted down the hallway. Both Ron and I had to hustle to keep up with him, the rest of the entourage close on our heels. We followed him down the old creaking stairs to the bowels of the building. The basement was a maze of brick rooms in various states of decay. I coughed as I took in the thick musty smell of damp dirt. Passing from room to room, we searched for any indication of paranormal activity. Our search was interrupted by the squelch of the two-way radio. It was Jan from base camp.

"Ron, we lost radio signal from the infrared camera to the base camp."

* * *

"Maureen, wait up," I said, as I responded to my wife's update over the walkie-talkie. "Crap. Well, there's no point in staying there. Why don't you join us?" *That's typical*, I thought. "It looks like they're screwing with us again." More often than not, paranormal investigation and electrical interference problems go hand in hand because it is believed that the spirits use the energy to manifest.

With that we continued our sweep. Walking down a long, dark corridor, we entered the farthest room on the right, the boiler room. We stopped abruptly in front of the massive cast-iron furnace, where we attempted to make contact.

"I can feel something," Maureen blurted out.

"I'm not picking up anything," I said, with an arcing motion of my EMF meter.

"I'm telling you, someone's here," she said, more insistently. "They're hesitant, not sure whether we can be trusted. It's almost as if they're skirting us."

I began haphazardly scanning the area in an attempt to catch the spirit. Reaching below waist level the meter came to life.

"I told you," Maureen interjected. "It's a little girl." She closed her eyes as if to concentrate. "She's playful. I think she has blonde hair."

Nick chimed in. "I don't know of any little girl that would have died here."

"That's okay. It doesn't matter. I'm telling you, she's here."

Agreeing with Maureen, I said, "Nick, we are the first team to really investigate the mansion. There may be spirits here that you don't even know about."

Maureen did say she was playful, so I attempted to provoke the child spirit. "If you're here, can you show us? Give us a sign." I thought for a moment. "Can you knock my cap off my head?"

We paused, giving her a chance to respond.

Nothing happened.

As if rushing to the spirit's defense, Maureen said, "I think she's scared. After all, she's not used to anyone knowing she's here."

Unable to get any more information from our reluctant visitor, I turned to the team. "I guess we're done here. Let's go upstairs."

We left the basement and continued our sweep of the house. With Nick still in the lead, we climbed the regal stairs to the second level, passing through endless rooms with little result, until we came upon Mary's room. Although my EMF meter remained silent, Maureen felt an energy swirling about her. Unable to make contact, we ventured on until we reached a set of massive doors. "What's this, Nick?"

"It's our Masonic Lodge. Want to see something cool?" Nick asked, his lips twitching up in a smile. "Check this out." Raising his arm, he gestured us to follow him.

We stood in front of a wall full of large wooden levers and watched as Nick, grabbing a fistful of wood, flipped each switch. Motioning us aside he threw open the door of the lodge, then summoned us into the darkness.

"Wait for it," Nick said, giddy as a schoolboy.

As if by magic the parade of lights began. From right to left, the old bulbs came to life, jumping from one bulb to the next, causing a domino effect of illumination around the room. We stood transfixed for a moment as the room swelled with light. The feeling of serenity passed over us as if we'd entered another realm. It was simply amazing. At each end of the hundred-foot-long hall stood three velvet thrones on platforms, and burgundy benches lined the sides of the walls. As we walked past the Italian tile portraying the image of Galileo, we approached the kneeling altar in the center of the room. "Wow. This is awesome." I said.

"Oh my God, the energy is so peaceful," Maureen added.

"You feeling anything here?" I asked.

"Yes. Safe." Maureen smiled. "They can't touch me here."

The feeling of euphoria resonated with the team; we all seemed at ease here. As if not wanting to leave, we lingered for quite a while. Never having had the opportunity to be inside a Masonic Lodge before, we were like kids in a toy store, eager to explore. The time flew by as we asked endless questions of our hosts. Soon, though, I realized it was time to move on. There was still so much to do.

Most of the group headed back to base camp while Greg, Nick's son-in-law, led me up a metal ladder to a door in the roof. Stepping over puddles of water we made our way to its edge. The view was breathtaking. The lights of the town illuminated the spires of the churches and the fog-covered mountains in the distance. *Awesome*, I thought. It was a picture-perfect view. We chatted for a moment, then turned to head back. As we walked across the tarred roof, we heard what sounded like footsteps sloshing in the water behind us. We quickly turned, only to be greeted by a rush of cold air and the beep, beep, beep of my EMF meter.

There was no one there.

We were alone.

Greg and I looked at each other, momentarily stunned.

We stood transfixed to the spot. Waiting for something, anything, to happen.

Silence.

Excited with what had transpired, but unwilling to wait any longer, we shrugged our shoulders and climbed down the ladder and headed back to base camp.

It was now nearing the "witching hour," two o'clock in the morning, the time, according to folklore, when the veil between the living and the dead is the thinnest, and creatures of the night are at their strongest.

"Team, let's finish this investigation," I said, as I reached under the table where I'd hidden the tarnished, silver candelabra. For the last few days, I'd been thinking of how I'd like to wrap up the investigation. But, knowing how strong Maureen felt about this little subject, I thought I'd spring it on her at the last moment. "What do you guys think about doing a seated communication by candlelight?" I said, barely able to contain the excitement in my voice.

Maureen spoke through a muffled yawn. "What, you're kidding, right?" She frowned at the white, half-melted-down candles and the pack of matches I'd just laid down on the table.

Ignoring Maureen, I turned to Nick. "Hey, wouldn't it be awesome to do a seated communication by candlelight, in the study?"

"Call it what you like, Ron, but it's still a séance." Maureen slowly studied the faces, scanning the room for a reaction. Although she didn't say it, I could tell by the look on her face that she was thinking about the many years she'd spent as a medium for séances. She'd warned me about her concerns weeks ago, when I'd mentioned my growing interest in having one. "Séances in the wrong hands can be extremely dangerous. Sometimes doors opened are not so easily closed. Not to mention what may slip through," she'd said. But not one to be easily dissuaded, and wanting to experience it all myself, I didn't let up.

"Come on. It'll be great." I did my best to guile Maureen, but so far, she wasn't budging. "Look, what could it hurt?"

"I'd be interested in trying it. I've never had the opportunity to be involved in one," Nick said. "I've only been able to see them on television."

"Me too." Sarah, Nick's daughter, joined in. "Oh my God, that would be incredible!"

"Fine," Maureen grumbled under her breath. "We'll have a

séance, but only if you take it seriously, Ron. It's not something to be taken lightly."

"You will? Great!" On some level, I was disappointed; I'd half expected to have to fight a little harder for it. Man, she must be tired. Now I felt bad. "You're sure you're okay with this?"

"Whatever."

Grabbing the candelabra, I made a beeline for the door. You have to strike when the iron's hot. The dining room was a large room off the foyer, with rich mahogany wainscoting. The temperature sensor in the room had read 66.6 degrees all night long. So it only seemed natural that, if we were going to perform a séance, this room should be the place.

Nick and I grabbed a round banquet table and placed it in the center of the room in front of the green marble fireplace. Positioning the infrared camera on the mantle, we adjusted the focus. While Nick and I organized the chairs around the table, Marc, our cameraman, set up the camcorder on the tripod in the corner of the room. Since everyone was partaking in the séance, we left base camp unmanned.

Maureen, after placing a variety of crystals and other items for protection on the center of the table, beckoned to the team to take their seats. "You guys are sure you want to do this, right?"

"What are you, crazy? Of course we do," I said, speaking for everyone present. I closed the pocket doors and turned off the lights, setting the stage for what was to come.

Taking a seat to the left of Maureen, I positioned the EMF meter, along with my 35mm and temperature sensor, directly in front of me, and then turned toward her, silently signaling for her to take over.

"Here's the deal," Maureen said. "Everyone please hold

hands. But I want to make sure you are aware of a couple things before we start. First and most importantly, never, and I mean never, break the circle until I say so. Think of our hands like a continuous chain of energy. If the chain is broken, even if you clasp hands again, you risk allowing unwanted spiritual energy to enter."

"So, if someone pulls their hand away, and even if they clasp them again, it's similar to a repaired part of a chain-link fence being the weakest link, right?" I asked.

"Yes," Maureen answered. She looked from me to those seated at the table. "This is why I don't want you to be caught unaware. It's pretty common that your body, because of the strong bond of holding hands, begins to feel odd. In fact, don't be surprised if you start feeling what I do. But please don't panic." Maureen picked up the salt that Nick had retrieved from the kitchen earlier and made a full circle around the table and all those who were seated. "The salt will help protect us from unwanted energies," she said, capturing the curious stares of all present. She took her seat once again. "Okay. Is everyone ready?"

With an air of uncertainty, the group collectively agreed.

We all joined hands.

"I hope you don't get offended, but we'll be saying the Lord's Prayer." Not waiting for a response she continued, "Our Father, who art in heaven…"

"We invite only spirits that do not wish us harm to enter this circle," Maureen finished.

The protection seemed to be working, maybe too well, for nothing was getting through. But it wasn't long before a banging shattered the silence. Startled, the group turned toward the pocket doors. "Did everyone hear that?"

"Yes," Nick replied, a quiver in his voice.

My EMF meter went off, and a familiar look of pain passed over Maureen's face.

The atmosphere in the room had changed. A cold air began to dance at our feet.

"Do you guys feel this too? My feet are freezing," Sarah said, shifting uncomfortably in her chair.

Maureen's words echoed in my brain. "Don't break the link." Lifting my left hand, I grabbed Janet's right hand and placed it over my own right hand, freeing me to grab the camera. I shoved it under the table and pressed the shutter. The light from the flash frightened the group. "My bad," I exclaimed, meeting nervous laughter.

I began asking questions with no reply. "Damn, looks like the protection is too good."

"Fine." Maureen called out as if to remedy the situation, "Okay, we will allow whoever is here to join us, as long as you mean us no harm."

Words we would later regret.

Anxious to continue, I began my questioning again. "Are there any spirits who would like to talk?"

Maureen slowly raised her head. Through a voice not her own, she replied, "Yes, why are you here?"

My heart began to thud wildly in my chest. I stared into her vacant eyes for the space of a heartbeat. "Who are you?"

"It—it—it's Mary," Maureen said through ragged breath, in that same strange voice.

A collective gasp filled the room. Raising my head; I looked up into the wide-eyed stare of the group. Ignoring the fear in their faces, I continued, "Is this your house? Did you die here?"

Maureen shook her head from side to side, then began rocking back and forth in her chair, her voice barely above a whisper, "Where's my John?"

Was she referring to John Widder? Curiosity piqued, I gazed at Maureen. Her face mere inches away, I looked into the abyss that once was her eyes. Repulsed by her look, I couldn't help but turn away momentarily. I had never seen her like this before. I said, "Did you and John have a thing going on?"

My meter immediately went dead.

The coldness that we had been feeling at our feet now filled the room.

Nick began fidgeting in his chair, all the blood drained from his face.

The silent veil was shattered.

Maureen bellowed, "GET OUT!"

Nick, as if unable to contain himself any longer, yanked his hands free and jumped to his feet. "My ass!" he screamed, running for the pocket doors.

I stood there in shock as everyone, with the exception of Maureen, ran for the door and out of the mansion. She closed her eyes, as if working things over in her mind, and sighed heavily before exiting the room.

Squelching my concerns, I remained behind. Still fascinated with what had just transpired, I took my EMF meter and scanned the area. Hmmm, little to no readings. When I placed it back on the table in front of where Maureen had been sitting, it went off the scale. With my hand I felt a cold spot, but the thermometer sitting only a few inches away was reading normal (68–70 degrees). Using a handheld laser hanging from a lanyard around my neck, I began taking temperature readings from different angles. They revealed that the temperature by my EMF meter was considerably different (52–54 degrees) from the temperature near the thermometer sitting on the table. Had we opened up a portal? Or was there a spirit still here? Without a moment to spare I began taking infrared shots and continued with the measurements of the area.

After a while the group began to drift back into the room, excited about what had just happened. Over the buzz of chatter, I decided to review the tapes. To our dismay, we discovered that the camcorder had shut itself off shortly after we had made contact.

Nick asked, "Does this happen a lot?"

"Not that often, but it never fails to impress me when it does. Sometimes the spirits don't want to be recorded."

We were all enthralled as we reviewed the infrared video, anxious to see what it had captured, when our concentration was broken by a blood-curdling scream. We jumped to our feet only to see Sarah running down the corridor and out the side door, hands flailing wildly in the air.

Above the sound of her screaming, we heard the high-pitched, shrill sound of the motion detector we had placed on the cellar door being set off.

While Greg went to check on his wife, Maureen and I could barely control our laughter at the sight of Sarah running down the hall, like a scene out of an old B movie.

Rushing to the cellar door, we found the motion detector flashing wildly in the dim light. Something or someone had set it off. Moments later, Sarah returned arm-in-arm with Greg, her face shining with embarrassment from her scare. "I was on my way to the bathroom when that thing—went off." She pointed to the motion detector. "I swear. I never touched it…"

In an attempt to recreate the scene, we reset the device and tried various methods to set it off, to no avail. With our fatigue getting the better of us, we decided to chalk it up as another unexplained event and call it a night.

RESULTS OF THE INVESTIGATION

Our two-and-a-half-hour journey to the Houghton Mansion was well worth our time. Through the evidence collected—photos, EMF readings, and electronic disturbances—we discovered that the mansion was home to several spirits. Besides finding the obvious spirits, Albert and Mary Houghton, the NEGP was the first to encounter the little girl in the basement. But the highlight of the investigation was the "seated communication by candlelight" (séance). Maureen's trance channeling of Mary exposed a possible love affair with chauffeur John Widder. We looked forward to a return visit to the Houghton mansion to unearth more corroborating evidence of this secret love affair.

episode nine

DANGEROUS PURSUIT

CASE FILE: 6252463
DANGEROUS PURSUIT

Location: Reading, Massachusetts.

History: 1950s white ranch.

Reported Paranormal Activity: Disappearing
and moving objects and unexplained property
destruction.

Clients: Rusty (owner), Moose (Rusty's friend).

Investigators: Ron (lead investigator), Maureen
(trance medium).

Running to the phone, I tripped over the hunting pack Stephen had left on the floor. "Damn," I said, reaching for the receiver before the last ring.

Barely audible, a voice echoed through the receiver. "Hello, Maureen."

"Hey, what's up?" I said to Ron.

"Are you doing anything right now?"

"Why?"

"I, uh—I got a call from this guy in Reading who needs our help."

"Now? Ron, it's the middle of the day, it's my day off, and I've got stuff to do." I couldn't explain it, but I was suddenly feeling a little apprehensive.

"I know, but he sounds pretty desperate. It won't take us too long, I promise." He continued, "I can pick you up in a half hour and we can be home before supper."

Not thrilled with the idea, but hearing the concern in Ron's voice, I said, "I'll be ready."

Within a matter of minutes Ron pulled up in front of my house. I opened the passenger door of his car and peered in to see his nervous grin. *Hmmm, what was he up to?* After our conversation on the phone, I couldn't help but feel there was something Ron wasn't telling me. He'd mentioned that the client's girlfriend had referred us, after attending one of our ghost-hunting 101 lectures, so that wasn't it. But I couldn't put my finger on it. Just because I'm sensitive, people make assumptions that I know it all. Unfortunately, that's not how it works. However, I wished this was one of the times it did work that way.

I slid into the passenger seat, closed the door, then said, "Ron, what's this all about? You seem a little secretive."

"I'd rather not say."

Moments later we pulled up in front of a '50s white ranch and parked behind a dual-wheel Ford with a gun rack hanging in the rear window. Standing next to the truck was a short stocky man, his black leather vest and white T-shirt highlighting the massive tattoos running the length of his muscular arms. Beside him stood a taller man smoking a cigarette, with his worn leather boot resting on the bumper. Feeling like we just pulled up in front of a biker bar and hesitant to step out of the car, I asked Ron, "Are you sure this is the right address?"

Ron pulled out a piece of white lined paper, took one look at the scribbling, then said, "Yup. This is it."

Stepping out of the car, leery at the sight of the two looming figures in front of us, I let Ron take the lead as we cautiously made our way up the driveway. Ron reached out his hand to greet them. "Hi, I'm Ron from the New England Ghost Project. You must be Rusty, we spoke on the phone."

He ignored Ron's greeting, looking past him, and gave me an icy stare. "Is that Maureen?"

Ron answered slowly. "Yeahhh."

He closed the distance between us, eyeing me like a pole dancer in a strip joint. "You the psychic?"

"Yeah. Hi, I'm Maureen."

"Here's the deal," he said boldly. "My house is trashed. I clean it up at night, and when I get up in the morning, it's trashed again." He looked at the guy with the cigarette. "Just ask my buddy Moose. He's seen it too. Come on, I'll show you what I mean." He led us up the brick walkway.

The minute I opened the door and took in the devastation, my gut twisted into a knot. Ron and I walked into the living room first, stepping over shards of broken glass and broken picture frames. "Wow, this room looks like it's been ransacked."

"Are you telling me a ghost did this?" Ron asked, in disbelief.

Rusty, the homeowner, growled, "Hell, yeah. I think it's a little girl." He thumbed his hand in the other man's direction. "Like I said, just ask Moose, he stayed over the other night to see what would happen. He's my witness."

A little girl? He had to be kidding. *What little girl would do this type of destruction?*

As if reading my thoughts, he said, "I think it's because she wants my attention."

Yeah, that's what they all say. What kind of fantasy world is he living in? Scratch that last thought, I don't think I want to go there.

Turning my attention to the task at hand, I asked, "Can we take a look at the rest of the house?"

"You've got to see the bathroom," he said, walking briskly into the small room on the left. "See this mirror? It has to weigh over one hundred pounds, and it was bolted to the wall. Look at it now."

Ron Kolek

An infrared shot of the mirror shattered in the bathroom. Was this the result of the little girl spirit? I think not!

As we stared at the shards of mirror blanketing the tiled floor I thought, *A little girl did this? Yeah sure.* One look at Rusty and I knew, this was a man who didn't like being wrong. Fearing that speaking my thoughts would send Rusty into a rage, I held my tongue.

"Wow, this is amazing," Ron said, as he stepped closer, glass crunching beneath his feet. He raised his 35mm camera and took some photos of what was left of the mirror.

Something told me Ron wasn't buying this either.

Ron glanced at me over his shoulder, "You want to see if we can make contact?"

"I suppose." Feeling a little awkward, I followed Ron into the living room. We stopped in front of the fireplace and cleared away bits of debris and broken sconces that lay shattered on the floor. I reached into my pocket, fumbling to remove my rose quartz pendulum from the front of my jeans. "Are we ready?"

I felt the burn of their stares as both men shuffled forward to get a better look. Usually I'm self-conscious, but now, standing here, pendulum at the ready, I felt nothing but sheer terror.

Ron stepped between us, almost as if he were taking a protective stance. Giving me a knowing look, he said, "Okay, let's do this."

Anxious to leave as soon as possible, I agreed. "Are there any spirits with us now?"

The pendulum swung counterclockwise: yes. Waves of energy began prickling my skin, indicating that the spirit was close by. I was surprised that the spirit was communicating so quickly.

Rusty spoke up. "I want to ask a question." Without waiting for me to respond, he asked, "Are you a little girl?"

Although the pendulum began to swing counterclockwise, indicating a yes, I felt the darkness behind its lie coming through. "This is no little girl."

"No way. You're wrong!" Rusty snapped.

Ron interceded. "You have to be careful. Spirits can lie." He waited a moment, as if waiting for a reaction to his words. "Sometimes they'll appear as little girls, so that you'll welcome them in, when they're not really little girls at all, but something more menacing that's trying to gain your confidence."

Rusty's face turned red with rage. "No, you're wrong. This is a little girl. She told me so."

In an attempt to appease him, I said, "Rusty, I can't say for sure if your spirit is a little girl. I can only tell you what I'm feeling." I paused. "Let's ask a few more questions, and see if I can sense her."

Moose spoke up in a smoker's voice. "Is she the one who took my wallet? If so, I want it back."

"Why? What happened to your wallet?" Ron asked, happy to change the subject.

"Well, the other night I stayed over here. I put my wallet on the kitchen counter, and in the morning it was gone." He continued, "That bitch took it."

As I listened to Moose, I couldn't help but notice that Rusty had his wallet chained to the belt loop of his dirty jeans. Evidently, *he* wasn't taking any chances.

"Okay." I began again. "Are you the spirit who took Moose's wallet?"

The response was a yes. In my mind's eye, although it appeared to be a little girl, I looked deeper. Behind the mask of a child, there was something else there. Dark. Angry. Filled with hate. Reading my thoughts, the entity grew in strength. It had been discovered, and it didn't want its plan unearthed.

My pendulum pulled straight down. It was apparent that whoever it was finished speaking with us.

"I have another question," Rusty screeched.

"I'm sorry, it's gone. We're not going to get any more answers today," I said.

Taking my cue, Ron said, "Would you look at the time. I think we should head out."

"Yeah. I think we're done here. At least for now," I replied, trying to hide my glee.

"No, I want to talk some more. Can't you make her come back?" Rusty asked.

"No. Besides, it doesn't work that way. If I get anything on the photos I took, I'll give you a call," Ron said, as he followed me toward the door.

Once outside, we all stood between the front bumper of the Ford and the Harley that was parked halfway into the garage bay.

"Hey," Moose said, "why do you think the little girl's breaking all our crap?"

The ringing of Rusty's cell phone disrupted our conversation. "Holy shit! See, I'm not lying about the spirit wreaking havoc in my life. When have you ever seen a caller ID look like this?" he said, sticking the LCD screen of the still-ringing phone in our faces.

My eyes became transfixed on the caller ID, which read 000-000-0000. "Oh—my—God," I said, bile rising in my throat. He was right; I had never seen anything like it. I couldn't say for sure whether it was of paranormal nature or not. What I did know is how it made me feel. One look at the odd number and gooseflesh riddled my forearms.

"Come here, Maureen. I want to talk to you for a minute." Rusty grabbed my arm, and all but dragged me past Ron's car to the end of the driveway.

I cringed. What the heck did he want from me? I glanced over my shoulder at Ron, who appeared to be in an awkward conversation with Moose. Rusty regained my attention by digging his fingertips into the soft flesh of my upper arm. "Ouch."

"Sorry, about that." He lessened his hold. "Maureen, can you come back?"

I looked up to the house where Ron and Moose stood, waiting. "Ron and I..."

"No. Not Ron. Just you." He spoke in a low, grating voice.

"I, ah, I—" He'd caught me off guard. I was at a loss for words, which, for anyone who knows me, seldom happens. "I don't understand," I said, close enough to gaze at the skull and crossbones etched into his flesh. Call me crazy, but I wasn't getting a warm and fuzzy feeling about this.

"I told you about the little girl. What you did in there, communicating with her, got me thinking." He hesitated. "I think the little girl was afraid of Ron. I bet she'll talk to you alone. Can you come back tonight?" he asked, a look of hunger on his face.

Tonight? What is he, crazy? I wasn't ever coming back.

"I didn't want to bring this up," he started. "I'm not sure it has anything to do with anything…"

"What?" I asked, the word slipping out of my mouth before I could stop myself.

Rusty, still gripping my arm, looked side to side, as if in search of a private moment. "I just got out of jail."

Almost afraid to speak, I asked, "For what?" My voice sounded hoarse, even to me.

"Murder," he said, his voice low. It sounded like a threat.

My body tensed in response. Slowly, cautiously, I removed my arm from his grasp.

Obviously reading my body language, he got defensive. "He was a friend of mine. I didn't mean to kill him. Just hurt him."

A wave of nausea washed over me, and I found myself wondering if he were so callous with the life of a friend, how would he treat his enemies? I chose my next words more carefully. "Rusty, I'm not avoiding you, but maybe it would be better if Ron and I came back with the rest of our team to do a full investigation."

"I don't think she likes Ron," he said again, and I could sense his impatience. "I only want you here." He paused. "What's your phone number? I'll call you tonight."

Call me? Oh no. No, no, no. The skin along my back and neck crawled, like there were a million insects doing the mambo on me.

Just then there was a sound from behind; I turned to see Ron walking toward us, with Moose in tow. "What do you say, kid? We have to get going before the traffic hits," Ron said.

I swallowed the lump forming in my throat. *Thank God.* I was never so happy for an interruption in all of my life. Rolling my watch over on my wrist, I checked the time. "Yeah, you're right, we had better get going." I forced an apologetic smile on my face, one that I didn't feel, and said, "Sorry guys, we really do have to go."

Ron pulled a business card from the back pocket of his Dockers, handed it to Rusty, and said, "Give me a call on the Ghost Line if you encounter any more issues. In the meantime, like I said before, I'll develop my film, and we'll see what we get."

We nearly ran to Ron's car and climbed in. I held my breath as Ron backed out of the driveway and onto the street.

"What was that all about?" Ron asked, as he put on his right blinker and pulled up to the stop sign. For a moment, Ron sounded like a little boy. A boy that had been the only one not invited to a classroom party.

"He wanted me to come back tonight, alone." I looked at Ron. "Without you."

"What are you, crazy?" Ron yelled. "You're not going back. Right?"

"No freaking way!"

"You didn't give him your number, did you?" Ron said, waggling his finger in my face. "Don't ever call him from your cell phone, home phone—anywhere…"

"No worries. I'm not calling him." I sighed heavily. "Did you know he just got released from prison?"

Ron turned, with a look of apparent guilt on his face, "Um, maybe?"

"What the hell were you thinking? I could kill you!"

"Well, he needed help. Besides, I thought you wanted to help people." Ron grinned sheepishly.

"Yeah, at what cost?"

RESULTS OF THE INVESTIGATION

Although we have no physical evidence, we believe the darkness behind the façade of a little girl was really the man that Rusty had murdered.

This was one of the most horrifying investigations we've encountered. It just goes to show, sometimes there's more to fear from the living than from the dead.

episode ten

THE STONE HOUSE

CASE FILE: 6231949
STONE HOUSE

Location: Undisclosed government location.

History: A field stone building, originally a
home, built in the 1890s. During World War I,
it became a home for the wives of servicemen. In 1959, the building was purchased by
a religious order for retreats and a home
for troubled boys. The government leased the
building in 1994.

Reported Paranormal Activity: Unusually high
attrition rate, electrical problems, unexplained noises, foul odors, cold spots, insect manifestations, and the uncomfortable
feeling of being watched.

Clients: Deborah (location manager), Evon
(Maureen's sister).

Investigators: Ron (lead investigator), Maureen
(trance medium), Leo (photographer), Ron Jr.
(investigator), Sabrina (Maureen's daughter),
Bety (Maureen's friend).

Laura Wooster

Ron returns to the now abandoned Stone House. Does evil still lurk there?

I slapped a coffee cup on the desk while I waited for the lethargic computer to boot. Another morning with the New England Ghost Project. *Damn, I hate mornings.* The cobwebs cleared in my head as I began to check my emails. As usual I scanned the list, looking for anything of interest, when one caught my eye. *Hmmm, what's this?* I read it out loud to myself, "A cry for help…"

To: ronk@neghostproject.com

From: Evon

Subject: A cry for help!

Dear Ron—Hi, this is Evon, Maureen's sister. She told me to contact you directly, so I am. I work at a government building where a lot of strange things have been occurring. Not only do we have an unusually high attrition rate, it seems that everyone is at each other's throats. At first we thought it nothing more than coincidence. But now, we're not so sure.

We have been experiencing horrific odors that appear out of nowhere and mysteriously disappear as quickly as they come. On several occasions we've had electrical problems, computer problems, and infestations of various insects.

As if that weren't enough, we've had a series of unexplained events, cold air swirling around our legs, knockings in the walls, and while on conference calls, the phone buttons will all light up, suggesting someone or something is listening in.

We're desperate. Please, please, please, help us to find out what is going on. The only problem is my manager wants this to remain anonymous.

We appreciate any assistance you can offer.

Please contact me as quickly as possible.

Evon

Realizing the seriousness of the situation, we accepted her challenge. And here's where our story begins.

* * *

Tension filled the air as we made our way up the winding dirt driveway. The moon hung low in the sky, illuminating the menacing stone structure, making the two front windows appear like a pair of evil eyes, lurking in the distance. An uneasiness swept over our group. As we exited the cars, I looked at my friend Bety and my daughter, Sabrina; since it was their first time out on an investigation with us, I attempted to gauge their reactions to our surroundings.

We cautiously entered the building.

"Hi, Evon!" I wrapped my arms around my sister, whom I hadn't seen for a month or so, and gave her a big hug.

"Maureen, so glad you came," she said in a quivering voice.

I turned to face Ron. "This is my sister, Evon, and her manager, Deborah."

"Nice to meet you," he said, extending his hand in a greeting. "Is there somewhere we can set up?"

"Yeah, you can use the conference room off to the left." She hesitated. "Would you like some coffee?"

"Yes, that sounds great," Ron said.

Typically I wait until we've walked the premises to get a feel for the place prior to making any judgments. This time it was different. I didn't need to walk through the old stone house. I'd barely stepped over the threshold when the first waves of trembling energy brushed across my forehead, sending a shiver up my spine. The eagerness for investigating that I'd felt a mere moment ago was replaced by sudden doubt. I was all too familiar with the risks associated with investigating the paranormal. It was one thing subjecting myself to the danger; it was another altogether to expose my own flesh and blood to it. I looked at Sabrina, my daughter, and for the first time since we'd left my house, I regretted bringing her along.

Moments after completing our setup, Deborah returned, mugs in hand.

"So, what's the story on this place?" Ron asked, scanning the surroundings.

Deborah handed Ron a cup of coffee. "In preparation for you guys coming I did a little research. The building is over one hundred years old and was originally built by a local businessman for his mistress." She paused for a moment to collect her thoughts. "It took two years to complete the house, and at that time, he married his mistress and moved in with her. Three months later he died mysteriously. During World War I it became a home for the wives of servicemen whose husbands were away. In 1959, it was bought by a religious order, which held retreats and had a camp for difficult children. We are currently leasing the building from the order."

No sooner had she finished her story than Leo, our photographer, yelled, "What the heck is this?"

While Leo was drinking his coffee, a large, fat fly appeared out of nowhere and, as if in some weird kamikaze trance, made a spiral nosedive directly into his cup. Was this some type of omen?

Ron started grabbing equipment. "Hey, Evon, would you mind giving us a hand?"

"No, not at all. What can I do?" Evon asked eagerly.

Ron handed her the remote infrared camera. "Take this. It's the infrared camera," he said, reading her quizzical gaze. "The monitors at base camp display everything you're seeing. So just make sure to keep it level and aimed at us."

We left Sabrina at base camp, and with Deborah in the lead, we walked through the foyer toward the back of the building and made our way up the carpeted stairs to the second floor offices.

As I walked into the large office at the end of the hallway, I felt a low-level current of energy hum across my skin, raising the hairs on the back of my neck. "Someone's here," I said. Ron, with his EMF meter in hand, began to sweep the area at shoulder height.

"Are you sure? I'm not picking up much of a reading."

Evon, clutching the mobile infrared camera, asked, "Ron, how close do you have to be to detect a spirit?"

"Fairly close with this type of meter," Ron answered.

I concentrated a little more. Instinctively, I knew why he hadn't gotten a reading. "Your meter is up too high. Here, around hip level." I gestured with an arcing motion of my hand. "It's a little boy."

Ron lowered the meter. The EMF meter blinked wildly "Wow. Look at that!" he said.

Suddenly I felt strongly that the young boy was trying to warn me.

I looked up into the concerned eyes of our guests. "Can you guys feel this? It's so thick. Heavy." I struggled to breathe, my chest constricting. The harder I tried to reach out to the little boy, the stronger the energy became, as if something or someone stood in the way. I ignored my gut instinct of impending doom and used my pendulum to reach out to the little boy once again.

"Is there anyone else here?" Ron interjected.

"Something's happening! I can't see you guys anymore. The monitor's all snow. Something's interfering with the infrared camera." Sabrina's concerned voice echoed over the walkie-talkie.

That's when the first strike of energy hit.

Suddenly feeling like a Mack truck had hit me, I stumbled. Before I was able to regain my posture, it struck again. The energy burned a trail of pain and numbness, traveling through my pendulum, up my arm, and into my chest. My heart about to explode, I doubled over in pain. As if I were in a tunnel, my mind became a blur; I could barely hear the muffled sound of the EMF meter and the snapping of Leo's camera.

I struggled to regain my body. Eyes closed, I became intent on expelling the dark entity.

Drawing on the aura of my emotions, my will strengthening, my consciousness clearing, I mentally pushed back. The entity, no longer able to maintain its grip, lessened its hold and retreated into the void. I silently said a prayer of thanks when the vicelike grip on my heart lessened. That grip was a feeling I recognized. It was demonic.

* * *

Stunned by what had just transpired, I reached out and grabbed Maureen's arm to help steady her. "What the hell was that?" I asked, straining to be heard over the sound of the EMF meter.

"Are you up to asking a couple more questions?" I felt awful asking, but the communication had been so strong, I hated to end things.

"Not really," she mumbled.

Maureen's friend Bety, eager to help, drew her pendulum out of her jacket pocket. "What questions do you want to ask?"

With that, the EMF stopped dead.

"Hmm. What's up with that?" I asked.

"He's gone," Maureen said.

I turned to Evon and Deborah, who were standing in the doorway, and asked, "Are you girls all right?"

"I'm not quite sure," Deborah said hesitantly. Then looking at Evon to see her reaction to what had just transpired, she said, "Sometimes when we are here at night, working late, we've been so creeped out that we've quickly gathered all of our belongings and fled the building."

"Wow. What was it that 'creeped' you out, do you have any idea?"

"I don't want to speak for everyone here," Evon said, "but it feels like 'something' is watching us, and not in a good way." Evon looked at Deborah for approval, then looked at me. "Do you know what it is?"

I thought for a moment on how to answer Evon's delicate question. The quiver in their voices told me they may not be ready to listen to the answer I was about to give. I decided to deal with it later. "Let's finish the investigation and see what we come up with." Ready to move on, I turned to Maureen. "Are you okay? Can you continue?"

"Yeah. I guess so."

"Good, let's check out the first floor."

A few moments later, as we passed through the foyer, Maureen stopped in her tracks. "It's the little boy. He's back."

With my meter in hand I scanned the area. "There are no readings. I think he's gone."

"No. Get down lower to the ground, Ron. I think he's playing a game with you." This time I knelt down and lowered the meter until it was a foot above the oak flooring. The flashing red light indicated he was there.

"Oh my God. I just saw him." Maureen pointed to a spot directly in front of where I held my meter. "He's there, kneeling down in front of you." Her voice thick with excitement, she said, "He has dark curly hair. Marcus. His name is Marcus."

After a few moments of playing what appeared to be a game of supernatural tag, I asked, "Does anybody have any questions for Marcus?"

"Yeah, I do," Bety said without missing a beat. Pendulum in hand, she asked, "Did you die here?"

Yes, came the reply.

I looked from Maureen to Bety, and was amazed to see that both their pendulums were swinging in unison.

My meter went dead.

"Ron, I think he wants us to follow him. Try over there," Maureen said, nodding in the direction of the door.

As I drew closer to the door, the readings on the meter got stronger and stronger. "Where does this door lead to?"

"Oh," Deborah said in a sheepish voice. "I forgot to tell you about the basement."

"What about the basement?" I asked.

"One day we came in," Evon said, opening the door to the cellar, "and there, on the top step, was a large dead black bird. A raven, I think."

"Ooh, do you know how it got there?" I asked.

"Haven't a clue, but it scared the bejeezus out of us."

Descending the stairs, I used the meter as a beacon in the darkness, following Marcus's lead with each blink of red light. Through narrow twisting corridors, with only the glow of my EMF meter and a small flashlight, we continued to follow Marcus through the dark, damp recesses of the cellar. We found a closet that no one even knew existed, a darkened area by a fuel oil tank, and a hole in the wall that led to nowhere.

It seemed evident that we were being guided for a reason. But why? Were these hiding places Marcus had used when he was alive or, worse, what he thought he needed now that he was in spirit? A shiver ran through me at that thought.

We left the cellar and headed back up the stairs. As we climbed the stairs, we felt a rush of cold air, which seemed to pass right through us. Collectively we knew that we were not alone.

It was time to regroup. We gathered together to discuss what we had observed and what actions could be taken. I pulled a pack of matches out of my shirt pocket and lit the candelabra to set the mood, then placed my EMF meter on the conference table.

"Ron, what are you doing?" Deborah asked.

"Just an experiment. I'm hoping that if a spirit enters the room, we'll get a reaction from either the EMF meter or the lit candles. You never know; it could happen." I smiled.

Deborah waited until the last of us had taken a seat to begin speaking again. "I didn't want to mention this before, but you know, when I did the research on the building I was saddened to hear of a tragic accident in the parking lot that took the life of a little boy." The flames of the candles danced and lengthened as she continued. "I believe he was brought into this house, where he later died."

Was his name Marcus? Was it the same little boy we'd communicated with earlier in the evening? I wanted to find out more, so I decided to make one more sweep. One by one we walked upstairs in silence, almost reluctantly. Our tight-knit group gathered in the hallway, huddling in the glow of my flashlight. The plaque over the door caught my attention; momentarily I flashed the light in its general direction. The sign read, "Shalom," but instinct told me what we were about to encounter would be anything but peaceful. Raising my laser thermometer, I began to take readings.

* * *

I stood there hugging my arms while Ron fiddled with the temperature gauge. That's when I felt it, waves of the same familiar yet uncomfortable energy roiling over my skin, causing the hair at the base of my neck to prickle. A swift-flowing, cool breeze swirled around our legs. One look at the wide-eyed stares of our hosts, and I knew they'd felt it too.

I looked past the others at Ron. "He's back," I said, signaling with a nod, then took my place by his side.

"Wanna make communication?" Ron said, his EMF meter blaring.

Reluctantly I pulled out my pendulum. It was him. I knew it. The same heaviness weighed on my shoulders. An onslaught of emotions welled within me, and feelings of hatred and loathing that were not my own filled me to the core. "Are you the same entity from before?" A resounding yes. After tossing back and forth question after question, a pattern began to unfold, and with it a feeling of uneasiness. There was something different, disturbing, about this entity. Ron sensed it as well and asked, "Do we know you? Have we met you before?"

The pendulum swung wildly: yes!

"Have you ever lived?" Ron continued.

We turned slightly to read the digital readout on the thermometer: 66.6 degrees. Evidently the entity was going for shock factor. I wasn't surprised.

"Not to worry," Ron piped in. "We've seen that before. Van Helsing fears nothing!"

Pleeeassse. I asked the question again. "Have you ever lived before?"

No. Once again the pendulum swung wide, then just as quickly as the communication had begun, it ended.

The thickness in the air that felt touchable a moment ago had begun to recede. Breathing a sigh of relief, I said, "He's leaving."

Truth be told, I'd asked the question twice in hope that I'd receive a different answer. But in my heart, I knew the truth. Whoever "it" was had never existed in human form. There are those in the paranormal and spiritual community that refer to this type of energy as "demonic." I, on the other hand, try to think of it as "negative energy." Am I deluding myself? Quite possibly. Just like when you break a pill that is too big to swallow, sometimes you do what you have to do to get by.

I reached out my hand in a gesture of comfort to my sister and found myself wondering if Ron was thinking the same thing that I was. Namely, *How the heck are we going to break the news to our hosts?* Never in my wildest dreams had I expected to encounter the darkness that we had tonight. Nevertheless, there are some things of this world that are not easily explained. This was one of them.

Once we all got back downstairs we presented the preliminary results of our investigation. We offered our hosts holy water with which to bless themselves and the premises, as a form of temporary protection, along with our recommendation to bring a man of the cloth in to assist in removing the entity plaguing their workspace. It's not a recommendation we offer lightly.

Although they were extremely grateful to have verification that the disturbances were not merely conjured by their minds, they decided to discuss the events of the evening amongst themselves and get back to us.

A week or so later I received a call from my sister. "Maureen, it's Evon. How are you doing?" She paused. "We received the pictures you sent us from the investigation, and, oh my God, they're freakin' scary."

She must have been referring to the photograph that was taken during our first encounter with the "negative energy."

"Yeah. Are you talking about the one with a skull-like image over my face? I know what you mean. It didn't make me feel too cozy either."

"Are you okay?"

"Yeah. I'm fine, Evon. Don't worry." I waited for a moment, almost afraid to ask. "How's Deborah doing? Does she want us to come back in?"

"Actually, that's why I'm calling. I think we're going to wait a while for things to quiet down." She continued. "We had a meeting and decided it's time for us to find a new location. Besides, the space is small and we're looking to expand."

I had my doubts about their reasons for leaving, but kept them to myself. "So, now what?"

"Well, we were wondering, when we move, do you think you can help us out? You know, so nothing follows us."

"We'll see what we can do. You know, it would probably be a good idea if we came back to do a cleansing of sorts."

There was something in her voice that told me I wasn't going to like what she was about to say. "Actually, Deborah felt embarrassed; she didn't want me to say anything. But the other night, right after the investigation she started to feel sick: migraine, nausea, and vomiting." She hesitated. "I told her it was a coincidence, but what do you think?"

The investigation had taken a toll on me as well: I had felt exhausted, lightheaded, and the area around my heart had felt sore and swollen, overworked, and stretched, like an old worn-out dishrag. Not knowing what else to say, I said, "Evon, please tell Deborah I'm sorry." I had a thought. "When I offered the use of the holy water I'd brought, do you remember if she used it?"

Evon was silent for a moment, as if contemplating what I had just asked. "No. She didn't." Her voice barely above a whisper, she added, "I know because I used it, then offered it to her, but she opted against it."

That explained it. At least to me. I would never force my beliefs on another, but Ron, myself, and the other members of the NEGP have run into similar "negative energy" situations and have no doubt that holy water is one of many choices of strong protection. I also believe it's the faith and belief in its power that make it so. I chose my words carefully. "Evon, please send my best to Deborah, and give us a call when you're ready to take action. We'll help you as best we can."

* * *

Months later, while waiting in an airport terminal, ready to board a plane on our way to meet our agent, Deidre, for the first time, Ron and I received an urgent phone call.

"Maureen, can you hear me? I'm sorry to bother you; is this a bad time?" Evon yelled. "My phone's cutting in and out. Crap,"

Evon said, her words quick and loud, like she feared her cell phone connection was about to drop.

Covering my other ear with my free hand, I struggled to hear over luggage wheels scraping on linoleum and the whirring of conveyor belts. "I've got a few minutes. What's up? Are you okay?"

"Well, yeah. Sort of." She hesitated. "We're moving to the new building today...Our team is here, and we were hoping you could guide us through a prayer. You know, to make sure nothing unwanted follows us."

I motioned to Ron to help me move our luggage to a more private, quiet part of the airport. Not an easy task. "All right, do you have the St. Michael prayer card I gave you?"

"Yes. But what do we do with it?"

Not comfortable with just whipping off a quick fix, I said, "Evon, Ron and I are just about to board a plane. Maybe it's best that we meet up with you guys when we get back."

"Maureen, please. Just tell me what I can do. Everyone's anxious, and like I said, we're picking up the last of the boxes."

Still uneasy, but realizing their predicament, I said, "Does everyone there feel comfortable creating a prayer circle?"

Her voice grew distant, as if she was holding her cell phone away from her ear. However, I heard enough of their conversation to realize they were all in agreement. "Okay, now, I want you to say the Lord's Prayer, followed by the prayer on the back of the St. Michael card I gave you." I waited for a moment, listening for any questions. When I didn't hear any objections, I continued, "Next, state that although you wish no harm on any beings residing there, you wish only for them to find the light, and that they can not, will not, do not, have permission to follow any one of you while you're leaving the building." I really didn't believe Evon and her co-workers would be followed; however, these situations are extremely delicate. And intent and belief in what can occur is at times a contributing factor of the end result. Doing my best to hide the concern in my voice, I then asked, "Does what I'm saying make any sense?"

"Yes, I think so. Maureen, thanks for your help." The sound of relief evident in her voice, she said, "Look, don't worry about us, we'll be fine. Have fun on your trip."

With that she hung up the phone.

That ended our association with the stone house. But I had my doubts about the dark entity. We had crossed paths before, and I had the sneaking suspicion we would meet again.

RESULTS OF THE INVESTIGATION

Since we investigated the stone house, we've been informed that the property has changed hands several times, through various developers, each one of them intent on bulldozing the stone structure to make way for a series of new homes. Unfortunately, it seems that "coincidental" accidents have plagued the builders: loss of money, missed deadlines due to failing equipment, accidents including broken legs, etc. Oddly enough, although the area around the stone house has been cleared, the structure still remains intact. Shortly after the investigation Ron was interviewed by *Woman's World* magazine. You can read his interview about the house in a reprint on www.neghostproject.com.

DREAM HOUSE

CASE FILE: 6258976
DREAM HOUSE

Location: Pomfret, Connecticut.

History: The original house, built in the 1700s, was later renovated and enlarged to the current structure. In the 1950s it was converted into a nursing home and later back into a private dwelling.

Reported Paranormal Activity: Apparitions, poltergeist activity such as broken glass, unexplained odors, and uneasy feelings of being watched.

Clients: Paula (owner), David (owner/Paula's boyfriend), Bridgette (Paula's daughter).

Investigators: Ron (lead investigator), Maureen (trance medium), Leo (photographer), Ron Jr. (investigator), Karen (EVP specialist), Jenn (investigator in training).

The *Woman's World* article about the stone house investigation had barely hit the stands when a woman from Rhode Island contacted me on the Ghost Line.

Her name was Paula and she and her boyfriend had just bought a second home in Connecticut. It was their dream house. They'd fallen in love with it. All had seemed fine until they started the renovations. That's when things began to happen.

Orbs began showing up on film.

ORBS

Although they are encountered quite frequently in paranormal investigations, there is no scientific proof of what they are. Orbs can be created naturally through water vapor or dust particles. However, many believe that these balls of light are the souls of those that have passed, while others believe orbs are a result of spirits drawing energy from the environment. Orbs themselves can be transparent or solid; their circumferences may display images within, such as rings and faces.

Paula had the sensation that she was being watched, and perhaps the most dreadful of all was a series of unexplained accidents that plagued visitors to the house. She dreaded going there alone. She also said that her boyfriend, David, wasn't himself at times, that he seemed different when he was at the house. While she spoke, I couldn't help but notice the fear in the quivering of her voice. She pleaded for immediate assistance to discover the source of the incidents. But unfortunately, getting our group together with such short notice is difficult at best. Everyone has their own lives and agendas. Understanding her need for urgency, I offered her a temporary solution to protect her and the house, hoping it would be more than temporary.

"Paula, is there a Catholic church nearby?"

"Yes, Ron. Why do you ask?"

"There are a couple of things you can do. Take a small container to the church, and fill it with holy water from the font. Take the holy water, and bless all of the doors and windows along with the four corners of the inside of the house."

"What should I say when I'm blessing the house?" she asked.

Although I've blessed homes and attended more than one exorcism with a Franciscan monk, I had to keep in mind that not everyone shared my knowledge. I suddenly had an idea. "No problem, Paula. I'll send you a copy of the St. Michael prayer. It's extremely powerful. In fact, Maureen and I use the prayer regularly for protection. You can also command the spirits to leave you alone. This works in a lot of cases." I paused. "But you cannot be afraid. If you show fear, that means you're not sure, which negates the whole purpose."

"I'll try anything at this point," she said. "When do you think you guys can make it?"

"Unfortunately we're not going to be able to make it for a couple of weeks."

"Okay. Although I wish it was sooner, I understand."

Before we knew it, two weeks had flown by and we found ourselves standing in the living room of the sprawling, circa-1730 colonial.

I scanned the room, looking for a place to set up base camp, but it was difficult to concentrate with the buzz of everyone talking in the room; Karen and Leo were in their own little world chatting away, oblivious to the group's needs. Paula was already speaking about her experiences to anyone who would listen, and I had no clue where my son was.

Maureen approached me. "Ron, I'm feeling the energy already."

I snapped at her, "Can't you wait? Do you always have to rush me?"

Her eyes sparked with anger. "You're such an ass at times."

"What did I do now?" I grumbled.

Without saying another word she did an about-face and stormed away.

Here we go again, I thought. It was like being married—we were fine one minute, and the next minute we wanted to wring each other's necks.

With Paula still yakking away, I spied Ron Jr. coming out of the den. "Ron, grab a camcorder and record this, will you? I'll take care of base camp."

Without missing a beat, and realizing she was now being filmed, Paula started the story from the top. "It all started when we began the renovations. At first we began to see shadows and had the uncomfortable feeling of being watched. When visitors have taken pictures, orbs have shown up. In one of the pictures, an orb the size of a beach ball can be seen under the kitchen table," she said, looking directly into the lens of the camcorder. "Things began to disappear and objects moved of their own accord." As if for acknowledgement, she looked past us into the kitchen where her boyfriend sat, then back at the camera. "In fact, when we first bought this place, we only came out here on weekends. One night while we sat on the couch in front of the fire, we agreed that it was time to purchase an antique fireplace screen, in keeping with the traditional décor. Now, keep in mind that we always lock this place up when we're gone. When David and I returned the following weekend, an antique screen, like the one we were talking about, had appeared out of nowhere." She hesitated, then yelled to David in the kitchen, "Honey, why don't you tell them about what happened to you?"

"You're doing fine; why don't you keep going?"

"No, you can explain it better than I can."

Still holding a cup of coffee, he entered the living room, although he seemed reluctant to speak, he began. "We're doing a lot of work ourselves, but we have some contractors to help us with the bigger projects. They've called me several times to ask me about the woman who watched them from the window, and if it was all right to still do the work with her there. At first I panicked, thinking someone had broken in. But when I asked the contractors to go in and take a look, they found no one there. There have been a series of so-called coincidental accidents that have happened to not only family members and friends, but the contractors as well, to the point that the contractors have quit, refusing to return. In fact, one night we had a housewarming party. Moments after leaving the house, a friend's car was T-boned by another vehicle. He spent the next several months in the hospital recovering from his injuries."

Finally finished with setting up base camp, I walked into the living room to join the team. "Okay, let's get this show on the road."

The chatter receded; the only sound to be heard was the gathering of equipment in preparation for the sweep.

Karen, our EVP specialist, holding the Panasonic D690 digital recorder in the palm of her hand, pressed the record button, and in a hushed voice, she said, "Testing, 1, 2, 3, testing." Seemingly confused, she attempted her test a second time. "What the hell? Ron, you're not going to believe this, but the batteries have been drained. And they're brand new."

"Did you bless them?" Maureen asked.

Karen gave a sharp nod, then said, "No." Digging into her kit, she pulled out another set of triple A batteries and quickly replaced the drained ones.

Maureen reached into her pocket and pulled out a clear plastic bottle embossed with a gold cross. "Why don't you let me bless them?"

Leo, camera clutched tightly in his hands, stood patiently behind Karen. "Maureen, would you mind blessing mine too?"

"No problem." Maureen moistened her finger with the holy water and quickly blessed the equipment. "We're all set."

Karen checked the level of her batteries, satisfied they were fully charged, and said, "Ron, I'm ready when you are."

"Paula, can you show us the rest of the house?" I said.

"Sure, follow me," Paula said, as she led us down a hallway toward the back of the house and up a set of stairs to the second floor.

* * *

Ron motioned for me to walk in front of him. Although the presence of a woman had reached out to me when we first arrived, the closer we got to the second floor, the stronger her influence became. Once we reached the top of the stairs, I said, "Ron, I can feel a woman here." I motioned to Leo. "Take a picture. Quickly."

While Leo clicked his 35mm camera, loaded with infrared film, I lifted my pendulum, closed my eyes, and began to reach out to the spirit.

"Are there any spirits with us now?" Ron asked.

The pendulum responded: yes.

"Are you a woman?" Ron continued.

Once again the pendulum responded with a yes.

With each question asked, I sensed the energy swirling about us, growing in strength, feeding off us to manifest. Our emotions intertwined, I felt her anger wash over me as if it were my own. In my mind's eye, I saw a quick glimpse of a woman struggling to maintain her grasp as her dead baby was being torn from her arms. With a lump forming in my throat, I said, "Ron, this woman lost her baby in childbirth." I gasped, "She's so angry." I glanced up at Paula. "First her baby, now her land."

"Oh, that explains why at night we hear a woman crying in anguish." Paula pointed to the next room over. "That's our bedroom, right there."

Ron, giving Paula a sign of acknowledgement, added, "Yeah, that makes sense. Why don't we go check the bedroom out?"

Continuing down the hallway, we entered the first bedroom on the right.

The spirit I had just felt had begun to distance herself. Although I still felt her presence lingering, it was nothing more than a faint thrumming of low-level current on my skin. Like the echoing of a train whistle in the distance, it faded into the background.

I had taken no more than two steps into the room when an icy hand gripping my leg stopped me in my tracks. "Ah, let go!" I screamed. "What the hell?"

Startled, Ron yelled, "What, what?"

I stepped away from the bed, backing up to the wall. "Something from under there grabbed my leg."

"Get out. Really?" He said as he dropped to the floor, lifted the bed sheet, and peered under the bed. "Maureen, there's nothing here."

"I'm telling you what happened. Here," I said, raising the pant leg of my faded jeans, "look at my calf. I'm not sure if we'll see any marks, but it feels like it's bruising already."

Together we walked to the bathroom, and turned on the light to get a better look.

"Wow, I guess you did feel something," Ron said, looking at the red handprint on my leg.

As we returned to the group, I tried to put what I'd just felt into words. An impression of the incident popped into my head, and instinctively I knew. "I think it was an elderly woman who had fallen off her walker and was reaching out for help."

I couldn't help but notice Ron's look of disbelief, but then Paula spoke up. "Well, actually, in the fifties, this building was a nursing home."

I smiled at Ron, "Did you hear that?"

"Yeah, yeah, whatever," Ron said.

I wasn't surprised at Ron's next suggestion. "Why don't we try to communicate?"

"What are we going to do?" Paula asked.

"We are going to make contact with the spirit and see if we can calm things down a bit."

"I'm up for that," Paula said. "So what do we do now?"

"Let's all sit on the floor and hold hands. This way the energy flows freely from person to person." Ron knelt down on the rug. Unable to sit Indian style, he adjusted his legs so that they were straight out in front of him, and then nodded for everyone to follow his lead.

Within moments we were all holding hands. The EMF meter, still on, lay eerily quiet in the center of the circle. Closing our eyes, we focused our intent.

"Are there any spirits here who would like to communicate? If so, show yourself now." Ron raised his voice to be heard above the sudden blaring of the EMF meter. "Thank you," Ron replied to the spirit.

Ron continued, "If anyone in this circle receives a message, just speak up."

A sharp pain sliced through my chest. Unable to breathe in deeply, I took short, quick breaths. "There's negative energy here. He doesn't like Bridget, he wants her gone."

"Who the heck's Bridget?" Ron asked.

"Oh my God, Bridget's my daughter," Paula said, her voice shaky. "That must be why, why—she can't sleep in this room."

Ron, picking up where he left off, continued. "They are only making changes in this house to make it comfortable. We ask that you not hurt this family, rather that you protect them."

The EMF slowed down, eventually stopping. The entity was gone.

We closed the circle, dusted off our butts, and continued our investigation of the building.

Walking two flights down through a narrow stairwell, we stepped off the last step into pitch-black darkness. "Where are we now?" Ron asked.

"In the basement," Paula answered.

I heard a slight ting of metal scraping, as Paula pulled the chain to the naked light bulb. "I want to show you the hidden room that David and I found." She gestured with her hand for us to follow. "It's over here. But be careful, there's not much light. David and I believe it might be part of the Underground Railroad."

We gathered in an area just in front of the door.

"It's right here, behind these pieces of wood." Paula pointed to a stack of wooden panels leaning against the wall.

Like peeling an onion, Ron and Ron Jr. removed one board after another. Layer by layer, they struggled with the weight of old beams and planks of rotted wood, until nothing was left except for a small wooden door, its edges masked by globs of mortar and stone. Together they pulled on the handle. It was stuck. Refusing to be thwarted, they yanked even harder. The door finally gave way. The sound of wood scraping on cement was like fingernails drawn across a chalkboard, causing my teeth to ache. I hung back and waited as Ron peered into the secret room. Realizing he needed light, he retrieved the flashlight from his rear pocket. Taking a moment to juggle the items in his hands to make room for the light, he aimed the beam in front of him, ducked his head ever so slightly, and headed into the dark abyss.

"Hey, Maureen, come take a look at this," Ron's voice echoed.

As I stepped into the secret chamber, I felt the first chilled breeze brush over my skin. After the rest of the group filed in, Ron reached his left hand out and yanked on the wooden door, sealing us inside and preventing any outside interference. I stood there, holding my breath in anticipation, as I watched the low light of the cellar fade into blackness. And I couldn't help but wonder about the door. Once inside, the door had closed behind us as easily as a hot knife cut through butter, like someone or something wanted us inside. How odd?

Now standing in utter darkness, I closed my eyes to focus my senses. Although I knew there were no more than five of us huddled within the secret chamber, it began to feel crowded. Almost too crowded.

I opened my eyes, struggling to see the silhouettes of our team in the darkness, but my mind looked past them, through them, until all I could see was the images of women and children, huddled in the corner of the room, gasping for breath. I stood there watching as streams of tears washed down their filthy, soot-soiled faces. My mind was transported to a different time.

Suddenly, my breathing turned heavy, raspy.

The air around me grew thick with smoke.

My chest tightened, constricted. I held my hand over my mouth to stifle the spasmodic cough. I took a sharp intake of air. It burned. I coughed again. The image slowly receding, I said, "Ron, I...I...I need to leave."

"Did you see something? Are you all right?" His voice sounded as thick as the air felt.

"The room is filled with smoke," I coughed, "and death." Ron Jr. pushed the door open. I left and all but ran up the cellar stairs, making my way to the front of the house and out the door into the night. Pacing back and forth, I inhaled and then exhaled slowly, struggling to clear the irritation in my lungs. If I hadn't known any better, I'd say I'd just exited a burning building. But that was impossible. I turned to stare at the house that from this vantage point looked fine. *Hmmm, looks are definitely deceiving,* I thought.

Not pain-free, but feeling somewhat myself, I went back into the house. Being empathic can be a challenge. Especially when I open up to communicate with spirits and end up wearing their pain and their suffering like a glove.

Karen's screech caught everyone's attention.

Ron, Leo, Ron Jr., and I ran toward Karen, who had been standing in the hallway, near a very large mirror, recording EVPs. Ron asked, "What's the problem?"

"All my recorders are empty!"

"You're kidding," Ron replied.

"No, I'm not. I've been recording all night. Oh my God, would you look at this one…" Karen held up one of her digital recorders, and angled it for us to see the screen. The numbers on the recorder were running backward, in reverse. "I didn't even push the button," she said, distraught. "They're erasing themselves!"

"Well, looks like we can forget capturing any EVP evidence," Ron muttered.

Ron's remark pushed Karen over the edge. She turned off her recorders. One by one she dropped them into her kit.

As a group we walked into the kitchen and took a seat.

David, his hand flat on the table, leaned over and said in a low voice, "I've had a few accidents here myself. I was on the stepladder fixing the trim against the ceiling, when out of nowhere someone unseen lifted the ladder and yanked it out from under me. I ended up with bruises and a fractured rib. Then, there are times I've woken up drenched, as if someone has poured a bucket of water on me." Still standing, he pushed away from the table, did an about-face and walked over to a well-lit room adjacent to the kitchen. The only room that we had yet to investigate. "There's more." He gestured with his hand for us to follow him. "Come here," he said. "I want to show you guys something."

Our morbid curiosity piqued, we followed him.

"One weekend I came to the house alone. I had way too much work to do, and Paula wasn't able to make it. So, after a long day of laboring, just before bed, I came down to the kitchen to get myself a drink and decided to use this bathroom, instead of the upstairs one."

I watched David's eyes glaze over as if he was looking at the bathroom, but not truly seeing it. As he began to retell the events of that night, his previously relaxed stance became rigid, guarded. "Well, I was sitting on the toilet, when the door began to open by itself." His smile turned into a grimace. "At first I was stunned, and then I got mad. I probably said some things I shouldn't have."

"Like what?" I asked.

Attempting to hide his embarrassment, he looked away momentarily. He gathered his thoughts and said, "I called them perverts!"

"Then what?"

"Then this." He stepped aside and let us take a look. There on the floor was a toilet bowl sheared in half. Well, not really in half. As I looked more closely I noticed that not a drop of water from the bowl had spilled. The only thing that kept the water from pouring forth and onto the floor was a sliver of porcelain, no thicker than that of a dollar bill standing on edge.

"Wow, that would be tough to pull off," Ron said.

"You didn't get hurt, did you?" I asked.

"No. It happened after I went upstairs to bed. I heard a loud bang, and when I went to investigate the source, that's when I found it."

Even though David's emotions were hard to read, I felt a swift, sudden onset of fear, and it triggered something in me. Just then an image of David being tipped over on excavating equipment popped into the forefront of my mind. "David, you also had an accident in the backyard, didn't you?"

"Yes. But how do you know?" He paused. "It scared the hell out of me, so I had some of my guys pack up the machines and drive them away."

"Was it a Kubota?"

"Yeah," he rubbed his chin as in deep thought, "how did you know that?"

I had no good answer for him, so I told him the truth. "I have no idea. It just popped into my head."

"Interesting," he said. "One minute I'm on the Kubota, the next, I'm tipped sideways." He said in excitement, "I had to jump out of the way or risk being crushed."

"David, that's sounds so terrifying. Thank God you're all right," I said.

"Maureen, Ron told Paula about a blessing she could do on the house. Do you know of a protection that I can use for traveling? These incidents have me a little on edge."

As coincidence would have it, prior to leaving for the day, I'd jotted down a few prayers of protection. One of them was for traveling. I dug into my pocketbook and handed him the prayer:

> *In the name of God I go on this journey.*
> *May God the Father be with me,*
> *God the Son protect me, and*
> *God the Holy Ghost be by my side.*
> *Whoever is stronger than these three persons*
> *May approach my body and my life; yet*
> *Whoso is not stronger than these three*
> *Would much better let me be!*

The grandfather clock chimed three times. With a two-hour ride back, it was time to go. As we left, we gave David and Paula the tools to protect themselves. We hoped that our investigation had answered some of their questions as to why their dream house had become a nightmare. And for now, our job was done.

RESULTS OF THE INVESTIGATION

This is one case where history and the paranormal go hand in hand. Our research showed us that the presence of the elderly woman could be attributed to the house once being a nursing home. And perhaps more dramatically, we later discovered that this area was the scene of several Indian raids in which settlers' houses were burned and families massacred. Was this the tragic event that Maureen relived in the secret room?

Since our investigation David and Paula have split up. His behavior at the house became more and more not his own, yet he failed to recognize it. He refused help, and now the dream house sits vacant.

episode twelve

THE SPECTRAL HITCHHIKER

CASE FILE: 6348765
SPECTRAL HITCHHIKER

Locations: America's Stonehenge, Salem, New
Hampshire; Route 28, Salem, New Hampshire;
and Methuen, Massachusetts.

History: Shrouded in mystery, America's
Stonehenge is a maze of stonewalls punctuated
with chambers. At four thousand years old,
America's Stonehenge is one of the oldest
megalithic sites in North America.

Reported Paranormal Activity: Sounds of drums
and chanting echoing in the night, unexplained
lights, blue mist, and shooting orbs.

Clients: N/A

Investigators: Ron (lead investigator), Maureen
(trance medium).

Ron and I pulled out of the parking lot of America's Stonehenge.

"Well, that was pretty mundane, ghost hunting in the afternoon. But at least we got the podcast done," Ron said, referring to our latest iTunes adventure. "Other than that one spirit who dogged us all afternoon, there really wasn't that much happening."

"Yeah, but he was pretty strong. Remember when we were standing around the sacrificial table? It was all I could do to not channel him."

"Well, why didn't you? Isn't that what we were here for?" Ron asked, his voice thick with sarcasm.

"Easy for you to say. I have free will like everyone else. The last thing I want to do is channel someone as nasty as that spirit. A Native American that sacrificed people by cutting their hearts out."

"And you know this how?"

I knew, like always, Ron was just trying to rile me up. "I know, because when we were standing by that big flat rock, the one with the groove carved around the edge to drain the blood, I had a quick glimpse of the spirit as he tore someone's heart out. It made me sick. I could feel his pleasure in the task."

Ron Kolek

A photo of the sacrificial altar at America's Stonehenge. Notice the groove in the stone used to drain the blood of the victims.

Suddenly, a tingle in my third eye caught me off guard. I pressed my finger to my forehead. "Hey, Ron, I'm feeling strange."

"Yeah, but when don't you?"

"No, I really mean it." I turned to look around, having the odd sensation that we were not alone. "Maybe I should have blessed the car. I think the spirit followed us."

"I don't think so. Come on," Ron said, denying the possibilities.

I heard the vague, familiar sound of rhythmic beeping over the music and Ron grumbling. "Shhh," I said, as I turned the radio down. The EMF meter in Ron's pocket had sprung to life.

"Oh, that's just the wires," Ron said, pointing to the telephone poles above our heads as we waited to turn onto Route 28.

But the energy pulsated in my third eye, making it challenging to concentrate on the road. And as we drove away from the wires and the EMF meter kept beeping, I said, "Wires, huh, Ron?"

"Well. Okay. Maybe not."

"Are you recording this?"

"I am now," Ron said, as he pressed the button on the digital recorder. "We're on our way home in Maureen's car. Who, by the way, didn't put any protection on it. And guess what's going on in my pocket?" Ron said as he held the microphone closer to his pocket, catching the incessant beeping of the EMF meter.

"Right now the energy is so strong, it feels like my head is going to blow off my shoulders as I'm trying to drive down Route 28 in Salem, New Hampshire," I said, my voice raised a couple of octaves above the norm. "This is not good!"

Over the continuous beeping of the EMF meter, Ron said, "Maybe this is his way of getting back at us for not allowing him to channel." He hesitated. "He's going to kill us both."

An involuntary sigh escaped my lips. "Ohhhhhhh, now's not a good time to channel." I mentally shoved back with greater force than I did at Stonehenge.

"Do you want me to drive?"

"No, I can handle it," I said, more determined than ever to remain in control.

Ron, sounding a bit nervous, said, "Okay, but don't channel." He reached into the duffel bag lying between his feet and pulled out the familiar blue bottle of "special blend."

SPECIAL BLEND

Ron's trademark method of protection. Reportedly a special mixture of liquid sage, holy water, and Jack Daniels (according to Ron) in a blue glass bottle with an atomizer. Only Ron knows the true ingredients.

Instantaneously the meter stopped, as if the spirits feared the mixture.

We looked at each other, wide-eyed, our voices resonating as one. "Oh—my—God."

"Oh, my...do you believe that?" I said.

"That's freaky," Ron said.

Suddenly remembering that we were recording the event for a podcast, I said, "Okay, we have to say what just happened here. I'm still feeling energy, by the way. I think he's in the backseat," I emphasized. "Ron whipped out the holy water and sage mix... and at that very second the EMF beeping stopped." I continued, "What does that tell ya?" My sentence broke off with a laugh. "That the spirit knows he's going to be spritzed." I glanced in my rearview mirror, the energy so strong I half expected to see him sitting there staring back. A little nervous, I said, "He's in the backseat, Ron, if you wouldn't mind spritzing there too."

Ron turned and began spraying over his shoulder. He looked at me. Reading my thoughts, his demeanor changed. His voice was now laced with concern. "Wow, this is definitely not good."

The energy began swirling around me, closing in as if the spirit were trying to escape being sprayed and was intent on sharing my body. It suddenly became difficult to see. My peripheral vision was getting hazy. I dug my fingers into the steering wheel and mentally pushed back once again. The sudden haze in my vision receded. There was no way I could allow this to happen. I was driving, for God's sake! "This isn't a joke, you know. I am totally serious." I became even more determined as I gripped the steering wheel tighter. "Don't worry; I am in control."

Ron fidgeted in the seat to remove the EMF meter from the front pocket of his jeans. He turned to me, holding the meter in the air. "You tell me this. How can my meter go on, when it's switched off?"

My jaw dropped. "Oh my God." Although the switch was turned off, Ron's meter was beeping wildly. I could hardly believe my eyes.

A sudden jolt of energy seared my forehead. "Ohhhh...I can feel energy," I yelled.

"Wait a minute," Ron said. He lifted the blue bottle once again. "I got the spritz."

I choked when I swallowed a mouthful of special blend.

"Can you drive and channel at the same time?"

"Ahh, I don't know. I've never done it."

"Do you want me to drive?"

"No. Why don't we say a prayer?"

As we began to recite the Our Father, I couldn't help but notice the sky in front of us. With each verse we recited, the cloudless sky, through the windshield of my Audi, began dramatically changing from blue to a deep crimson to flaming orange. "Ron, check that out," I said, giving a quick nod.

"Holy shit!"

The energy seemed to subside, but I wasn't convinced. I was nervous to keep driving, and I was hungry, so I told Ron we were pulling over.

Once in the Wendy's parking lot, Ron asked, "What now?"

"Well, I don't know. You think we should spray the car with the special blend?"

"Probably."

With all four doors open, he began dousing my black leather seats with spray. I cringed; what the hell was I thinking? My poor leather seats.

We went into Wendy's, ordered, and found a table.

Ron said, "So, now that I'm thinking about it, we may have only chased him out of your car and into the parking lot...What do you think would happen if he followed you home?"

I scanned the room, replaying Ron's question in my mind. Hmmm. I shrugged my shoulders as I took a bite of my cheeseburger. "It hasn't happened while working with you yet, but when it does, I'll let you know."

Little did I know these words would come back to haunt me.

RESULTS OF THE INVESTIGATION

Although America's Stonehenge was relatively quiet, aside from the annoying Native American spirit, the trip home was full of excitement. By carelessly forgetting to protect our vehicle, we unintentionally invited an unwanted guest along for the ride. Although we were able to protect ourselves from the spirit's advances, his energy was so strong that later, when Ron attempted to replace the battery in his EMF meter, the leads were found fused to the battery.

episode thirteen

THE CONCORD COLONIAL INN

CASE FILE: 6498923
CONCORD COLONIAL INN

Location: Concord, Massachusetts.

History: The Inn, rumored to be built on a
  Native American burial ground, is comprised
  of three buildings and sits across from
  Monument Square in historic downtown Concord.
  The left side of the building is the oldest,
  built by Captain James Minot prior to 1716.
  In 1799, the right side of the building was
  built, the home of Henry Thoreau and his
  aunts. The center building was used during
  the Revolutionary War to store weapons. In
  1855 it became a boarding house, and in 1900
  it became the Colonial Inn.

Reported Paranormal Activity: Room 24 seems to
  be the focus of paranormal activity. Although
  some guests clamor to sleep in haunted Room
  24, staff and others refuse to enter. Doors
  open and close by themselves, books fly off
  the shelves, and full-bodied apparitions have
  been seen.

Clients: Arthur (head waiter).

Investigators: Ron (lead investigator), Maureen (trance medium), Leo (photographer), Linda (Leo's wife), Janet (Ron's wife), Clay (tech manager), Janet (Clay's wife).

Laura Wooster

Ron and Maureen at the Concord Colonial Inn

Maureen and I sat with our laptops in the crowded, haunted Room 24 of the Concord Colonial Inn, anticipating another remote episode of *Ghost Chronicles*. It was 9:55 p.m., five minutes before we were due to begin, and our guest had yet to arrive. David Grossenburg, the manager of the inn, had invited my wife and me to spend the night, but first we had to do the show. The other members of the NEGP sat on the bed, waiting. As I shifted in my chair, a soft knock interrupted my train of thought. I breathed a sigh of relief when the door opened and I realized it was Arthur, our guest. Finally. Pulling out the chair, I quickly motioned for him to take a seat. Not trying to hide the irritation in my voice, I said, "Cutting it close, aren't we?"

"Well, I was busy downstairs with…"

I cut him off. I really didn't care. There was no time for explanation. "It's showtime."

Our producer, Erik, echoed over the headset, "You're live."

"Good evening everyone, welcome to another edition of *Ghost Chronicles Live*, on TogiNet. I am Ron Kolek, your host, the gatekeeper to the realm of the unknown, the unexplained, and the unbelievable, New England's own Van Helsing. With me tonight, as usual, is my co-host, psychic investigator for the New England Ghost Project, the Queen of Pain, Maureen Wood. We're broadcasting live from the haunted Concord Colonial Inn in Concord, Massachusetts, and our special guest is Arthur, the head waiter.

"So Arthur, you've worked for the Concord Inn for more than twenty-five years. I'm sure out of everyone here, you must have some great ghost stories that you can share with our listeners."

"Oh my goodness, yes." The words rolled off his tongue. "I'm sure I have one or two."

Maureen's shoulders bunched up like a kid waiting to hear a haunted campfire story. She leaned in closer to the microphone. "Oooh, tell us, please."

I looked at Maureen. She frowned as if she knew what my next words were going to be. As always, Maureen was eager to jump right into the meat of the stories, without setting the table. Dismissing her words, I continued, "They'll be plenty of time for that later. For now, could you share a little bit of the history of the Inn?"

Arthur lifted the microphone off the table and held it to his mouth. "Well, this house was built by John Thoreau, Henry David Thoreau's father. Henry David Thoreau lived here from 1835 until 1837. In fact, the front parlor I walked you through earlier this evening is rich with history."

"How so?" I asked.

"Thoreau's aunts, two sisters on his father's side, would meet in that room and discuss the evils of slavery with locals and like-minded members of the First Parish Church, over there across the green," he said, pointing toward the window. With the darkness of the hour, there was nothing to be seen but his reflection staring back. "Noted people took part in these meetings: Mr. Pitney, who wrote an antislavery book, and who now has a street named after him on Beacon Hill; Frederick Douglas, the great black emancipator; and Senator Charles Sumner, who, because of his antislavery beliefs, was caned over the head on the Senate floor."

Arthur puffed out his chest and adjusted his bow tie, as if in preparation for the words to follow. "The seeds of the Thirteenth Amendment of the Constitution, which abolished slavery, were planted in the downstairs parlor. It's a very *spirited* room. You never know what's going to happen, but it all happens when it's supposed to."

The moment Arthur said "spirited," the battery light on my laptop began to blink wildly, indicating I was about to lose power.

In panic mode I reached behind me, only to find that I was still plugged in. *What the hell? A low battery is impossible; the computer's plugged in*, I thought. Trying not to interrupt the flow of the show I gave a knowing nod to Maureen to take over as I frantically began to check the connections. It was too late. Arthur's voice trailed off as the laptop died.

"Hurry up, connect, connect, connect," I yelled at Maureen as she scrambled to bring up the network and connect to the studio on her laptop. Clay, our tech specialist, jumped off the bed and picked up my laptop, adjusting the settings. Then he unplugged the power cord and visually inspected it. "It looks fine to me."

"Maureen, are you up yet?" I asked, frantic.

"Almost, give me a minute," Maureen said.

I swapped the microphones and headsets from my laptop to Maureen's just as our connection went through and the station answered. "Erik, are we up and running?"

"What happened? One minute you were there, then you dropped," Erik asked.

"I was running off the wall current when the battery died and my laptop lost all power."

"Did you bless your laptop? I did," Maureen said smugly.

"Bite me," I replied, more than a bit irritated. But she was right—I hadn't blessed it. Ghosts tend to not be able to mess with blessed objects. Paranormal activity had most likely drained power from my laptop, and her blessed machine was still up and running.

"Okay guys, you're on in five, four, three, two, one, go." Dead air replaced the sound of Erik's voice. I pointed at Maureen, giving her the cue to come back on live.

"We're back," Maureen said.

"I apologize for that little mishap," I told our listeners. "But you know, that's what happens when you deal with the paranormal." *And you broadcast in a haunted location.*

"Are you ready for a ghost story?" Arthur asked.

"Shoot," I said.

He rubbed the bottom of his chin. "It was November, Thanksgiving, three years ago now. I was waiting on stations five and six, in the dining room where you ate tonight. Thanksgiving is one of our biggest days; we serve over twelve hundred meals in four hours. There is a lot of pressure on all waiters to keep up with the pace, you have to keep it moving or risk ruining the rest of your day.

"I was waiting on four parties of eight. When one party finished, they handed me a credit card for payment. I hurried over to the cash register to swipe the card." He mimicked the motion with his hand. "When suddenly…bingo, gone, zappo, it disappears right out of my hand!"

"Seriously?" Maureen asked. "What did you do?"

"I panicked. I began getting upset. Where was it? What happened to it? Where had it gone? There I was, with dishes coming out of the kitchen, stacked up high, customers waiting. And the gentleman whose card had just vanished into thin air was staring me down, watching the whole thing. So I dropped to my knees and looked all over the floor. I looked to my left, to my right, and still, no credit card.

"The credit card machine sits on top of a wooden cabinet with doors that are always kept closed. The worst thing you can do as a waiter is to lose someone's credit card, the second worst thing is to do it with them watching you."

I wondered where he was going with this. "So then what?"

"For some odd reason, I decided to look in the cabinet. I bent down on the floor once again, opened the door, and voila! There it was. Tucked in the back of the cabinet. But the problem was, the only way into the cabinet is through the front door, and it had been closed, all night."

"Arthur, that is fascinating," Maureen said. "Evidently the spirits wanted you to know without a shadow of a doubt that *they* had taken the credit card."

"We've had some professional psychics here and they told me that a male spirit was playing games with me. He didn't mean any harm. Apparently it was his way of trying to stop me from taking things so seriously."

"Is that what they were trying to tell me when they took my forty bucks at the Windham Restaurant?" I said, thinking back to the night that I'd tossed some money onto the table to take care of the bill, only to have it go missing a moment later, never to be seen again. I found myself getting aggravated all over again.

"Have there been any other ghostly events that you'd like to share with our listeners?" Maureen asked.

"Well, will you look at the time?" We were seconds away from the half hour and at any second Erik at the station would be plugging the commercial break. Quickly, before losing the air, I said,

"We're going to take a break right now, and when we come back, Arthur is going to share another ghostly tale." I smiled at Arthur, "You can hang on, right?" He nodded in response.

Maureen looked up from her laptop, and grinned. "So, you didn't need my laptop, huh?"

"Whatever."

With the last remnants of commercial fading off into the distance, Maureen said, "We're back. And for those of you just tuning in, we're here at the haunted Concord Colonial Inn. Before the break Arthur, the headwaiter, was just about to share another ghostly tale with us. Arthur?"

Arthur grinned. "Well, let me tell you about another spirited event. It took place in the dining room, not far from where you ate tonight, on February 21 of this year, which I think is Lincoln's birthday. That Sunday, the Sons of the North, the Union Army, a fraternal organization, had brunch here for their annual get-together. Normally, for all big meetings, I set the guests up at round tables and place the podium in the center of the room, for easy viewing. For some unknown reason, for the first time in twenty years of setting up functions, I decided to place the podium next to the grandfather clock instead."

"I take it something happened?" Maureen asked, her voice thick with anticipation.

"Yes. The guests were finishing up dinner, and we began to serve dessert. The chaplain of the group stood up to speak. I've heard a lot of benedictions in my time, but this was an outstanding, eloquent speech. Then, at the end of his speech, before the opening of the prayer, he asked that everyone bow their heads in a moment of respect and honor to the fallen president." Arthur hesitated. "At that instant, in that very second that everyone bowed their heads, the grandfather clock started to chime. With the podium so close to the clock, the microphone echoed the sound, which in turn reverberated around the Inn. The clock chimed twelve times…The only problem was, it was two in the afternoon." As if to emphasize his point, he continued, "The clock was in perfect working order. It was the first and only time it ever happened."

"Wow, that is unbelievable," I said. "Can you believe it, though? It's time for us to say goodnight. Arthur, thank you so much. You certainly know how to tell a tale."

"Thanks, Ron. It's been a pleasure."

"We want to thank the manager of the Concord Colonial Inn, David Grossenburg, for making this all possible. Tune in next week, when we will be joined by Steve Wilson and Black Betty from the Spirit Light Network."

"Ron's referring to my friend, Bety Comerford. Why do you always call her that?"

"It's just every time I think of her, that song pops in my head. You know, the one from Ram Jam, 'Black Betty'?" I go into song. "Whoa, Black Betty, ram-A-lam. Whoa, Black Betty bam-A-lam…"

"She's gonna kill you." Maureen said, chuckling.

"Whatever, the line is getting longer by the minute. Well, look at this, it's time to say…"

"Good night and God Bless," we said in unison as the show ended.

* * *

Ron stood up from the chair and walked Arthur to the door as I made my way to the bathroom. Feeling exhausted, I leaned over the sink, the cold water rushing over my hands. I slowly raised my head and glanced into the mirror. Startled, I stumbled backwards. I reached out and grabbed the towel bar to keep myself from tumbling over. My reflection was gone, replaced with the image of another woman. Unable to do much else, I stood there, staring into eyes that were not my own. Her jet-black hair was pulled up in a bun, a stark contrast to her pale, triangular face. Her small hands were folded in front of the soft blue bodice of her gown. Her striking green eyes stared at me longingly, as if she wanted to speak, but didn't know how. I opened my mouth to scream, but no sound came out. My heartbeat thudded. Finally finding my voice, I said, "I'm sorry. I can't understand you. What do you want?"

I blinked and she was gone.

I thought of yelling for Ron, then changed my mind. What good would it do now? He would rush in, meter in hand, and attempt to communicate. No. That wasn't happening. I was exhausted and just wanted to go home. Breathing a sigh, I shook my head slightly to clear the cobwebs, then leaned over the sink and looked up in the mirror again. "Gross." My normally olive skin, with the exception of dark circles forming beneath my eyes, looked like death warmed over. Great.

I exited the bathroom and walked smack dab into Linda, Leo's wife, who had been waiting outside the door.

"Maureen, it looks like you've seen a ghost!"

"Well, I…" I waved my hand dismissively. I was about to explain, then thought better of it. I didn't want to get into it now.

I crossed the room to Ron. "Ron, there's a…"

Ron interrupted me, "Maureen, I meant to ask you earlier, but forgot. Why didn't Steve make it to dinner tonight?"

"This isn't Steve's idea of a night out." I turned to look at Jan, who, looking exhausted, was pulling a toothbrush and toothpaste out of her overnight bag. She and Ron would be staying the night.

I took it as a sign that it was time we called it a night. I put on my jacket. "You know, you're really lucky that Jan is part of the group. Who knows, maybe Steve will become a believer someday. I think he just needs to experience things for himself."

"Yeah. I guess," Ron said. "Oh, you were going to say something?"

"Yeah. There's a woman with dark hair in the bathroom."

"What?" Ron asked.

"I'm serious; she just appeared in the mirror out of nowhere."

At my words Ron dove on the bed. "Oooh, baby, come and get me."

"You are crazy." I laughed out loud. "You never know. You should be careful what you wish for, Ron."

"How so?" Ron grinning from ear to ear, sat straight up on the bed.

"Yeah, you know when you're watching a scary movie and the guy is kissing a beautiful woman, " I raised my hands and wiggled my fingers in the air. "Then, 'boogada, boogadda, boogadda,' she turns into a ghoulish demon." I laughed.

Ron wrinkled up his nose, and smirked. "Whatever."

I suddenly began to feel even more exhausted than I had a moment ago, if that was even possible. "Gang, I'm out of here."

After I'd gotten into my car, I pulled a little bottle of holy water out of my canvas bag. Typically, I bless my car with holy water to prevent any unwanted visitors. But it was 1:45 a.m. and I was tired. Besides, usually I do it before I get into the car, and I'd forgotten. At this stage, it seemed pointless—I was already in the car. Plus, I hadn't felt any negative energy, so I shouldn't have anything to worry about. I threw the bottle back in the bag and stepped on the gas.

As I pulled away from the Concord Inn, my third eye began to throb. *What's up with that*, I thought. But I was too tired to think about it more.

Once I got home, I realized I should take out the sea salt and do a cleansing, but again, I was tired and felt physically incapable. I dragged myself to bed. Before my head hit the pillow, I was dead to the world.

SEA SALT CLEANSING

An ancient method of removing residual energy. Sea salt and spring water are mixed together and either poured over one's body or placed under the head of the bed to draw away negative energy while a person sleeps.

I woke up, greeted by my husband's angry stare.

"What's the matter with you?" I asked, rubbing the sleep from my eyes.

"What's the matter? What's the matter?" he spat out. "I'll tell you what's the matter. When you go on your little 'ghostly' adventures, you had better sleep in another room!"

Since I'd slept so soundly—it was the best rest I'd had in years—I was at a loss as to what he was referring to. "Why? What happened?"

His eyes grew wide. "You...you brought something home with you."

"Come on, Stephen. Really. What's going on?"

"Last night, I heard you when you got home and climbed into bed. But I fell back asleep."

"Go on."

He stared at me hard as if he didn't know how to say it. Then he began, "Well, you started rubbing my back and I thought, *Wow, she should go investigate more often.*" He frowned. "Then, the next thing I knew, I was up on my elbows with you beneath me. I was kissing you, holding you. I closed my eyes. When I opened them, I'd shifted over you enough that light from the streetlight was coming through the curtains. Then, bam! Right in front of my eyes, your face shriveled away, until it was nothing but a skull with eye sockets!"

For a minute I was stunned. I looked at the way his eyes watered as he retold the story, reliving it a second time. Not knowing what else to say, I asked, "Are you sure you weren't dreaming?" as the memory of the night before began to come together in my mind: the woman in the mirror, the conversation I'd had with Ron and Clay, the "boogada, boogada, boogada" thing.

"No, I wasn't dreaming. I was still up on my elbows when I turned to my left, and you were there, sound asleep, oblivious to everything. It hadn't been you at all. Then when I turned back, the skull was gone..."

Intuitively I knew the woman in the mirror had followed me home. I was torn, one part of me felt bad that he had endured such an ordeal. The other part of me was happy that he'd finally experienced something paranormal. Maybe he wouldn't think me crazy after all.

I waited for my husband to leave to run some errands, when it was safe, I called Ron and blurted out my husband's "little indiscretion." After his laughter subsided, I asked, "So, Ron, did you get lucky?"

* * *

"Excuse me?"

"You know, did you capture anything?" Maureen asked.

"After you guys left, I did some base readings with my EMF meter. Although I was picking up some low-level readings, there really wasn't much to write home about. But here's the thing. After I finally fell asleep, I was awakened by what I thought was the shaking of the bed. I looked at Jan, who was curled up like a newborn baby, oblivious to what was going on."

"Did you see anybody?"

"No. But then it happened again, so I grabbed my EMF meter. The readings were definitely higher than before I went to bed."

"Who sleeps with an EMF meter on the nightstand?" Without waiting for a response, she said, "You do, evidently. Ron, do me a favor... please don't tell anyone else about his 'little indiscretion,' Steve will kill me."

"I promise I won't. Scout's honor," I said. But in truth, I never was a very good Boy Scout...I continued, disappointment in my voice. "I went through the footage of the night, and guess what?"

"The bed was shaking."

"No. Before it happened, the tape on both camcorders had run out."

"Maybe that was the plan," Maureen said. "So what did you do?"

"Nothing. What could I do? I gave Jan a kiss on the forehead and went to sleep. But I have something neat to tell you."

"What?"

"After breakfast, I was interviewing the girls at the front desk for the iTunes podcast. You're not going to believe this...They told me when the guys from the TV series *Ghost Hunters* came here and investigated Room 24, they saw a woman with dark hair as well." Ron paused. "So I guess it was a productive night after all. The radio show was a success. You saw the woman in the bathroom. I got my bed shaken, and just maybe, Steve was left with a deeper understanding of what the paranormal is all about."

RESULTS OF THE INVESTIGATION

We found little physical evidence on our investigation of the Concord Colonial Inn, other than a photograph taken during the radio show, which revealed an unusually large number of shooting orbs. Even though a shaking bed woke Ron, we were unable to verify it through video, because both camcorders ran out of film prior to the event. But the most intriguing evidence was Stephen's tryst with the spirit of the woman that followed Maureen home. Although he found it terrifying, most paranormal investigators would give their right arms to have that experience.

DANCING WITH THE DEAD

CASE FILE: 6437463
DANCING WITH THE DEAD

Location: Quincy, Massachusetts.

History: An old mill building converted into several businesses, including a dance studio.

Reported Paranormal Activity: Shooting orbs and mists caught on film.

Clients: Wendy (proprietor).

Investigators: Ron (lead investigator), Maureen (trance medium), Leo (photographer), Jeff Belanger (author and paranormal investigator), Rob (particle engineer).

The Ghost Line rang with a call from Jeff Belanger, the founder and chief cook and bottle washer of Ghostvillage.com.

"Hey Ron, what's happening?" he asked, in his familiar jovial voice. " I take it you haven't had a chance to review the video clips I sent you."

"Ah, that would be a no, but I'll check it out right now." Punching a few keys on the keyboard, I found Jeff's email. I pressed a few more, and a video popped up on the screen. The heavy beat of nightclub music blared through my computer speakers as I sat, momentarily mesmerized by the scene before me. "Wow! Is that what I think it is?"

"Yup, and you, my friend, are going to owe me, big time. If you're interested, I can hook you guys up."

"Are you serious? I'll tell you, Jeff, I've never seen anything like that before. I'd definitely like to get a closer look. If you know what I mean." I laughed out loud. Not wanting to let this opportunity slip through my fingers, I said, "We're going to be in Lawrence on Friday doing the radio show on WCCM. How about we hook up after the show?"

"That works for me. Say around seven? I'll email you the directions."

I hung up the phone. As far as I was concerned, this was going to be a great case. But how the hell was I going to tell Maureen that we'd be investigating the source of strange lights at a "pole-dancing" studio?

Leaving out a few details, I convinced Maureen to go along. So after the radio show on Friday, we had a quick bite to eat and left in Maureen's car for our trip to Quincy, Massachusetts. We followed the directions Jeff had emailed me and in about an hour we arrived at the studio. We parked next to a blue compact car and were immediately greeted by Jeff.

"Hey, Ron and Maureen, glad you could make it. This is my neighbor Rob," he said, nodding in the direction of the tall man pulling some type of equipment from the trunk of his car. "Rob's an engineer," he continued. "He works with particle-measuring devices."

"That's neat. Where is this place?" I replied.

"Just follow me," Jeff said, as he led us through a small wooden door into the old brick mill building. Once inside we followed him up three flights of stairs, but my eyes were drawn to the black and pink walls adorned with boas, hats, and bordello-type decorations.

Before we had the chance to enter the studio, a scantily clad woman with short auburn hair rushed out to greet us at the top of the stairs. Her lily-white skin was a stark contrast to the thigh-high black boots and black miniskirt. "Hi, I'm Wendy. Welcome to Gypsy Rose Dance Studio," she said in a bubbly voice.

"Hi, Wendy, I'm Ron and this is Maureen, our psychic investigator."

"Hey," Maureen said, looking a little uncomfortable.

Wendy looked from Maureen to me and said, "Has Jeff told you what's been going on?"

"Well, I saw the video and it's pretty cool," I replied.

"What video, Ron?" Maureen asked, her voice rising an octave.

Not even giving me a chance to answer, Wendy spoke up. "You know this a pole-dancing studio, don't you? I tape all my classes and rehearsals and when I do, I get these little lights that dance along with me. They're really neat. If you want I can show you the video while the boys set up the cameras. By the way, Maureen, do you want a costume? I'm sure I have one in your size."

Heat rose in Maureen's face and her eyes flicked from person to person, as if there wasn't a place big enough for her to hide. "Costume? Nah, I think I'll pass. But thanks anyway."

Maureen in a costume! I thought. In all the years I have worked with Maureen, I have never thought of her in a sexual way. Maybe a partner, a friend, and even a sister. But definitely not as an object of sexual desire. I was as happy as she was when she declined.

I walked by Jeff and Rob, who were setting up the camcorder, and continued to the far side of the studio. I blinked. My eyes needed to adjust to the hot pink walls and several wall-size mirrors that made the room appear bigger than it actually was. Two metal dancing poles ran from the hardwood floor to the suspended ceiling.

"Okay, guys, I'm ready when you are." Wendy strutted over to the boom box she had left on the floor in the right-hand corner of the room. "I'm going to start dancing like in the video. If you accidentally catch a glimpse of 'something,' and I don't mean paranormal, I apologize in advance." She smiled, then asked again, "Are we ready to go?" As if receiving the acknowledgment she was waiting for, she placed the CD in the player and pressed the button.

* * *

A lump formed in my throat as I looked at Ron and the other guys, their eyes glued to Wendy, barely blinking as if they were afraid to miss out on "something." Almost immediately her body began swaying with the beat, pulsating to the point where she and the music became one. We watched intently as she twisted, twirled, and spun around the brass poles to the heavy beat of the music. Each move, each thrust of her body, made me feel more and more uncomfortable. In my mind, I knew she wasn't a stripper, but for the life of me, I had begun to feel like the only woman, a voyeur if you will, at a strip joint, while men drooled at the abundance of bare flesh.

Ron Kolek

Wendy dances to the beat of the music in an attempt to excite the spirits.

Ron peered into the viewfinder of the camcorder. "Oh, I'm seeing something," he said over the pounding of the music. "It's the light anomalies, they're back."

I glanced at Jeff, with Rob peering over his shoulder. Jeff acknowledged seeing them with a nod of his head and a thumbs up. Well, I think that was what he was signaling.

Ron removed the EMF meter from his red duffel bag, gingerly stepping further into the room as if not wanting to disturb the sensuous performance of our host.

The EMF meter blinked sporadically, and the CD quickly ended.

"Hey, Ron, take a look at this," Jeff said, pointing to the camera's viewfinder. "Don't they look like the orbs in the video?"

Ron bent over to take a closer look at the small LCD screen and said, "Yeah, kind of, but not nearly as bright."

"Rob and I are going to try some experiments to see if we can reproduce them," Jeff continued.

"Great idea. Wendy, can you dance again for us?" Ron asked.

My back stiffened and I glared at Ron. I had just endured seeing more of Wendy than her gynecologist had and I wasn't looking forward to another round. As if Ron was reading my mind, he said, "Come on, lighten up, will ya? It's all in the name of science."

Science, my ass.

She smiled, and it looked genuine enough. "Sure," she replied, as she put another CD in the player.

She began to move in sync with the music. In one quick motion she flipped herself upside down, wrapped her legs around the pole, and spun like a corkscrew to the floor.

Jeff and Rob started their experiment, dropping bits of dust in front of the lens, in an attempt to "debunk" the light anomalies on the video.

Wendy completed her dance routine. Curious as to the results of Jeff and Rob's experiment we hurried over to take a look. Ron and I waited as Jeff rewound the camcorder, and then replayed it for us. Jeff glanced at a sheet of paper where he'd written down the exact timing of each anomaly and when they occurred, then stopped at the first sequence of numbers. "Here, you see this." He pointed to the LCD screen. "It's a little difficult to see, but we were able to reproduce an orb similar to what Wendy got on her video."

Ron and I took another step closer to the video recorder. "You may have been able to recreate the orb, but no way is it reacting the same way as they did in Wendy's video." Ron looked at Jeff again, and continued. "You think? I mean, in Wendy's video the light anomalies cascaded around the pole."

Jeff thumbed through the remaining sequence of numbers that he'd noted earlier, and when done he said, "Yeah, I guess you're right. I mean, we proved that dust can make the same orbs, but they are definitely not moving in the same manner."

Moments later, Jeff and Rob began to check on the results of the particle-measuring devices that they had previously set up.

Suddenly the air shifted, the atmosphere thickened. It was almost touchable, electrified. "Ah, Ron, I think someone's joining us."

Ron looked at his silent EMF meter. "Really? Well, I'm not getting anything," he said as he stuffed the meter in the front pocket of his Dockers, went over to one of the poles and started spinning around it, mimicking Wendy's moves.

I began to pick up on sexual energy that was not my own. Ewwww, there was a spirit becoming attracted to Ron. "Ah, someone likes you," I said.

He smiled.

"But it's a man," I said as Ron's smile faded away to near panic.

Just then, in mid-twirl on the pole, the EMF meter went off in his pants' pocket. Through the pale fabric, the constant red glow of the EMF meter told the story.

"Is that a ghost you're picking up on, or are you just happy to see me?" I laughed out loud.

As I struggled to control my laughter, I said, "I caught a glimpse of a tall black man with a funny hat. He's telling me he likes to come to the studio to listen to the music and watch Wendy dance."

"Like a pimp?" Ron asked.

"No, more like a transvestite." The second I said "transvestite," the intensity of the energy escalated, growing stronger and stronger by the minute, as if the spirit knew I'd recognized he was there. My third eye vibrated. Pulsated.

"Can you channel him?" Ron asked.

"Give me a minute." I closed my eyes, blocking out my visual sense, and forced myself to concentrate on the black man who was rapidly approaching. In the quiet of my mind, I asked him to tell me what it was that he wanted.

He answered my question. A visual of Ron twirling around the pole stood in the forefront of my mind, and with it an overwhelming feeling of desire. "Gross! Sorry, Ron. No, no, no, no. No way. I have my limits." I shivered inwardly. Like the shaking of an Etch-a-Sketch, I struggled to erase my mind of the spirit's desires. "Ewww. Nothing personal, Ron, but he really likes you, if you know what I mean. And that, my friend, is more than I want to see."

Ron thought about that for a second, then said, "Okay if you don't want to channel him, let's try something else. How about doing a contact circle?" Ron asked.

"Well, as long as I don't have to channel him, I'm good with it."

Ron turned to Wendy, "Want to try it?"

"Sure, how's it work?"

"Okay let's all sit in a circle on the floor, hold hands, and try to make contact as a group." Now sitting, Ron said, "All right, Maureen, can you begin?"

Using the method I'd learned when I was sixteen to help get myself and others into a relaxed state, I counted down. I started from twenty-one, counting backward all the way down to one. Lastly, I lowered my voice and finished by counting us down through the colors of the rainbow, "Ten-red, six-yellow, five-blue, three-green..." I inhaled then exhaled, sensing that everyone was ready to make communication. I said, "If there is a spirit here, please give us a sign."

Over the whir of the camcorder the silence was deafening.

"If there are any spirits here please give us a sign of your presence," Ron's voice echoed my previous question.

Suddenly, there was a bang. It sounded like it was coming from the door directly behind us, in the adjacent room. Ron jumped to his feet, ran over to the door, and pushed it open. He quickly snapped a photo with his 35mm. "There's no one there," Ron said as he scrambled back to the circle.

"Ron, I'm really not feeling a presence anymore," I said.

Not ready to call it a night, he said, "Come on, Wendy, Maureen, let's go into the other room where we heard the bang and see if we can use your pendulum there to get some questions answered."

Reluctantly I followed Ron and Wendy into her side parlor, a place where people could take a respite on soft cushiony chairs while others danced. We dragged three chairs over the black and white linoleum and small scatter rugs and placed them in a small circle. As we sat in the dark, once again the door made the same noise as before.

Jeff, having heard the noise at the same time we did, closed the distance between us and the other room. He commented, "Hey guys, I think that sound may be coming from the heating system."

"That makes sense. We've seen similar phenomenon on other investigations, and on some occasions it turned out to be a vacuum or the heat turning on," Ron said, flipping the on switch to his EMF meter.

I held my pendulum tightly between my thumb and forefinger as we asked questions of the spirit. Nothing. "I don't think he's here either."

In an attempt to liven up the moment, Wendy jumped to her feet, "Hey would you guys like to see a trick?"

"A trick?" I said, almost afraid to ask.

Like flies to flypaper, the second the guys heard the word "trick" they dropped what they were doing and rushed to her side. I wanted to laugh. I don't think I would have gotten this type of reaction from them if I'd just yelled "Fire!"

"We're men of science." Ron's grin widened again, and this time I thought his face would crack. "Inquiring minds want to know."

Wendy took a crisp twenty-dollar bill out of her pocketbook, and then turned to her mesmerized audience. "Now watch," she commanded. She folded the bill lengthwise and placed it on the chair. "Without the use of my hands I will pick up this twenty-dollar bill," she said. Turning her back to the chair, she glanced over her shoulder as if calculating her stance. Wendy adjusted her miniskirt. In one quick motion she sat down on the chair, and bounced back up.

"What's the trick?" Ron asked.

She smiled. "This," she said, as she reached her right hand between her butt cheeks and pulled out the twenty-dollar bill. She waved it in the air, like an honor guard raising a flag in a parade.

She walked over to me. "Maureen, would you like to try it?" Without waiting for an answer, she said, "Look, I'll even make it sanitary." Wendy took the twenty-dollar bill, unfolded it, then folded it in the opposite direction. "There, now it's all ready for you."

I felt the heat rising in my cheeks. "No, that's okay…"

Jeff, not one to refuse a challenge, jumped at the chance. Within seconds he was standing with his back to the chair. "So what do I do?"

Wendy let out a hearty laugh. "When you feel your bum hit the chair, squeeze your cheeks together."

Jeff sat down, then stood up. The folded bill remained on the chair.

"One more try," Jeff said, as he took the plunge yet again. "Wahoo!" He screeched as he reached his hand behind and plucked the twenty-dollar bill out of the seam in his jeans.

We all started clapping.

Jeff, addressing the smiling onlookers, said, "It's always good to learn a new skill; that gives me something to fall back on in bad economic times."

Laughter filled the studio as we began to pack our equipment.

Although I'd felt a little embarrassed during the show, Wendy was a genuinely nice, fun-loving person, and I found myself feeling way more comfortable as we made our way out the door than when we'd first arrived.

"Maureen, do not open your car yet!" Ron said as he circled my Audi, blessing the windows with holy water. Then, after spraying a healthy portion of "special blend" over himself, he said, "Okay, I think I'm good."

"I'd say. That's a little overkill, isn't it?"

"Let's just say that our friend the transvestite is one hitchhiker I don't want following me home."

I couldn't help it—just hearing him say it made me throw back my head and laugh.

RESULTS OF THE INVESTIGATION

We've had a lot of interesting cases in the past, but never a case like this. There were surprises at every turn, or should we say "twirl." Wendy the pole dancer, we later found out, authored two books: *Pole Dancing for Dummies* and, much to our surprise, *The Deaths of The Popes*. Jeff and Rob were able to reproduce similar light anomalies, but could not reproduce the movement that was seen in Wendy's video. We concluded that Wendy's studio was in fact haunted. The twist came when Maureen sensed the spirit of a black transvestite, who was more infatuated with Ron than Wendy. Since this investigation, Wendy has moved, and to her delight, it appears the spirit has followed her.

episode fifteen

THE LIZZIE BORDEN HOUSE

CASE FILE: 6321947
THE LIZZIE BORDEN HOUSE

Location: Fall River, Massachusetts.

History: On August 4, 1892, Mr. and Mrs. Borden were murdered with an axe. Lizzie Borden, their daughter, was accused of being the murderess. However, Lizzie was put on trial and acquitted of all crimes.

Reported Paranormal Activity: Impressions in the beds, guests who have reported being touched, orbs and mists in photographs, unexplained noises, and voices of the dead (EVP).

Clients: Lee Ann (the owner), Emily (tour guide).

Investigators: Ron (lead investigator), Maureen (trance medium), Laura (photographer), Ron Jr. (investigator), Jim (EVP specialist), Gavin (Welsh psychic), Martin (Gavin's manager), Byron (UK investigator from the ghost-hunting group, Haunted Devon), Pippa (BBC correspondent).

Lizzie Borden took an axe
And gave her mother forty whacks.
And when she saw what she had done
She gave her father forty-one.
~Author Unknown

I did my best to push the popular Lizzie Borden rhyme to the furthest recesses of my mind. It made me nervous, although I knew the rhyme was an over-dramatization of the actual events of August 4, 1892. I distracted myself by chatting with Gavin Cromwell, a psychic visiting from Wales who was accompanying us to Fall River. With foreign guests in town, Ron called Lee Ann, the owner of the Lizzie Borden House and a former guest on *Ghost Chronicles*, to see if we could host a UK/US investigation of one of America's most haunted sites.

"I sense there was a large shed or barn in this exact spot," Gavin said as I slid the car into a parking space behind the Lizzie Borden Bed and Breakfast, which was now closed for repairs.

Laura Wooster

The infamous Lizzie Borden House in Fall River, Massachusetts

Unlike Gavin, the only sense I was getting was one of foreboding. No matter how many investigations I've been on, I am never sure what we will encounter. Unsure how to answer him, I remained quiet as we made our way to the small brown clapboard building to our left.

"Good evening, everyone, I'm Lee Ann. So glad you all could make it."

Over the clamor of voices I heard bits of Ron's introduction of Gavin to the host. "He's a psychic visiting us from Wales."

I gazed around at the shelves piled with Lizzie Borden paraphernalia: various sizes of stained-glass ornaments in the shape of hatchets, Lizzie Borden hatchet earrings, baseball hats and T-shirts with macabre sayings, bobbleheads, water with a Lizzie label, and other items too numerous to even mention.

Lee Ann pulled out a small bottle with what appeared to be sand in it. "Our new hottest seller: authentic brick dust. It's collected from the decaying bricks of the haunted basement of the Borden home." She held out her hands like Vanna White displaying a letter. "Look, we tag each one with a stamp of authenticity. Not only that, but the proceeds benefit the renovation of the property." She grinned as she placed the bottle in Gavin's hands then, covering his hands with her own, she gently squeezed her hand closed. "Tell me. What do you feel?"

"Oh my God," Gavin said in his thick Welsh accent. "It's very powerful, isn't it?" He placed his free hand to his temple and closed his eyes. "Well, I never." Eyes still closed, he gently shook his head from side to side. "My goodness, the basement is a very scary place."

Lee Ann's eyes sparkled. "It is a very scary place. But I won't give anything away." She raised her head and looked around the room, then looked back at Gavin. "I can't wait until you've finished with your investigation. I so look forward to hearing what you pick up."

I took my place behind Gavin as we began the investigation. That way I had an opportunity to compare another psychic/medium's impressions to my own. My own little experiment.

Not more than two steps into the hallway of the house, I felt an overwhelming sense of evil oozing out of what I presumed to be the basement. As if Gavin and I were connected by an ethereal string, we reacted in unison, sidestepping the open door to our right. I took a series of short, shallow breaths as I tried to relieve the pressure of what felt like a hundred-pound weight upon my chest. Hoping to escape the sudden onslaught of discomfort, we hurried into the kitchen.

"Wow, Maureen, did you feel that?"

"Yeah. That was horrendous. My chest is still killing me." Then I felt something else. "Gavin, are you getting anything here? I'm feeling the presence of a woman."

He began to stumble around the kitchen, moving back and forth with his fingers to his forehead. "I'm getting the name Abby."

As Gavin spoke of Abby, sending out a cosmic calling card, my third eye began to throb. I looked at Gavin and thought of our drive over. He'd told me that he owned a Lizzie Borden doll that he was fascinated with. Without being certain of how much prior knowledge of the gruesome murders Gavin had, I held my tongue. As for me, growing up in Massachusetts I'd have been hard-pressed not to hear the tales. Rather than compromise the investigation with names that I already knew, I decided to keep them to myself. What I didn't know, however, was where in the house the crimes were committed.

With my thoughts and the pressure in my forehead spiraling out of control, enveloping my whole face, I began to feel as if I were wearing a mask, looking through eyes that were not my own. A sudden onset of emotions coursed through my body, burning me to the core: anger, hatred, repulsion. Over the sound of blood pumping in my own ears I vaguely heard Ron's voice as I struggled for control.

"Gavin, what's the problem?" Ron said as he entered the room.

"I don't know. Look at her. She's..."

Ron interrupted, closing the gap between him and me. "Maureen. Now's not the time." We weren't ready for me to trance channel—we weren't even set up yet.

The anger within me growing, my head raised slowly of its own accord, staring through the mask into Ron's eyes. "Leave me alone!" I said, barely conscious. The words gurgled, torn from my throat.

I felt Ron's hand on my shoulder. Sickened by his touch, I jerked away. "Don't—touch—me." My anger festered like a pus-filled wound.

"Maureen." Ron pushed forward.

Once again repelled by his touch, I stumbled backwards. A sharp pain seared my lower back as I collided with the potbellied stove. My hand frantically searched for the hatchet I'd seen earlier, nestled in the basket on the floor. One part of me wanted to drive it into his skull, while the other part of me struggled for control. "Ron, get away from me!" I bellowed, clenching my fists, "Get away. I just want to kill you right now."

Ron took a step backwards, while Gavin and Martin, Gavin's manager, quickly retreated to the far corner of the kitchen. Bending at the waist, I squeezed my eyes shut, struggling to control the urges that possessed my emotions. Reclaiming my soul, I mustered my free will, and with a mental shove, I evicted the vile presence invading my body. I looked up at Ron once again, this time through my own eyes, no longer through a mask.

"Are you all right?" Ron asked.

"Yeah. Sort of."

"Why don't we take Maureen out to get some air?" Martin said.

He gingerly approached me, taking me by the elbow and ushering me back through the short hallway and out the side door. Gavin followed.

A burst of cool air hit me in the face as we exited the building, a refreshing relief to my labored lungs. After a few deep intakes of breath, my body slowly regained strength. I'd only been here a short time, and I had already experienced far more than I really wanted to.

Martin slowly approached me and said, "Maureen, are you okay? You scared the bloody hell out of us."

I turned and caught the wide-eyed stares of Gavin and Martin, "The cool air is helping a lot. Thanks."

Gavin, feeling less nervous, joined in the conversation. "That was actually quite disturbing, Maureen, to see you like that. There wasn't any warning at all; it hit you like a ton of bricks. You just fell into a trance, taking on the energies. I'm beginning to understand what's happening here. The energy is so thick. It's not good, not at all."

We heard Ron's voice through the door. "I guess we ought to go back in," he said.

Gavin and I walked into the parlor. This time, feeling a little braver and more prepared, I closed my eyes to get a feel for the environment—and shuddered as a searing pain shot through my head. What was I thinking? Empathic abilities and murders don't mix. I grabbed the left side of my head. It felt like my head was splitting open.

"This is horrendous. Maureen, I'm so glad I don't feel their pain like you do," Gavin said, as he picked up the 5x7 picture frame from the side table.

I walked up beside him, peering over his shoulder at the gruesome sight of Andrew Jackson Borden, Lizzie's father, his body slumped to the side of a Queen Anne–style couch. Blood and gore spilled out of his head, splattered on the wallpaper. "Gross."

"Oh my, would you look at this?" Gavin pointed from the picture to the green velvet couch we walked past as we entered the room. "Lee Ann, is this the original couch that Mr. Borden was murdered on?" he called, his voice loud enough to carry into the next room.

Lee Ann leaned into the parlor. "No. It's an amazing copy though, isn't it? Actually, I spotted the frame on eBay, bought it, then had a local guy do the reupholstering." Stepping into the parlor, she leaned over and lightly caressed the couch. "He did a great job, don't you think?"

The throbbing finally lessening, I replied, "I'd say." It was true; the replica was nearly identical. In fact, the more I looked around the room, then back at the photograph, the more I noticed how meticulously the home had been restored. The flowered wallpaper. The heavy, velvet drapes. "Wow, Lee Ann. Did you do all the restorations yourself?" I asked.

"Pretty much. I've tried to capture the authenticity of the place. You know, to give our guests a genuine, unique experience."

I thought about all of the people who were clamoring to spend the night in the Borden home and shuddered.

As we walked into another sitting room, I found that although I felt some energy, it wasn't nearly as strong as in the parlor. That had me thinking. "Gavin, what is your impression of the area where Mr. Borden was murdered? To me, it feels like his energy is nothing more than a memory. It's residual. More like a horrific imprint of his murder than an actual haunting."

Gavin nodded. "Yeah. I don't think Mr. Borden is still haunting this house."

Ditto, I thought, as I listened to the sound of gear clanging off the dining room table. While Ron Jr., along with Ron and Jim, our new EVP specialist, continued setting up base camp in the adjoining room, Gavin, Laura, our photographer, and I amused ourselves with the array of period clothing hanging in the front hallway. Finally, getting antsy, we headed for the stairs to venture onto the second floor.

"What are you doing?" The screech of Ron's voice stopped us short.

"What? We're getting bored. I mean, really, Ron, it's already after seven-thirty."

"Byron and Pippa from Haunted Devon aren't even here yet. And we're not starting without them—after all they are my guests."

"Fine." This was getting ridiculous. Gavin and I were eager to explore.

No sooner had we retraced our steps back down the stairs than a knock resounded at the front door. Relieved, I smiled at Byron, the UK investigator, and Pippa, his girlfriend, a news reporter for the BBC. It was great to meet them since I had only seen them on our Halloween videocast, a live Internet video broadcast shown on Halloween with three ghost-hunting groups—the New England Ghost Project, Haunted Devon (UK), and Haunted Australia—conducting simultaneous investigations in three different countries.

After a quick swapping of pleasantries, we walked into the parlor and began our investigation. Ron spoke into the microphone. "We're in the parlor where, supposedly, Mr. Borden was murdered."

Ron Jr. bellowed, "What do you mean 'supposedly'? This was the murder room."

"And how do we know that?" Ron asked.

"I don't know, genius, maybe the evidence photo sitting over there might be a hint."

The sound of laughter broke the growing tension in the room.

Then Ron continued. "Gavin, what are your impressions of this room?"

Gavin pointed toward the kitchen. "Whoever did this came in through that door, and to me, I've got to say, it feels like a male energy doing this killing. But upstairs, that might be different. This one was killed first, the other one, later."

"What about you Maureen?"

"Truthfully, I felt how he died, more than anything."

Without saying a word, Gavin walked up to the bookcase and picked up the photo of Lizzie Borden and studied it. "I think she was a lesbian."

Ron gazed at Lee Ann for her reaction.

With raised eyebrows she said, "Hmmm. That's interesting."

"Okey dokey. Moving on. Next room." Ron said.

As we entered the next room, Gavin stopped. "I hate this room with a passion. I don't like it. Immediately when I walked in, I felt like a blanket dropped on me."

Since I had shared the same feeling, I added, "Yes, it's a heaviness all around you, like you're walking through a wall of energy."

Gavin took several steps to the far corner of the room and stood next to a Victorian table lamp. "I feel that this was a room where they came to socialize." Stopping short, he peered out the window and said, "I sense a female spirit, who comes to the house and peers in. She's an acquaintance of the Bordens. She comes to the house often, but can't or won't come in. That's all I'm getting in this room."

Looking at Gavin and I, Ron asked, "Where to next?"

"I don't know," I said. "Since we didn't make it past the first floor for the past three hours, and we have no idea what's upstairs, why don't you guide us." I said, not trying to hide the irritation in my voice.

Ron wrinkled his nose, then said. "Fine. Be that way."

Jim, our EVP specialist, suggested, "Why don't we go to the third floor? When I was setting up the IR camera I had a feeling that I was being watched."

"Sounds like a plan." Ron said.

* * *

I took the lead, with Maureen, Gavin, and the rest of the group close behind me as we made our way to the third floor.

We walked down the narrow corridor to the front of the house. Upon entering the room I caught an odd whiff. "Is it just me, or does anyone else smell this?"

The remainder of the team meandered past me, sniffing the air as they walked around the rich mahogany bed.

"Yeah. It smells very antiseptic, like blood, I don't know," Maureen said with a puzzled look as she sniffed the air again. "Like a hospital."

"Very, very steroid, isn't it?" Gavin added in his thick Welsh accent. I looked at Ron Jr., sure that Gavin meant "sterile."

"Yeah, but what's the smell?" I asked.

"It smells like a hospital," Maureen said.

"Ether?" I guessed.

"Yes, that's it," Maureen said, nodding in agreement.

With the smell still permeating my nostrils, I decided to explore it more. "Jim, hand me the UV light."

ULTRAVIOLET LIGHT (UV)

As in the television show *CSI*, UV light can be used to identify traces of blood and other fluids. It is also utilized by some paranormal investigators to illuminate dust particles, to rule them out as a source of orbs.

Jim reached into the holster on his belt and handed me a small ultraviolet flashlight. I switched it on and scanned the carpet and the rest of the room for hints of blood or other bodily fluids. Without finding a trace, I stopped my scan and asked the two psychics if they were picking up on anything.

Maureen answered, "I feel someone was sick in this room."

"I feel a female energy," Gavin said. He put his fingers to his chin and said, "I'm getting a name, not a first name…its Sulliban, or something like that."

"Sullivan?" I said.

"Yes, that's it. She's not the one who was sick. She's a servant." He paused, his eyes moving as he searched his mind. "I am picking up on a lodger, a boarder. I know it's a bed and breakfast, but this was before."

"I wonder, can you get confused by different time periods?" I asked. "I know we have found some places that are haunted by spirits who have lived at different times."

"Yeah, absolutely," Gavin said. "The older the place, the more layers there are, and it can get confusing at times."

Maureen spoke up. "You know what's interesting? My ears are fluttering like there's talking, talking…" she said. "There's some kind of confusion going on." She paused for a moment. "Combined with the sick person I mentioned before, it doesn't feel good up here at all."

"When you first entered the room, you got a 'swoosh' of energy. Now that you have been in here for awhile, is it different?" I asked.

"Yes, my body is getting used to it. It's sort of leveling off," Maureen said.

"Like when you go into the water, your body gets used to the temperature," Gavin added.

"All right, let's try some EVP work now," I suggested.

Jim placed his recorder on the bed where I had sat down and waited for the room to become quiet before beginning to ask questions. He started, "Are there any spirits here that would like to speak with us now?" A few seconds passed. Next he asked, "Can you please let us know you're here? Give us a sign." After a moment of silence, he continued, "This is my recorder; can you please tell us your name?"

"Hold everything. Did anybody see that?" I said, looking around the dimly lit room. There was no reply. "I just saw something run across the bed. Not a person, but maybe an animal," I said, searching the befuddled faces of the team. "Ron," I said to my son, "did you see anything through the camcorder?"

"No, I didn't see a thing," he replied.

We asked a few more questions and then ended our EVP session. As we walked out of the room, Maureen said to me, "I don't know if Jim got anything on the recorder, but when he was asking the questions, I could hear a high-pitched whine like they were trying to respond."

Byron joined in our conversation. "I thought I heard a cat," he said.

"That's interesting," I replied. "There's supposed to be a ghost cat here."

We entered the last room on the right, adjacent to the top of the stairs, a small bedroom where the ceiling matched the slope of the roof. I knew I would have a problem standing, so I sat on the end of the twin bed. Byron, also tall, joined me. Maureen, bent over by the low ceiling, said, "The energy is different here. I feel like my heart just skipped a beat. There's anxiety here, but not like the other room."

Gavin spoke up. "I'm getting the name Mary or Martha." Gavin was snapping his fingers, as if trying to get a mental grasp on it. "She seems a bit put off. People are talking about her, and she wants to get something off her chest."

"Why don't you try to contact her?" I said.

"Okay," Gavin replied. "I can't say if her name is Mary or Martha, but the name Sullivan comes into play. I feel lots of static in here. My skin's all tingly. Ms. Sullivan, can you please make a noise to let us know you're here? Bang something. Give us a sign." Fingers spread wide, Gavin clawed at the air. "She's feeling really anxious."

"Skittish," I added.

"Yes, she's skittish, like she's not sure," Gavin said.

"As if she doesn't know who she can trust?" I asked.

"Yes, yes, that's exactly it. She doesn't know if she can trust us."

Pippa said, "Ms. Sullivan, we mean you no harm. Can you please affect someone in the room? Touch someone please."

I sat waiting for a reply, when once again my "psychic nose" kicked in. "Does anybody smell anything?" I asked.

Ron Jr. answered, confirming the blank stares of the group. "There's no smell in here."

"There is," I said as I sniffed the air. "I smell rose, kind of powdery, like a rose powder."

Gavin took a deep breath. "I have a hard time smelling anything with this bloody cold," he cried.

Pippa, sitting on the floor in the back of the room, said, "Let me try, maybe she doesn't like men."

"Feel free," I said.

She began, "Ms. Sullivan, we have the utmost respect for you, and we mean you no harm. We want to help you. Can you please make a noise or give us a sign that you are here?" She continued her query. Silence was her only answer.

Maureen soon drew closer and said, "I think she's trying, but having a tough time. She doesn't have enough energy." Then she paused. "I smell it too. It smells like baby powder only different… I know! It's the powder they used in the old days. A rose dusting powder," she said as she made a swirling motion with her hand in the air.

"It's funny," I said. "I smelled it before, then it went away, and all I could smell was Gavin's leather."

"Leather?" Gavin replied. "I have no leather on. Ron, you cheeky boy. I would never wear leather."

"That's weird," I said. "I really caught the strong odor of leather."

"Maybe someone else dropped in," Maureen said with a smile.

"Hey, Ron," Martin asked, "do the names make any sense?"

"Not to me," I replied.

"There are some photos behind me on the floor," Maureen said.

Jim left his perch in the back of the room and crawled over to look at the photo sitting on the floor in front of an old steamer trunk. Illuminating them with his small flashlight, he read a name, "Bridget Sullivan."

"Really?" Gavin said.

"Good job, Gavin. At least you got the last name," I said.

"Ron, the energy is waning here," Maureen interrupted. "I think we should go downstairs."

* * *

I descended the stairs to the second floor, following behind Ron and Gavin. With no more than the beam of the flashlights and camcorders guiding our way, we passed through a series of rooms, feeling little to no energy. We continued down the hallway until we reached what Lee Ann referred to as the John V. Morse room, a comfortable-sized bedroom facing the street.

"Okay, I want you and Gavin to walk around this room and tell me what you feel." Ron motioned with his flashlight. The narrow beam of light sliced a path over the room, brightening the white cotton bedspread that was swallowed by darkness.

Gavin and Maureen give their psychic impressions of the events that transpired in the John V. Morse bedroom.

Suddenly feeling like a trained monkey performing for an audience, Gavin and I walked around the far side of the bed. I began to feel the swirl of energy encircling us. Almost in unison we said, "Someone's here."

My breathing became shallow, labored. I sighed heavily. "Gavin, are you feeling this?"

"Yes." His voice sounded distant as the energy closed in on me.

"Why don't you two hold hands?" Ron said. "Let's see what you can pick up as a team."

Hesitantly, almost as if we both were afraid that we'd somehow hurt each other, we took a step, closing the gap between us. Slowly, we reached out and took each other's hands in our own. I closed my eyes and focused my intentions. A spirit was with us. Of this I had no doubt. But who? Was it Lizzie? Abby? Mentally I reached out. Suddenly, my world began to spin out of control. It was too late to turn back now. My consciousness faded into the background.

* * *

I stood closer to Maureen and Gavin. Her body swayed. She raised her head slowly. Her eyes were piercing. It was the look I'd seen many times before. It was no longer just Maureen.

Camcorder rolling, seizing the moment, Byron spoke up in his heavy British accent. "If you're here, can you step forward for us?" He paused, only for a second. "Can you let us know that you're here?" Barely pausing, "Can you step through. . .okay, do you want to speak to us?"

No response could be heard except the sound of Maureen's labored breathing.

"Hold up," I said to Byron, realizing that Maureen needed time to adjust to the alien energy pulsating through her body.

As she raised her head, she stared at me. By the look in her eyes, I knew it was no longer Maureen. "Who's with us now?"

Eyes now closed, Maureen inhaled deeply. A series of moans escaped her lips. Sighing heavily, she lowered her head, slowly shaking it from side to side. In a voice not her own, she spat, "Dirty girl."

"Who are we speaking with?" I asked.

In a throaty whisper, barely audible, she said, "Abigail."

"Abigail," I said, repeating her name. "Do you have something you want to tell us?"

Maureen inhaled. Exhaled. She sighed deeply once again. She groaned. "Never turn your back." Penetrating eyes met my stare. "In this house," she finished with a hiss.

Not wanting Gavin to become a hindrance, I leaned in and whispered in his ear, "Let her go."

All too eager to comply, Gavin quickly released her hands and scurried to the edge of the room.

I addressed Maureen once again. "Abigail, why are you still here?"

Her breath raspy, once again she began shaking her head side to side. Her voice thick with emotion, she replied, "I—can't—leave."

Touched by her sorrow and eager to understand, I asked, "Do you want to leave?"

She slowly moved her head from left to right, pivoting on the balls of her feet. Her body swayed to and fro. She stumbled backwards.

One look at her awkward movements and I realized Maureen, teetering on the brink of consciousness, was losing the battle. My arm reached out to steady her.

Her breathing stopped for a mere moment as an inaudible gasp escaped her lips.

"Abigail," I repeated. "Why can't you leave?"

Agitated, Maureen drew a long agonizing breath, tearing away from my grasp. She retreated backwards, mere inches from the wall. Doubling over, her body rocked up and down. She expelled a sudden, high-pitched moan, obliterating the growing murmurs of the onlookers. Just then her body stiffened. Her eyes were engaged one moment and haunted the next, as if vanishing behind a mask. The entity had taken control.

Maureen was gone.

"Abigail. Abigail!"

She turned to her side. Her body writhed in pain. She coughed, choked. Wet gurgling sounds emanated from deep within her throat, as if she was vomiting. Violently she dropped to the floor, screaming, kicking, gagging, as retching sounds continued to spew forth.

Reacting quickly, I tossed the microphone on the bed and dove to the floor. I grabbed her flailing legs. My only reward was a kick to the groin. I gritted my teeth as I heard her head slam against the wall. I reached for her legs once again, pulling her away. Leaning my weight on her I screamed, "Maureen! Maureen!"

Still gurgling, gagging, spewing, to all in the room she sounded as if she were puking.

"Where's the light? Get a flashlight over there," Ron Jr. cried out from the back of the room.

"No. We're using infrared, it could screw 'em up," I commanded. Maureen whimpered as I continued to wrestle with her convulsing body. "Maureen! Maureen!" I repeated, as I placed my hand on the side of her head. "Abigail, leave. Leave this body. It's not yours." I repeated, "Leave this body, it's not yours."

Maureen's body went limp for a fraction of a second.

When she regained consciousness, her body jerked in response. She bolted upright. The palms of her hands digging into my chest, she shoved me back. "Get—off me. Get off me. Get off me," Maureen cried. As I stood up, she cowered in the corner, both hands clutching her head. "My freaking head. It's killing me!" She cried out. "Oh my God. It hurts."

"Did it feel like forty whacks?" I chuckled, in an attempt to lighten the moment.

"Ha, ha." Maureen grimaced as she continued to clutch the back of her head. She looked down at her bare feet. "Where are my shoes?"

I knelt down and ran my hands along the pile of the carpet. "I don't know where they are," I said. Grabbing a flashlight I looked under the bed. "How the heck did they get way over there?" I lay down, chest on the floor, and stretched to reach them. "Here." I tossed them to her.

Maureen pushed up on her hands, then dropped back down.

Realizing her plight, Gavin hurried over and placed his hands in front of her. "How about a bit of energy to get you going?"

A few moments later, Gavin stood up, reached out his hand, and helped Maureen off the floor.

Ron Jr. turned on the bedroom lights and walked over to where Maureen and Gavin were standing. He looked at the carpet. "There's nothing there? I could have sworn you threw up."

"Maureen," Byron screeched. "Look at this."

Maureen and Gavin stopped talking between themselves and turned to look over Byron's shoulder, at the faded photograph hanging on the wall.

"Oh my God, Maureen," Gavin said, pointing at the picture, then at the flowered carpet beneath our feet. "You almost landed the same way Abby did."

Maureen, looking a bit stunned, said, "'Oh my God' is right. That's disgusting." She hesitated. "Ron, come here. Take a look at this."

I went to see what the buzz was about. Looking at the photograph, I said, "Wow, that's great. A dead body. Now let's get going."

Maureen sighed heavily.

"What? What's the matter?" I looked at Maureen once again, then stopped short. "Are you okay? Seriously, you're not looking so hot."

"Well, actually, I'm feeling like crap." She turned her wrist over. "It's after ten o'clock, and I have to get up at five for work."

"And your point?" I grinned. But I knew where she was going with this. She had stayed way longer than originally planned. Not to mention the beating she took.

"I'm going to get going. I have a long ride home." Maureen looked around the room. "Sorry, guys."

"Would you mind dropping me off at the hotel?" Martin asked.

"No problem. Let's go." With that she and Martin headed downstairs.

With Maureen gone, we continued our investigation. Emily, a tour guide for the B&B who had just arrived, led us to the basement.

"Gavin, what are you feeling?" I asked.

Gavin paced back and forth across the dirt floor. "The darkness I felt before when Maureen and I first entered the house is gone now."

"What do you mean it's gone?" I asked. "It just disappeared?"

Gavin replied, "Ron, as I'm sure you must know, the energy can move around. Here one minute, gone the next. Sometimes not restricted to one room, or the house for that matter. In fact, it takes a lot for a spirit to manifest. The energy can dissipate as the night goes on."

"Oh, then they're not much different than we are," I said.

Gavin half laughed. "No they're not. Oh, wait, I'm getting something," he said, putting his fingers to his temple. "A coffin?"

He twisted at the waist, turning to look at the rest of us. "Yes, I think there was a coffin here at one time."

Emily said, "Come with me." She motioned for us to follow.

Curious, we hurried through an opening in the basement wall, entering a small, cluttered room. There, to our astonishment, tucked into the corner was a pine coffin.

"Oh, do you believe this?" Gavin said.

"It's not a real coffin. It's one that we use for Halloween decorations." She smiled. "But the fact that you picked up on it is cool, just the same."

Just then my EMF meter blared, startling the group. "What's that?" Gavin asked.

"Oh, that's nothing." I said as I took the meter and raised it to the wires running along the rafters. "It's just the wires. Electrical wires are a natural source of EMF."

Gavin frowned, looking a little disappointed.

I still wanted to try some experiments to contact the spirits, so we cut short our investigation of the basement. As we stepped into the kitchen, we found Lee Ann.

"How did it go down there?" she asked.

"Not too bad. Actually, I did pick up on the coffin you have stashed away." Gavin beamed.

Lee Ann looked a little puzzled, then her eyes sparkled. "Oh, my Halloween decorations."

"Lee Ann, do you have a small table?" I asked. "I want to do a little experiment."

"Table tilting?"

"Yes." I watched as the look of pride washed across Lee Ann's features. Evidently she'd had experience with this before.

> ### TABLE TILTING
> Developed in the 1900s as part of the Spiritualist movement. The participants sit around a table, join hands, and attempt to reach out to the spirits. The spirits respond by moving, levitating, or knocking on the table.

Lee Ann brought a small octagonal wooden table up from the basement and placed it in the middle of the front parlor. Lee Ann, Pippa, Gavin, and I sat at the table. Ron Jr. was viewing the room on the monitors of the base camp, while Laura took up a position in the far corner of the room. Jim, manning the camcorder, stood over my shoulder. Byron, his camcorder in hand, took a seat on the couch. Laura dimmed the lights as I turned on my EMF meter and placed it in the center of the table, hoping it would detect any fluctuations in the magnetic field of the room. Placing our fingertips on the table, we began.

Laura Wooster

Ron, Pippa, Gavin, and Lee Ann attempt to make contact with the spirits of the Lizzie Borden House via table tilting

Gavin spoke: "I call upon all spirits around us tonight. I call upon all spirits in this house. I invite you to draw closer to this table. Tilt this table, move this table. I call on all spirits, whether male, female, or child, to draw closer. Use all your energy to make this table move."

Jumping in, I said, "We mean you no harm. I know it is difficult, but please try. Use our energy. We give it freely."

Gavin said, "All spirits in this house, please come forward and let us know you're here."

It didn't take long before I could feel a gentle hypnotic rocking of the table beneath my fingertips. Someone was here. My heart beat slowed in sync with the rhythmic sway of the table.

"It's rocking!" Gavin cried. "Whatever spirit is here, can you make it go faster?"

My eyes closed; somehow, not sure how I was doing it, I mentally tapped into the spirit circling the table. "Patience, patience, she's trying," I whispered.

"Which spirit is here?" Lee Ann asked over the creaking of the table as it swayed.

"Abby's here," Gavin said. "Byron, can you ask the questions?"

"Sure," he replied. "Abby, if you are here can you please make the table move faster? Show us you are here. Show us you can communicate with us. Please." The table rocked, harder and harder, creaking and moaning.

"She's showing herself to me," Gavin said. "She is not showing herself as she looked normally, but the way she looked when she was murdered. Like she just got up from the spot. She's between Ron and Pip, right in front of that lamp." The rocking grew stronger; our fingers barely touched the table.

Pippa spoke, "Abby, do you want us to know that Lizzie did this to you?"

"For the record," I said, "Lizzie was proven innocent. So she didn't do it. Did she?" The rocking of the table stopped as if it were held down by some supernatural force. Evidently, Abby did not like my statement. "Oh, wow, did you see that?"

"Abby, if Lizzie killed you, could you please make the table move again?" Pippa asked. No sooner had the words left her lips, when the rocking returned. It appeared she was confirming that Lizzie had murdered her.

"I know this is going really well," Byron said, "but maybe we ought to try glass swirling. It requires less energy."

> **GLASS SWIRLING**
>
> Introduced by the British, it involves placing a glass rim-down on a table. Each participant places a finger on the bottom of the glass. The spirit, using the energy of the group, moves the glass in response to questions.

"I don't know, Byron. I have never seen so much energy like this before. I'm barely touching the table and look at it rock," Pippa said. "Let's try something. Everyone take their fingers off the table." Lifting our fingers, it immediately went dead. "Put them back down." As we did, the table began to rock. "See, she's using our energy."

A thought popped into my head. "I feel she's getting tired. Why don't we try the glass swirling?" I paused. "Thank you, Abby. We really appreciate your help." The table went dead.

Removing my EMF meter, we replaced it with a short drinking glass, positioning it in the center of the table.

Gavin began, "I want everyone to picture a band of white light surrounding us. Enveloping us. Protecting us." After a moment of silence, we began.

Pippa said, "Everyone, please place the very tips of your fingers on the glass. Like this."

We all mirrored her movements. "We would like to call Abby forth. We know that you want to communicate. We know you have a story to tell. Can you please step forward?" Pippa said softly, as the glass began to slide across the table toward Lee Ann.

"She's drawn to you," Gavin said.

"Thank you, Abby," Pippa said. "Can you bring the glass back to the center of the table?" As if on command, the glass complied. "Thank you, Abby. Can you make the glass go in a circle?" Again, as requested, it began moving in a circular pattern around the table.

Byron spoke up. "Abby, can you show us where the church is?" Without pausing, the glass moved toward Pippa. "Is that right, Lee Ann?"

"Yes," she said.

"Show us where Doctor Bowen's house is." The glass moved toward Gavin.

"That's right," Lee Ann said, with a look of astonishment.

We continued to test the spirit in regards to directions, with mixed results.

Gavin interrupted. "She's getting frustrated with our direction game. And you know what, I'm sensing that she didn't feel accepted in her home."

As the glass circled the table in a clockwise direction, I asked, "Abby, if you didn't feel comfortable in this house, please make the glass go in the opposite direction."

Without missing a beat, it turned in place and moved counterclockwise.

Gavin spoke up again. "Abby, the woman I sensed earlier, the one who visits here, is either a friend or relative."

Pippa asked, "Abby, is the woman who visits here a friend?" The glass stopped moving. "Is it a relative?" The glass began to move again, denoting a yes.

Lee Ann chimed in, "Mrs. Borden, stop for a minute, please." The glass responded as asked. "Mrs. Borden, was it your sister, Sarah?" The glass began to move in a circular motion, another yes.

I asked a question. "Abby, do you mind all these paranormal investigators coming in here with their cameras and equipment?" The glass spun wildly, then tipped over and rolled toward me. "Oops, what does that mean?" I asked.

In response, Lee Ann picked up the glass and gently placed it back in the center of the table. "Mrs. Borden, please move the glass if you like these investigators coming here." The glass immediately responded by moving in a wide, circular motion on the table.

Gavin piped in, "I sense she likes us here because she has a story to tell."

Pippa resumed her questioning. "Abby, are you a religious person?" The glass moved more forcefully. "Did you like going to church?" The glass moved with even greater force until it tipped over once again. As an eerie silence fell over the room, a church bell began to toll in the distance. Dong. Dong. Dong. Twelve times.

Lee Ann picked up the glass, once again placing it back in the center of the table as she said, "Mrs. Borden, last year when I was up in the guest chamber making the bed, was that you who passed through me?" Once again the glass moved in a circular motion denoting a yes response. "Thank you, Mrs. Borden. I will try to talk with you more often."

Pippa asked, "Mrs. Borden, is there any truth to the rumor that Mr. Borden abused his children?" The glass stopped. "Is there any truth that he was unfaithful?" No reaction.

Gavin intervened, "I don't think she is comfortable with these questions. Ask her something else."

I asked her, "Mrs. Borden do you like the way the house is kept?" The glass moved quickly around the table.

"Mrs. Borden, do you find it rather humorous that people come to visit here?" The glass moved faster and faster. It became more and more difficult to keep our fingers on the glass. One by one they fell off, until only Pippa and I remained. The glass, spinning wildly close to the edge, fell off.

Lee Ann said, "I have one more question." Reseating it, we placed our fingers back on the glass. "Mrs. Borden, do you appreciate the way I keep your house?"

As the glass began to move quickly around the table, I turned to Lee Ann. "Of course she does! She absolutely adores you. Watch this. Mrs. Borden, do you like Lee Ann?" The glass took off, spinning faster and faster, until it pushed off the table, into Lee Ann's lap.

Gavin spoke up. "Mrs. Borden, I know you are getting tired and so are we, but could you please answer one more question? Did you get along with Lizzie?" The glass jerked, barely moved. "I think she's too scared to talk."

I said, "Let it rest…" The glass slowly moved off the table. As far as I was concerned, we were done.

"Thank you, Mrs. Borden. We really appreciate you talking with us," Pippa concluded.

Exhausted, with an hour-and-a-half ride home, it was time to call it quits. The team began to break down base camp and the rest of the equipment, while I made small talk with Lee Ann in the kitchen. Suddenly I saw blood beginning to drip from my hand. To my surprise, there was a small cut on my hand.

"How did you get that?" Lee Ann asked.

"I really don't know. I don't remember cutting it on anything," I said. Reaching into my duffel bag, I retrieved the first aid kit. Finding the last bandage, I placed it on my hand.

"Ron, do you want to stay the night here?" Lee Ann asked.

"No, thank you." I smiled, then walked out the door toward the car. As I opened my car door, the overhead light revealed more blood on my hand. *What the hell is this?* Unable to figure it out, I looked closer. There, beneath the gushing blood, was another slice in my hand. Knowing I had no more bandages I returned to the house, lights now out. I banged on the door. Lee Ann answered. "Do you have a bandage?" I held my hand up. "Not sure why, but I'm cut again."

Once in the kitchen I cleaned the wound, while Lee Ann went in search of a bandage.

As she handed it to me, I pointed to my hand. "Take a look at this. It looks as if someone put a razor to it."

Lee Ann leaned in for a closer look. "Wow. Are you sure you don't want to spend the night?"

"No, thanks," I said, struggling to hide the sarcasm in my voice. "I think I've had enough of the Lizzie Borden House for one night."

RESULTS OF THE INVESTIGATION

It was exciting to be able to arrange an investigation in such an infamous location for our foreign guests. The prevalent spirit of the night seemed to be that of Mrs. Abby Borden. Although most of our evidence was collected through spiritual methods such as trance channeling, glass swirling, and table tilting, the spirits were present nonetheless. Maureen's channeling revealed the pain of Abby's death and a glimpse of her killer, who Maureen believed was Lizzie. Gavin's insight into the death of Mr. Borden revealed a male accomplice.

THE HOUSE THAT WENT TO POT

CASE FILE: 6231980
THE HOUSE THAT WENT TO POT

Location: Bow, New Hampshire.

History: The original house was built in 1740. Over the years, additions were tacked on to accommodate hired hands who worked the adjacent apple orchard. Since then, the house and additions have been merged, and the structure has become a single family home.

Reported Paranormal Activity: Orbs, unexplained organ music, the sound of a baby crying, light bulbs burning out almost daily, insect infestations, and the sudden appearance of words scratched into the woodwork.

Clients: Frank (homeowner), Samantha (Frank's wife).

Investigators: Ron (lead investigator), Maureen (trance medium), Karen (EVP specialist), Janet (Ron's wife).

Press: Rita (reporter for *Andover Townsman*), Tim (Rita's photographer).

quickly glanced at the email attachment, which revealed a mundane photo of a brick oven with what appeared to be a pie plate in front of it. But as my eyes began to focus, I soon realized that it wasn't a pie plate at all, but rather an extraordinary-looking orb.

I was never much of an orb person. You've seen one orb, you've seen them all. But this one was somehow different. For reasons unbeknownst to me, I decided to call the woman who sent me the email.

"Hello, Samantha?" I said over the crackling in the telephone receiver. "This is Ron Kolek from the New England Ghost Project."

"Oh, I am so glad you called. I would really..." she said as her voice faded into the static on the line.

"I can barely hear you. Is there something wrong with your phone?" I inquired.

"No, it's the ghost. He does all kinds of stuff like this. It's terrible," she said, her voice once again barely audible. "I would really like to talk to you. Do you think you could come to the house?"

"Sure, where do you live?"

No reply. The phone went dead.

Frustrated but undaunted, I called her back. After the second ring she answered. "Hello, Samantha?" I said quickly, before we were cut off again.

"I'm sorry," she said, her voice a little clearer now. "The ghost does this all the time. I'll email you the address; it's just outside of Concord, New Hampshire. But there's a catch: you'll have to be here no later than Saturday, because we have to move out by Sunday." She paused, sounding a bit hesitant to continue. "The bank is foreclosing on the house."

"That's not much time, but I understand. We'll be there Saturday. I look forward to meeting you and hearing more about the house." I hung up the phone. I found myself oddly curious. Why would someone even care to have their home investigated when they were losing it? Was she looking for verification, or just crazy? I guessed there was only one way to find out.

Four days later, we arrived at our destination, a sprawling farmhouse with an attached barn. As the tires of the Subaru kicked up the stones from the gravel driveway, I wondered how old the house was. Then I saw a white sign against the yellow clapboards: 1740. No sooner had I opened the car door than I heard the familiar sound of tires crunching against gravel. I turned to see a black sedan pulling up behind us. It was Rita Savard, a journalist, and Tim, her photographer, from the local newspaper the *Andover Townsman*. Rita was writing an article on the Ghost Project and I had asked her to tag along.

We were greeted by a heavyset woman with salt and pepper hair who looked a bit beaten, like a child who had her lunch money taken by the school bully.

"Hi, I'm Samantha. You must be Ron," she said, barely able to muster a nervous little smile.

I introduced the group, and we followed her to the wooden porch, through the creaking screen door, and into the house. As we entered the kitchen, we were approached by a man whose long, gangly arms swung as he walked, lending him an air of oafishness.

"Hello, I'm Sam's husband, Frank," he said in a quiet, educated voice, which was a stark contrast to his appearance. "Glad you could make it."

I made the appropriate introductions and then started in with the questions. "Samantha, why don't you tell us a little about what has been happening here?"

"Well, it all started when the house we were living in, in Massachusetts, burned down. We had no choice but to look for a new place to live. This place looked perfect; I called the realtor and made an appointment to see it. We fell in love with it. Even though the price was suspiciously low, we bought it.

"When we first moved in, we found pennies and other coins face down on all the windowsills. We thought that the previous owner had placed them there for good luck, so we collected them and put them in this jar," she said, as she took an old jelly jar off the mantle of the brick fireplace. "Maybe we were wrong. Our problems began when the septic system failed. Shortly after that, orbs began appearing in photographs, like the one I sent you. Light bulbs burned out almost daily. I called an electrician, but he couldn't find anything wrong with the wiring. Next we began to experience cold spots throughout the house, so cold you could see your breath. We also had infestations of various bugs." She sighed heavily. "Our luck went from bad to worse. Frank lost his job. The bills kept piling up. And finally, the bank foreclosed on the house."

Although we couldn't help them monetarily, I was glad we had decided to take on this investigation. If, as I suspected we would, we found paranormal activity here, I could at least let the couple know they weren't crazy.

I said, "Anything else make you believe you have a ghost?"

"Well, in addition to the photos, we also hear things: a baby crying and, perhaps even stranger, organ music. We have no neighbors, and there is no organ in the house." She brought her hand to her chin, as if in deep thought. "There are other things too. Would you like to see?"

"Sure." I looked at our two friends from the newspaper and asked if Rita was ready.

Rita, with her head down, scribbling the last of her notes, paused and looked up. "I'm ready when you are."

"Okay, let's rock. Samantha, would you lead the way?"

We followed her down a narrow hallway to the well-worn staircase at the back of the house. The boards of the stairs moaned beneath our weight. We followed her up the staircase and down another corridor to a room on the right. I ducked as I passed through the small door into a rather narrow room. Judging from the height of the ceilings, I could see that this house wasn't built for tall people. Samantha led us to a window overlooking the back of the barn.

"You see this?" she said, pointing to a dark spot on the yellowed pine floor. "It's blood, and no matter how hard I try, I can't remove it."

"Well, how do you know it's blood?" I interjected.

"When it first appeared, it looked like fresh blood. I was frantic. I thought someone had cut themselves. But everyone was fine, and there was no reason for it to be there. And there's more," she said, as she motioned to the door we just entered. "Close it."

Janet, who was closest to the door, slowly pushed it shut, its old iron hinges screaming in response. "Oh my God," she said. "There's writing on it."

I quickly made my way to the door. There, to my surprise, were several words scratched or carved into the rough-hewn wood.

Maureen leaned in closer. "What's it say, Ron? I don't have my glasses."

Studying the marks etched in the wood, I said, "This one says 'die' and this says 'kill you.'" Looking back at Samantha I asked, "Who wrote these?"

"No one," she replied. "They just appeared out of nowhere one day."

I raised my 35mm, checked the flash, looked in the viewfinder to make sure I had the shot, and pressed the shutter. Nothing happened. "What the heck?"

Maureen chuckled. "Did you bless the camera, Ron?"

"Would you shut the hell up?" I stammered. *Man, if I hear that one more time, I'm going to strangle her.* I raised the camera once more and snapped the shutter. "There, see? It worked."

"You're such an ass," Maureen said.

Suddenly Maureen pulled me aside and spoke in a low voice, for only me to hear, "There's something off about this place—and her."

"What do you mean?" I asked.

"I don't know. I just can't put my finger on it."

Unable to get any more answers, I looked at Maureen and spoke up for the group to hear. "What do you think? Are we done in here?"

* * *

I met Ron's gaze. "Yeah, I'm really not picking anything up in here."

"Okay," Ron said. "Samantha, let's move on."

Moments later we were in the next room, a small bedroom with torn flowered wallpaper, white trim, and a wide pine floor, painted brown. The floor was so dark it looked nearly black. Standing in the corner was a lone piece of furniture, an oval, mahogany, freestanding mirror.

It didn't take long for Ron's EMF meter to go off. Like so many times before, it confirmed what I already knew: that there was an entity in the room—or, to be more precise, two. I reached into my jacket pocket and removed the quilted pouch protecting my pendulum and crystals. I pressed the silver chain between my thumb and forefinger and asked the usual questions aloud: What is a yes? What is a no? What is a maybe? Are there any spirits with us now? Are you female? And so forth.

The spinning crystal pendulum revealed that there was a little girl with us and a little boy as well. By the sudden light and airy feeling I was picking up on, I knew that they were in a playful mood.

"They're gone," Ron exclaimed as his EMF meter went silent.

"No, Ron. They're here," I said as a quick smile shot across my lips. "They want to play with you."

Ron began poking the air with his EMF meter looking for signs of our elusive playmates.

I stood there, nearly bursting out laughing as I watched Ron running to and fro, chasing the readings on his meter. "Ron, hurry up. She's behind the mirror, giggling. I can hear her."

* * *

The spirits of the twins try to elude Ron behind the freestanding mirror. An infrared shot reveals what appears to be spirit energy.

Ron darted behind the mirror as his face grew red. Was it the glow of the EMF meter, or was he embarrassed about something? Soon I could tell by the familiar beeping that he'd caught her.

"Wow, I think I found her," Ron said with satisfaction. His victory was short-lived, though; his meter went dead.

"She's playing a game with you. I can hear her clearly. But it doesn't make sense."

Ron stepped out from behind the mirror. "What doesn't?"

"She's saying, 'Run and hide.'"

"You mean hide and seek?"

"That's what *I* think. But in my mind, I hear them saying it differently."

"Do you want to try to communicate with the pendulum?"

As if the children were all too eager to communicate, an onslaught of thoughts and images bombarded my mind. It was becoming difficult to speak. The energy in the room suddenly intensified. If I didn't know any better I'd have said the room was becoming smaller by the minute. Constricting, suffocating me, like the crush of an eighteen-foot boa. With my pendulum still in hand, I gave a sharp nod to Ron.

He stepped to my side. "Maureen, what are you picking up?"

Before he finished his statement her name popped into my mind. "Beth. They call her Beth."

The EMF meter came to life once again.

"I'm picking up the name Thomas. It's her brother."

"No. Michael." Ron stopped short. Then he looked at me with a blank stare. "I don't know where that came from," he said, with the look of embarrassment evident on his face.

I gave Ron a knowing smile. Working side by side with Ron, our energies mingled; his psychic awakening was bound to happen. "I think they died here, of fever," I said.

"Are they buried here?" Ron asked.

Before I could answer, Frank's voice broke the silence. "You know what, there's an abandoned cemetery in the woods."

"Ron, I think they want us to go find their graves," I said.

"Road trip." Ron grinned.

I looked down at my black leather clogs and cringed. "Ron…"

"What? Where's your sense of adventure? Who wouldn't give their right arm to go crawling through the woods to an abandoned cemetery, at midnight, no less?"

"Me."

"Oh, zip it." Ron chuckled, then walked away.

Before I knew it, I was tramping through the woods, following directly behind Ron.

After what seemed like hours but couldn't have been more than twenty minutes, our flashlights illuminated a moss-covered stone wall cloaked in darkness.

"We're here," Frank announced.

I stood and stared at the seven-foot wall. "Yeah, but how do we get in?"

"This way." We followed Frank's lead as he strode along the tapering wall. Finally we stood in front of the wrought-iron gate leading to the forgotten graveyard.

Ron raised his hand, the beam of his flashlight scanning the tombstones on the ill-kept grounds. "Let's go." Walking as if he had blinders on, eyes only for the stones in front of us, he climbed over the rusted gate. He turned to us, "You guys coming?"

Ron Kolek

The crew of the New England Ghost Project discover the abandoned cemetery deep in the woods.

Not eager to follow Ron up and over the gate, the rest of us walked along the side, until we found an opening, a four-foot span of fence missing. Without a flashlight I gingerly maneuvered my way around fallen headstones and cringed as the soft ground squished beneath my feet. "Ron, where are you?"

"Right here."

Straining to hear, I followed the sound of his voice until I stumbled over him as he knelt in front of a headstone. To break my fall I reached out and grabbed the rough, cold surface of the marker in front of us. "What the heck are you doing? Are you trying to bury me here?"

"That could be arranged," he chided. "Actually, I'm doing a rubbing. Here, hold this. Make yourself useful."

I held the corner of the paper. "What are these for?" I asked, as Ron, using the edge of the pencil, scribbled back and forth.

"For the research arm. I want to see what they can dig up." He laughed at his own joke. When finished, he rolled the paper and moved on to the next stone, repeating the process.

"Maureen, you picking up anything?" Rita called out.

"No, I'm not feeling much of anything," I said as I walked over to Rita and her photographer. "For the most part, cemeteries as a rule are pretty quiet. Then again, we have some great pictures from a few of them. Maybe it's all about timing. For instance, on Halloween, we spent the whole night in a burial ground and nothing happened."

Rita frowned as I heard Ron's voice in the background. "Maureen, come here, quick. Check this out."

With Rita and her photographer in my wake, we hurried over to Ron.

"Touch these and see if you get any impressions," Ron said as he knelt down beside two small tombstones, their engravings too weathered to read.

As I listened to him, I felt compelled to lay my hands on the cold slabs of granite. The palms of my hands tingled in response, but before I could get a sense of it, the energy faded as quickly as it had arrived.

"Do you think the kids are buried here?" Ron asked.

"I really don't know. I'm not feeling anything concrete."

"All right, I think we're done now. Let's get back to the house," Ron said as he stood up and headed back toward the rusted gate.

"Hey, Ron, where are you going? No need to climb over the gate, we found an opening. This way." I motioned for him to follow.

As we made our way back through the dense brush, Ron turned to look over his shoulder. "Look, there's a light in the cemetery." He peered at the group, as if mentally making a note of everyone present. "We're all here, right?"

"Well if they weren't, do you think they'd speak up?" I laughed.

Ron, ignoring my comment, whipped his 35mm out of his jacket pocket, and clicked the shutter before he took off on a run.

We hurried after Ron as he scurried through the darkness, back to the cemetery. But just as we reached the wrought-iron gate, the light disappeared.

Unable to find the source of the light, we made our trek back into the woods and to the house. But our investigation was far from over. We assembled in the dining room. There was plenty of room, since there was no furniture.

We stood in a circle and chatted about the light that we had seen in the cemetery. Samantha, who was to my left, reached out and clutched my forearm, emphasizing her words. With her touch, a throbbing pain, emanating from her hand, worked its way up my arm and thundered into my chest. Repulsed by her touch, I pulled away. Not wanting to embarrass the woman, I forced a smile, then walked across the room and stood by Ron. Earlier in the night I'd felt something was out of sorts with this house, this woman. Now I couldn't help but wonder what it was. "Samantha, I was just wondering…is there anything else that you haven't told us?"

She lowered her eyes to the floor as she shifted her weight from side to side.

From the way she reacted, I didn't need to be psychic to realize there was more to the story.

"Well, Maureen, I, uh…well, back when I lived in Massachusetts, I used to enjoy a little pot now and then. You know, just to relax…"

"And?"

"Once, while I was toking, I started fooling around with the Ouija board." She glanced up at me, and then nervously looked at her husband. "I made contact with the spirit of a man named Paul. He seemed pleasant enough, and through the board I found out that he was curious about what I was smoking. So, I invited him inside of me, sort of what you do Maureen. You know, so he could experience it for himself…"

No, that is nothing like what I do. "Samantha," I interrupted her. "It's not a good idea to invite a spirit in when you don't know what you're doing." What I do is dangerous enough, never mind inviting a spirit to reside inside of you for any extended length of time. It could lead to possession. And it's never accepted by the paranormal community to be under the influence of drugs while making contact with the dead.

As if to break the tension of the moment, Ron asked, "So what happened next?"

"Not long after, our house burned to the ground."

The unexplained pain I'd felt from her touch was beginning to make sense. "Samantha, we can help you. It's not healthy to walk around with another person's soul in your body. If you want, we can bring someone in to help you. Don't you think it's a little coincidental that after making contact with Paul, your world turned upside down?"

"No. It's just bad luck. Besides, he likes it in here. And so do I—he's my friend. Whenever there's a sale at Macy's going on, he tells me about it. I don't want him to leave."

As I stood there, mouth agape, Ron chimed in. "So, how do you communicate with Paul?"

With a sudden sparkle in her eyes, she said, "Come on, let me show you."

We followed her into the next room, which held nothing but a small desk with a computer, a chair, and a floor lamp. Samantha took a seat, splayed her fingers over the keyboard, bent her head as if in deep thought, and began to type.

Not sure what we were witnessing, Ron began taking pictures as the rest of us stood and stared in disbelief.

When she finished typing the last word, she spun around in her chair and met our gaze. "See, these are his words, not mine."

"Oh, so it's sort of like automatic writing," Ron said.

Interested in what Ron and Samantha were talking about, Rita, with pen and pad in hand, engaged Samantha in conversation as the rest of us gathered our belongings to call it a night.

In the process of loading our vehicles, Ron was caught off guard as Samantha gave him a brisk hug. Next, she latched onto Karen. Realizing I was next, I ran around the other side of the car and jumped into the backseat, waving good-bye through a closed window. No way in hell was I letting that woman touch me again.

A month later while sitting around a table at the Windham Restaurant, we went over the results of the investigation in a team meeting.

Ron leafed through his notebook. "Janet, did you guys find out anything about the cemetery?"

"Yes. Five of the graves in the cemetery were those of children, including twins."

"What about the twins? Do you have their names?"

"Yes, you're gonna love this. Elizabeth and Michael Thomas," she said with a knowing smile.

Ron stopped short and nearly choked on his beer. "You're kidding me. Michael. Do you hear that, Maureen? Janet said Michael!"

Ron always said he was as psychic as a brick. "Psychic as a brick, huh?" I said.

"Whatever," he said with a beaming smile. "I found out something interesting too. I did some research on the pennies Samantha found on the windowsills. It's an old Polish tradition to put pennies on the sills face down to ward off the Devil and his minions. Their greed attracts them to the pennies. Having the pennies face down ensures the Devil's confusion, thus distracting the Devil and his minions from tormenting the homeowner. And the English also place pennies on the windowsills to ward off negative energy and ghosts."

"Maybe someone should call and tell Samantha to put the pennies back on the windowsills," I said.

"What for? She doesn't live there anymore," Ron responded.

Oh yeah, that's right. I'd forgotten. Not wanting to sound crude, I kept my next thought to myself: if Samantha continued to carry Paul around like a second skin, pennies would be the least of her worries.

RESULTS OF THE INVESTIGATION

We learned several interesting facts from our investigation: the names of the twins were verified by research along with the location of their graves in the abandoned cemetery. The game of "run and hide" we later verified as an antiquated reference to hide-and-seek. And last but not least, we learned the dangers of indulging in mind-altering drugs while communicating with the dead. Sometimes you make your own luck, good or bad. And as for Samantha and Frank, we hope they are doing well, but we never heard from them again. We would have loved to have gone back to further investigate why the twins still haunt the house; however, the bank and the new owners were not open to the idea.

episode seventeen

WOOD ISLAND LIGHTHOUSE

CASE FILE: 6232396
WOOD ISLAND LIGHTHOUSE

Location: Biddeford, Maine.

History: In 1806 the U.S. Government purchased eight acres on Wood Island for the erection of the lighthouse. In 1858 the 45-foot stone tower that replaced the wooden structure was completed. The last lighthouse keeper on record was in 1986. In 2003 the Friends of Wood Island Lighthouse took over the care of the tower and keeper's house.

Reported Paranormal Activity: Apparitions, ghostly writing, and strange noises.

Clients: F.O.W.I.L. (Friends of Wood Island Lighthouse): Sheri (historian), Judy (secretary), Kathleen (chairman of outreach), Terry (lighthouse keeper's wife).

Investigators: Ron (lead investigator), Maureen (trance medium), Leo (photographer), Ron Jr. (investigator), Karen (EVP specialist), Thermal Dan (investigator).

Press: Doug Belkin (*Boston Globe* reporter), Gloria (Doug's girlfriend), Fred (Doug's photographer).

I turned my back to the wind and stared behind us. Streaks of purples and pinks hung low in the sky. If I didn't know any better, I'd have sworn the brilliant hues were clinging to a ball of fire. A ball of fire that was now chasing the horizon, peeking behind rows of pristine cottages that hugged the banks of the channel, bringing with it a cloak of darkness. Instead of allowing myself to fully enjoy the moment, I chastised myself. On the surface, this was a picture postcard moment, a moment more suited for lovers than paranormal investigators. To the unsuspecting eye, it would seem like a dream come true. But to me, it meant we were on our way to a haunted location with no escape. And the closer we got to our destination, the tighter the knot in my stomach was becoming. *Am I crazy?* My husband often asks me why I do what I do. I can't quite put it into words. It's who I am. I'm drawn to the spirits, and they to me.

I raised the collar of my winter jacket but knew it wouldn't do any good. The deep, bone-penetrating cold I was feeling since we'd shoved off was inside me, a cold that no number of blankets, or ninety degree weather for that matter, could stifle.

Over the rustling wind and flapping of the nylon flag, I yelled to the captain, "How long until we get there?" I wasn't quite sure he'd heard me, since I could barely hear myself.

"Not too long, about twenty minutes or so." He pointed directly in front of us. "Right there, that's Wood Island Light.

Can you see it? We'll be landing on the south side of the island. You'll have to walk three-quarters of a mile down a boardwalk to get to the keeper's house." As if reading my thoughts, he said, "Sorry, but the rest of the island is too rocky; there's no way for me to land the boat."

"Marvelous," I said.

Just then, seemingly out of nowhere, I felt the first sign of a disturbance in the air. The atmosphere shifted as a sizzle of energy glided over my skin, sending a trembling wave from the base of my neck to the tips of my toes. I looked from my right to left, but the only thing I saw was a single small island off the starboard side. I couldn't be certain, but I didn't think the energy I was picking up on originated from Wood Island. Although fast approaching, we were still more than a mile away.

Ron seemed to sense it too. He turned and looked me in the eyes, as if waiting for a reaction. "Yeah, I feel it too." I smiled inwardly at the thought of how much Ron's intuition had grown since we'd been working together.

Ron closed the distance between him and the captain, and then pointed to the very same island. "Hey, Sean, what island is that?"

"Negro Island. Back in the old days, it used to be a trading post." The captain's voice came in bursts above the constant thrum of the motor and the breaking of waves against the *Light Runner*'s aluminum hull.

Instantaneously the motor stopped short, cutting out completely. "What the—?" Sean paused and looked over the port side into the water, to see if we'd hit anything. He scurried to the rear of the boat and raised the outboard motor. To his surprise, a rope, which looked like a relic from an old ship, was tangled in the propeller. "This is strange. In all the times I've gone out to the island, I've never had this happen."

After about five minutes, like Captain Nemo, he freed us from the leviathan that held us from our journey. Back at the controls, he pushed the button until we heard the familiar roar of the engine. We were on our way again. "That was strange," he said.

Kathleen, one of Sheri's helpers, grabbed a handful of railing, then took a seat next to me. She leaned over and said, "I've been meaning to tell you, I love your earrings. Where did you buy them?"

Forgetting I had them on, I fumbled with them. "Shoot, I forgot to take them off." Then, realizing I hadn't answered her question, "Sorry, I'm not sure where he bought them. They were an anniversary gift from my husband." Not willing to risk breaking the fine filigree silver earrings by storing them in my overnight bag I left them on and did the only thing I could do—tighten the clasps.

The boat slowed. "We're here," Sean said, as he positioned the boat as close to the ramp as possible. "Would someone mind getting out to hold the ropes?"

"No problem," Ron said, as he and his son Ron Jr. stood at the bow of the boat. They jumped off and onto the ramp and held the boat in place while Sean manually cranked the winch, lowering the front of the boat until it lay flat against the ramp.

Together we pitched in, and in no time all our gear—sleeping bags, blankets, pillows, base camp and investigation equipment, and coolers filled with lots of food and drink—was piled high on the dock.

Sheri waited for us to sort out the gear and then led us down the narrow boardwalk toward the lighthouse. I was thankful that someone was forward-thinking enough to have brought a heavy-duty hand truck and cart. With a sleeping bag under my left arm, I grabbed the cart, dragging it behind me. Even over the clanking of the wheels on the planks of the boardwalk, I felt a low-lying energy, like a pot simmering, waiting to boil. I knew there were spirits lurking, waiting to pounce. "Ron, do you feel anything?" I asked.

An aerial view of Wood Island, the boardwalk, and the lighthouse.

"Yeah. Old."

"I feel anxious. Agitated." I paused, then for a moment I stood perfectly still, listening to the crash of the waves against the rocks and feeling the roaring ocean wind as it whipped through my hair. "I sense someone running, trying to get away. It's as if they're trying to hide."

Ron stopped walking, turned, and then said, "There'll be plenty of time for that later. We have—all—night." He grinned. "Now, can we get a move on? I'm freezing out here." Dismissing my words, he picked up his pace and briskly walked ahead. When he reached midway, he stopped short, peering over the side of the narrow walkway, and yelled, "Holy crap! Would you look at that drop."

I caught up to him and looked over the edge. Feeling a bit woozy, I looked away. From where we stood there was at least a fifteen-foot drop down to a, well, not-so-soft area. I suddenly felt sick. The knot in my stomach tightened some more. God, I hated heights. "I thought you wanted to 'get a move on,'" I said, wanting nothing more than to get away from this spot, even if it meant spending the night at the keeper's house with no heat. *It's all perspective*, I thought.

Regaining our stride, we continued to our destination. The nearer we got to the lighthouse, the louder the screeching of the seagulls, until it felt as if we had just stepped into a scene from Alfred Hitchcock's *The Birds*. Exiting the woods, we got our first glimpse of our home for the night: a weather-beaten cape with an enclosed walkway to the formidable tower of the lighthouse.

Ron Kolek

Our first glimpse of Wood Island Lighthouse, our home for the evening.

Pretty soon we had base camp up and running, and, to keep the frost out of our bones, nearly everyone was already on their second cups of hot coffee. Not me, I wasn't a coffee drinker. The last thing I needed was more buzzing in my brain.

"So where to first?" I asked Ron, as he stood chatting with Kathleen and Judy, the two volunteer members of the Friends of Wood Island Lighthouse preservation group who tagged along to help Sheri with whatever we needed. God bless them. Sheri had contacted the Ghost Project after we had conducted an investigation for the Friends of the Portsmouth Lighthouse in New Castle, New Hampshire. She wanted us to investigate the spirits of Wood Island and ultimately present our findings for an organization fundraiser.

He looked at Sheri. "Do you think you could take us up to the top of the lighthouse?"

"Yeah, but if we're going to go, we should do it now. I wouldn't want someone who's tired trying to climb those winding cement stairs. Even inside the tower, without a railing, they're treacherous. And I only recommend a small group of you go up. There's minimal room at best."

Doug, the reporter for the *Boston Globe*, stood at the ready, pen and paper in hand, as if smelling a story in the making, with his photographer, Fred, right behind him.

"Great, let's go. Maureen, you coming?" Ron asked.

With that, Sheri led us out of the kitchen, through the narrow hallway, and into the base of the lighthouse. Midway up the winding stairs, my heart began to thud in my chest, like a frantic bird batting its wings in a cage. I paused to catch my breath, breathed in slowly, out slowly. The feeling of anxiety and panic I had felt earlier was returning.

"Maureen, what's going on? Tell me what you're feeling," Doug said.

"It's a woman, I feel her panic, her pain," I said, as a tear slipped down my cheek.

"Maureen, are you going to be all right to make it up here?" Ron's voice echoed from above.

"Yeah," I choked back a sob and finished climbing the stairs. Once at the top we made our way up a metal ladder and through a hole in the ceiling. We stood shoulder to shoulder around the massive bulb at the top of the lighthouse, staring through the thick glass at the setting sun and listening to the waves crashing on the rocks.

Due to lack of space, Fred the photographer remained perched halfway up the ladder that led into the opening in the floor.

"You picking up anything here?" Ron asked, as he waved his EMF meter in front of me.

To answer Ron's question, I opened up my mind and mentally asked if there was a spirit present. Using my thoughts like a beacon, I felt a spirit approach us. Its energy roiled over my skin, and his thoughts seeped into my mind. "It was an accident. I—I didn't mean to do it," I said, through raspy breaths.

"Do what? Who are we speaking with? What did—you—do?" Ron asked.

* * *

I looked at Maureen, who was clenching her teeth. "It wasn't my fault," she cried.

Her stare was far off, distant. One look into her eyes and I knew that although she turned to look at me, she wasn't seeing me at all. I looked at the distance between her and the opening in the floor. Crap. This could be bad. "Maureen, not here. It's too dangerous," I called to her, but the only response I received was a loud rhythmic sighing, a sound to me that whomever was here was trying to take her over. I grabbed her elbow in case she stepped too far to the right. She'd be a goner for sure, and she'd take poor Fred with her. "Maureen, come back. Come back!"

After a few agonizing moments, she exhaled deeply, blinked a few times, then turned to me again. She was back among the living. Although she hadn't spoken yet, I could see it in her eyes.

"I'm okay. He...he wanted to speak so badly," Maureen said.

"I know, but he'll have to come find us later." I pointed at the trap door. "All you'd need is to take a wrong step, and you're history. Come on, let's get out of here while the getting's good."

I nodded at the reporter, indicating he should go down the ladder first. Maureen, still visibly shaken, followed. I held her arm and guided her through the opening. Yelling to Doug below, I called out, "You have her?"

"I'm fine, Ron," Maureen said.

Sheri and her team greeted us in the kitchen. "We were able to see a little of what happened up there on the base camp monitor," Sheri said, her voice thick with excitement. "Did Maureen know about the history of this lighthouse?"

"No. I didn't tell her anything," I said.

"Wow, should I tell her some of the things she hit on? It really fits," Sheri said.

"No. Let's wait until we're done with our investigation. Then you can fill her in." Although she seemed a little disappointed, she agreed. I didn't want Maureen to have any preconceived ideas when she was channeling.

I walked from the kitchen into what, in the past, must have been the dining area. Now the only things in the room were some lawn furniture: a large wooden picnic table and a couple of chairs. I guess there wasn't a need for anything else in a building that's primarily used for day tours. Brrrr. That included heat. "This can be our safe room," I said.

"Safe room? Ron, what are you talking about?" Sheri inquired.

"It's a meeting place where we choose to ignore the spirits."

SAFE ROOM

A designated place in a haunted location, where the team can assemble to be free of all the monitoring devices associated with an investigation. Especially useful on overnight investigations.

"Ron," Maureen poked me in the arm, then said in a voice only I could hear, "where do we sleep tonight?"

"Ah, sleep's overrated," I said. "Besides, when do you think you're going to have time for sleep?"

"Oh, I—will—find time," she said. "If I don't get sleep, I get bitchy."

I bit my tongue.

"Okay, you guys ready for round two?" I said. I stood there with my EMF meter and temperature gauge. "Who wants to go to the attic?" I paused, looking around the room, waiting for volunteers. "I have an idea. Karen, Leo, you come with me. Maureen, why don't you stay here and take a break?"

"Sounds like a plan," Maureen said, then, not missing a beat, she turned to Terry and picked up where she'd left off in their conversation.

Fifteen minutes later, in darkness, the three of us sat Indian style on the rough-hewn beams and sparse boards that made up the attic floor. Well, two of us sat Indian style; I, on the other hand, shoved a piece of weathered cardboard box and unused insulation aside and sat with my legs straight out. My rickety knees would have none of it.

"All right, Karen, why don't you do some EVPs, then we can take a moment of silence and see if we get any response?"

Karen turned on her recorder, placed it on the floor in front of us, then said in a calm, steady voice, "Is there anyone here that would like to speak to us? We would like to thank you for this opportunity to be here with you tonight."

Silence. Well, as silent as it could be with the wind whistling through the cracks in the wall.

I glanced down and noticed the red light; the voice recognition indicator was lit up like a stoplight. Someone was trying to communicate. *Cool*, I thought.

I could barely make anyone out. Only when they shifted their positions did I see black silhouettes, a shade darker than the expanse of the attic. Yet I couldn't be sure if it was them or a trick of my eyes as they adjusted to total darkness.

Suddenly, out of the corner of my eye a green light flicked atop the roof rafters and along the wall. "Did you see that?" I asked.

I couldn't see anyone as Karen and Leo turned to look around us, but I felt their movement as the boards beneath me creaked.

"Oh, wow. Look at the green lights!" Karen screamed.

It wasn't just me. Amazing! The green lights were zipping this way and that, dancing back and forth, over our heads and down around our feet. We sat, mesmerized, like kids watching fireworks for the first time, until they just stopped.

"I don't see them anymore," Karen said.

"If there's anyone here, can you please give us another sign?" I asked.

We sat patiently in the darkness, with only wind and the grumbling of Leo's stomach breaking the silence.

"If there's anyone here, can you please give us another sign?" I asked again.

This time my question was answered.

The green light brushed my cap and shot across the room toward Karen, weaving its way through her hair. Almost instantaneously Karen's voice echoed my own. "Did you feel that!"

"What? I didn't feel anything," Leo said.

When does Leo feel anything? I used to think that I was as psychic as a brick, but compared to Leo, I looked like one of America's most documented psychics of his time, Edgar Cayce. Pushing myself up to my knees, I turned on my flashlight, scanning the area. But no matter what angle I looked from, there was nothing there. "Whatever touched us is gone." With our bones aching from our awkward positions, we decided to call it quits and made our way back downstairs. Karen and Leo filled everyone in on what had just happened. As far as I was concerned, no amount of explanation would do it justice. What we had witnessed was something extraordinary.

I took a seat next to Maureen, who was finishing up a salad. "*Still eating?*"

"What do you mean, 'Still eating'? I just started," she laughed.

Following suit I scarfed down a sandwich and some chips, then said, "Okay, I think it's time for the basement. Let's go."

Maureen turned her wrist over. "Are you kidding me? It's only eleven o'clock? It feels more like two in the morning."

"That just means we have more time to investigate. I think we should do more overnights like this." The way Maureen rolled her eyes, I could only assume she wasn't having as good of a time as I was. "Ah, lighten up, will ya?"

Maureen didn't respond, but the heat of her stare told me all I needed to know.

We gathered at the top of the basement stairs, then descended into the dimly lit cellar that at that moment could have doubled as a freezer. My sleeve brushed against the rusted oil tank as we took our places, ready to communicate. I looked past Maureen to where Karen and Leo stood. "Why don't you guys stand over here a bit more." I pointed to a spot in front of the storage shelf, which housed cleaners and painting supplies. "Right over there."

Before we were completely ready, Maureen said in a low, guttural voice, "He's here." This night was hopping. With my EMF picking up fluctuating readings, I turned to Maureen. "Can you take out your pendulum?" I paused. "Leo, start taking pictures."

* * *

I took out my pendulum.

He was back. The same man I'd felt while we'd stood in the lighthouse. I held my pendulum between my thumb and forefinger. The spirit's thoughts becoming my own, I said, "I didn't mean to kill him. It was an accident. Everyone is blaming me."

"It's him." Ron's voice echoed my sentiment. "Who did you kill?" Ron asked.

Like a puppet on a string, I felt my head turn toward Ron of its own accord, "Who—are—you?" The words, thick with emotion, rolled off my tongue.

"We are here to investigate this lighthouse. More importantly, who are *you*?"

Ron continued with his questions, but before I knew it, and as if we'd insulted the entity, he was gone. Just as quickly as he'd left, a woman's presence appeared. "There's someone else here," I said. "It's a woman. She seems disoriented. She doesn't know where she is." Her energy felt thick, touchable even. As I reached out to her with my mind, a sharp stabbing pain started at the base of my skull and seared through to the front of my eyes. I pressed my fingers to my temples, which were now throbbing. "Oh dear God." As hard as I tried to get her name, I couldn't. "I think she was struck with a blunt object on her head." Still confused, she was unable to think clearly. I was suddenly filled with overwhelming sadness. My chest grew heavy. Weary. "I'm ready to go upstairs. Now."

Through it all I heard Leo snapping a series of pictures with his 35mm camera. As we exited the basement, I found myself wondering what, if anything, would show up on the film.

With no rest for the weary, we immediately bundled up and went outside onto the boardwalk. Thermal Dan, our thermal imaging specialist, Leo, Ron, and I headed back toward the dock to see if there was any activity. Ron was in the lead, with Dan and I following close behind. Dan slowly made a sweeping motion with his handheld, heat-sensitive/thermal-imaging camera. "What the heck is that?" he said.

Ron backed up a few steps, as he and I peered over Dan's shoulder. There was nothing visible to the naked eye, yet on camera a dark black image, a stark contrast to the light gray background, was zipping past us, swooping down, first from our left, then our right.

Intrigued, I stepped in for a closer look. That's when something hit me. I grabbed my head. "What the hell was that? Something just hit me in the head."

"What? What hit you?" Ron asked.

"I don't know, it felt like I just got smacked in the temple."

We walked a few more feet, and *bam*! I grabbed my head again, half expecting to find blood. "What the hell? It hit me again!"

"You're kidding, right?" Ron frantically looked from side to side, while Dan scanned the horizon.

Undaunted by what happened and curious, we pushed on.

We didn't take more than a few steps before it happened again. I'd never had the butt end of a gun smashed into my temple, but if I did, I'm sure it would feel like this. The pain was excruciating, as Ron and Dan's voices faded into the distance.

I dropped like a rock.

* * *

"Maureen, what the hell are you doing?" I'd been so consumed with the black shadow that I hadn't even realized Maureen was on the ground. Until, that is, she began writhing and screaming. Her fingernails dug into the soft, weather-worn boards as she frantically crawled like a crab on her belly. "Maureen!"

She'd already slid her body across four feet of boards and was getting dangerously close to the drop-off I'd spied earlier in the day. Without waiting to see what she was going to do, I reached into my pocket, pulled out the little vial of holy water, and dove onto her. Turning her onto her back while holding her in place, I moistened the tip of my finger with the holy water and made the sign of the cross on her forehead. Returning the vial to my pocket, I placed the palm of my hand on her head and determinedly whispered, "I command you to leave this body. It is not your own. Leave in the name of Jesus Christ. I command you to leave."

For what seemed like hours but couldn't have been more than a few minutes, she was eerily still. Her back rose and fell with each heavy intake of breath. "Maureen, are you back with us?" I shook her gently. "Maureen, answer me."

She looked up at me through heavy-lidded eyes. "Yeah, I'm fine. Thanks. I'm getting my ass kicked tonight." She shook her head as if to clear the cobwebs. "It felt like the same woman from the basement."

"What the hell happened?" I asked.

"I don't really know. One minute I was watching that black thing, and the next I felt something swoop down and hit me in the head. I think she was showing me how she died. I think she was hit by a blunt object, maybe the butt end of a rifle, right here," she pointed to her left temple. "She was running for her life." She swallowed hard. "I was running for my life."

"Yeah, it almost looked like you were trying to crawl away from an attacker. It looked pretty scary." I glanced at her tear-filled eyes. "Why don't you go back to the house and take a break. The rest of us will finish up out here."

Leo, who had been hanging back until now, said, "That sounds like a good idea. Come on Maureen, I'll walk you back."

* * *

As I walked with Leo back to the house, the skin beneath my fingernails was stinging so badly I wanted to scream. It felt like I had had tiny matchsticks shoved underneath them. The pain must have shown on my face, because the second I walked into the dining room, Kathleen, one of Sheri's helpers, ran over to me. A nurse by trade, she said, "Are you okay? What happened to you out there?"

"I, um, fell." She looked at me, disbelief evident in her eyes. That's when I looked down at my jeans and noticed a large green stain stretching from my hip to my ankle. How the heck did that happen? I went into the bathroom with Kathleen at my heels.

"Let me see your hands," she said.

I spread my hands out and held them up to the light. Slivers of pressure-treated wood, along with layers of dirt and moss, were wedged beneath my fingernails. No wonder I was in pain.

Kathleen grabbed her medical supply kit and within minutes

she had removed all the splinters. Before bedding down, I sat and chatted with Sheri and the other ladies.

Sheri looked at me, cocking her head to the side, then leaned in toward me, staring at my left ear. "Oh no...Maureen," she said, in a hushed tone. "You're missing one of those lovely earrings." Reaching up, I touched each earlobe. Darn it, she was right, my anniversary gift was now lost. I thought of what I'd just been through. If I'd lost it outside, I could kiss that earring good-bye. Surely it was gone for good.

Before I had a chance to dwell on my loss for too long, Ron and the rest of the group shuffled into the dining area. I slid closer to the ladies, making room at the picnic table.

"Ron, is now a good time to share the history of this place?" Sheri asked.

He stood for a moment and looked around the room, as if realizing the team was too exhausted to continue investigating. "Go for it," he said.

She began, "There have been numerous reports of hauntings. However, the information I think you picked up on, Maureen," Sheri glanced in my direction, "is the tragic events surrounding the murder-suicide. You see, a man by the name of Fred Milliken, described as a 'giant' of a man, lived on Wood Island with his wife and three children for several years in the 1890s. He was a game warden and a special policeman who had allowed a young lobsterman by the name of Hobbs to take up residence on Wood Island." A hush settled over the room. Everyone was mesmerized by the story Sheri told. "According to the newspaper reports, on June 2, 1896, young Hobbs visited Old Orchard Beach. After becoming intoxicated, he headed back to the island. He told a friend he was going back to the island to visit Milliken. Only he took his rifle with him, for the purpose, he said, of shooting some birds." She paused to take a breath. "Upon his return, Milliken, realizing Hobbs was drunk and carrying a rifle, ordered Hobbs to hand over the weapon. Hobbs refused. When Milliken approached, he was shot in the abdomen and died forty-five minutes later. Hobbs, distraught over what had happened, returned to the small rented shack located behind the keeper's house. He then put the same rifle in his mouth and pulled the trigger. The bullet passed through his head and lodged in the ceiling."

The grisly tale was beginning to take shape.

"Maureen, I think you picked up on Hobbs. You know, when you said that 'he felt guilty' and that 'it was an accident' and that he hadn't 'meant to kill him.' It's just so sad. Why do you think he's still here?"

"More than likely it's the guilt. Evidently he's refusing to let go of it. The information about Hobbs and Milliken makes a lot of sense. But I wonder who the woman is that I picked up on?"

"Well, that just tells me that we need to come back for another visit," Ron said with a sheepish grin.

"We'd love to have you back," Sheri and the volunteers chimed in.

"Sounds like a plan," I said, struggling to keep my eyes open. "But for now, I'm exhausted. If you don't mind, I think I'm going to try and get some sleep."

"Not at all."

"I don't know why, but I'd like to go down the boardwalk again," Ron said.

"You can go if you want to, but I'm not. I'm going to bed." I grabbed my sleeping bag and tucked myself into a corner of the room in front of the broken radiator. It looked like a good place to hide for a little while, if that was at all possible. I snuggled deeper into the sleeping bag, stuffed my jacket under my head for a pillow, and prayed for sleep. I began, however, to feel a prickling sensation dance atop my scalp, like a thousand little electrified fingers poking and prodding, searching for my attention. In my mind I begged the spirits to let me have a few hours' sleep. Completely exhausted, I managed to push them away, and the last thing I remember was the murmur of voices and the slamming of the kitchen door as Ron led the group into the night.

* * *

I left Maureen curled up like a fat cat and led the remaining members of our expedition toward the other side of the island. As we walked through the darkness, we came upon a spot where the ground was level to the boardwalk. An eerie calmness filled the air, as if we were shielded from the outside world. I reached into my pocket and pulled out my pendulum (yes, I have one too), and attempted to make contact. "Are there any spirits here with us now?"

The bobber of rhodonite swung counterclockwise, indicating a yes.

"Do you want to show us something?" I asked.

Another yes.

With greater intensity, the pendulum began to move to and fro, in the direction of the woods. "Oh, I think it's trying to guide us somewhere," I said. "That way, into the woods. Who's game?"

With the exception of Dan, the rest of the group remained on the boardwalk.

Stepping over thorn bushes and ducking under low-hanging limbs, we followed the pendulum to a clearing void of underbrush.

The hollow almost appeared to be the ruins of a homestead. Once again I began to ask questions. "Did you live here?"

Yes, the pendulum responded.

I continued to ask questions and found out that someone indeed had died, and not only died, but was murdered. The rest of my questions were unanswered as the pendulum came to a dead stop. Other than hearing a few noises, little else happened. I wondered why we had been led there. I had a sneaking suspicion that I would find out, but not that night. It was getting late, or, should I say, early, as it was heading toward the morning. We decided to return to the lighthouse.

* * *

I awoke to the murmur of Ron's voice and coffee percolating in the kitchen. *Doesn't he ever sleep*? I thought.

"Good morning," Kathleen said, as I stirred from my sleeping bag. "How did you sleep?"

"Just ducky," I said. "How about you?"

"I got a few hours' sleep." She smiled, and it seemed genuine. "I'm not sure if you remember, but you talked in your sleep. It was a little creepy. You sat up straight as a board and stared right through me. Then you said, 'Peter, is that you?'"

"I did?"

"Well, the odd thing is, the last keepers of this lighthouse, before they moved out and realized the place was haunted, used a Ouija board. And, during the questioning, what name do you suppose came out?" Without waiting for me to respond, she said, "Peter!"

"Wow. That is weird." Mentally exhausted I could only focus on one thing. Getting home to the warmth of my bed. But that wasn't happening anytime soon. "Kathleen, what time is it?"

"It's six-thirty. We have another hour and a half before the boat shows up."

"Thanks," I said. After freshening up, I pitched in with everyone as we packed up our gear. "Can you keep an eye out for my earring?" I asked them. I took the lone earring off and placed it gently in my shirt pocket.

"Sure," Sheri replied. "If we don't find it now, we won't be returning again until the spring. But you never know."

"Thanks."

All thirteen of us walked outside. Although the air off the ocean was freezing, the skies were a brilliant blue. I walked down to the ledge behind the lighthouse and watched the waves crash over the rocks. I had survived the night. And now the scenery before me almost made up for losing my earring. Almost.

Although I was disappointed, I was never so happy to see captain Sean and the *Light Runner*. Anxious to leave, we quickly loaded our gear and boarded the boat.

Once home, I shared my experiences with my husband, finishing with an apology for losing half of his anniversary gift. I then placed the remaining earring in my jewelry box for safe keeping. Who knew, perhaps in the spring I'd be lucky and the Friends of Wood Island Lighthouse would find it. It could happen...

Two weeks later, I woke up one morning to find the silver filigree earring sitting on the top of my jewelry box. My heart thudded wildly in my chest as I held the earring, opened my jewelry box, and, to my surprise, found the other one. My mind raced with the possibilities. I found it difficult to comprehend. How could I lose an earring over two hundred miles away, and have it appear out of nowhere?

I guess that, dealing with the paranormal as long as I have, I should know that anything is possible...

* * *

Several weeks later, the Ghost Line rang. "Hello, New England Ghost Project, Ron Kolek speaking."

The caller seemed hesitant to speak. An awkward silence hung in the air between us. "Uh, you, you're going to think I'm crazy," a man's voice finally said.

"You'd be surprised, I've heard it all," I chuckled, trying to relieve the tension in the air.

"Well, it's difficult to describe. First of all, let me say that I'm from the Midwest and know nothing about the East Coast. Last night I had this dream...about an island, off the coast of Maine, called Wood Island." He paused, then continued. "It was quite disturbing. There was a colonial family being held in a house, no, a shack, on the island. They were terrified. Each member of the family was slowly slaughtered one by one. It was horrifying."

"That does sound disturbing. But I have to say, why are you calling me?"

"Well, there's more. When I woke up, it disturbed me so much that I did a Google search for 'Wood Island' and found its site. Scanning the site, I found a link to your site, then nearly spit out my coffee when I saw your photo."

"Thanks. I tend to have that effect on people."

"No, seriously, you were in my dream. Which is why I was compelled to call. I don't know why, but I think you should know about this."

As I hung up the phone, I immediately began to think about the hollow in the woods. Had I been led there to uncover a secret? Or was there a mystery to be unearthed? Only time would tell...

RESULTS OF THE INVESTIGATION

Ron and Karen simultaneously witnessed a parade of unexplainable green lights in the attic. High levels of EMF readings were recorded in the lighthouse and throughout the keeper's house. Maureen made contact with two spirits: a woman who has yet to be identified, and a man who, because of his guilt and remorse, appears to be the lobsterman, Hobbs. While investigating the island, Thermal Dan captured a black shadow swooping down with his thermal camera, moments before Maureen began to trance channel the spirit of a frightened girl trying to escape. And last but not least was the reappearance of Maureen's earring two weeks after the investigation.

Although our investigation revealed many of Wood Island's secrets, it is still shrouded in mystery. Was the caller's dream a prelude to voices yet unheard? In order to put these unanswered questions to rest, another journey to Wood Island will be needed.

CONCLUSION

Ron, with his down-to-earth scientific approach, and Maureen, with her psychic insight, have taken you on a journey into the realm of the unknown, the unexplained, and the unbelievable. You were there alongside them while they unraveled the mysteries of each and every case. You witnessed the dangers of the unknown and the risk associated with communicating with the dead. But more importantly, you've learned why Maureen is known as the Queen of Pain and that Ron, well, he's just...a pain.

These seventeen episodes are a sampling of true cases from a selection of over three hundred investigative files of the New England Ghost Project. Although team members have come and gone, the true spirit of the NEGP can be seen in each and every case we investigate. Whether it's helping the living or dealing with the dead, we hope that this book provided you with a unique perspective into the lives of people touched by the paranormal.

> *From ghoulies and ghosties*
> *And long-leggedy beasties*
> *And things that go bump in the night,*
> *Good Lord, deliver us!*
> *~Scottish Prayer*

ABOUT THE AUTHORS

About Ron Kolek

Ron Kolek is the founder and lead investigator of the New England Ghost Project. With a degree in environmental science, he was the ultimate skeptic. However, a near-death experience changed all that. No longer blinded by his skepticism, he now uses his scientific background to seek the truth about the paranormal. In addition to producing and hosting *Ghost Chronicles* on Ghostvillage Radio, iTunes, and PodCast Alley, he also produces and hosts two weekly, one-hour, live radio shows (*Ghost Chronicles Live* and *Ghost Chronicles International*) on TogiNet.com and Para-X Radio. *Ghost Chronicles* previously aired live for three years on WCCM, 1490 AM in Lawrence, Massachusetts. Ron was also a contributor to Jeff Belanger's *Encyclopedia of Haunted Places* (2005), Thomas D'Agostino's *Haunted NH* (2007), Kalyomi's *Ghosts from Coast to Coast* (2007), and Chris Balzano's *Picture Yourself Ghost Hunting* (2008), and has previously written a monthly paranormal newspaper column for over six years. He has been on every major New England television station and has also been the subject of a German television documentary.

About Maureen Wood

Maureen Wood is a fifth-generation psychic/trance medium. Since as far back as she can remember, she has communicated with the deceased. At the age of fifteen, she was introduced to a woman who studied with Laurie Cabot (official witch of Salem, Massachusetts). This woman took Maureen under her wing and guided her in ways to not only understand, but also control her gifts. Also at the age of fifteen, she served as a medium for adult séances. She has practiced, studied, and instructed metaphysical studies for more than twenty-five years. Maureen is currently the lead psychic/medium for the New England Ghost Project and co-host of the popular radio shows *Ghost Chronicles* and *Ghost Chronicles Live*. Maureen was a contributor to Jeff Belanger's *Communicating With the Dead* (2005), Roxie Zwicker's *Haunted Portland* (2007), and Chris Balzano's *Picture Yourself Ghost Hunting* (2008), and has also written a monthly paranormal newspaper column. Like Ron, Maureen has also appeared on every major New England television station and has been the subject of a German television documentary.

If you would like to contact either Ron or Maureen, you can find them on their website at www.neghostproject.com. You can also listen to *Ghost Chronicles* live on www.TogiNet.com, www.GhostVillage.com, Para-X Radio, and iTunes.